The Brit

C000175970

In memory of my father and to my mother,
who encouraged an interest in architecture
from my earliest childhood

The BRITISH HOUSE

A Concise Architectural History

Edmund Gray

DRAWINGS BY F. BUDIMAN

BARRIE & JENKINS
LONDON

First published in Great Britain in 1994
by Barrie & Jenkins Ltd., Random House,
20 Vauxhall Bridge Road, London SW1V 2SA

ISBN 0 7126 4589 6

Typeset by 🗚 Tek-Art,
Addiscombe, Croydon, Surrey
Printed by Clays Ltd., St Ives, plc.

Acknowledgement for illustrations is generally made in the captions, but in addition,
the figures on pp. 92 and 102 are reproduced by courtesy of the Trustees of the British
Museum and that on p. 23, by kind permission, from *English Historic Carpentry* by
Cecil A. Hewett, published in 1980 by Phillimore & Co. Ltd., Chichester, West Sussex.
Thanks are due to the British Museum Press for drawings by Simon James (pp. 10,
11), to Margate Museums, Thanet District Council for the photo on p. 61, to Oxfordshire Department of Leisure and Arts for the figure on p. 31, and for Crown Copy-
right material to the Royal Commission on the Historical Monuments of England
(RCHME), for figures on pp. 38b, 41a, 45, 98, 107, 119b; to the Royal Commission on
the Ancient and Historical Monuments of Scotland (RCAHMS) for a figure on p. 14,
and to the Royal Commission on the Ancient and Historical Monuments of Wales
(RCAHMW) for figures on pp. 38a and 52b; also, for extra drawings, to Catherine
Lowdell (pp. 66, 69a, 78a, 82, 90a, 96, 97a, 105a, 113a, 135, 150c, 154, 163c, 166a, 170,
171b & c, 181c, 183, 184), Helen Lowdell (pp. 52a, 56, 100, 158b, 180), Mopsa Metter-
nich (pp. 16, 41b, 44, 51b, 74a, 79, 146), Rodney Paull (90b) and Guy Shackle (pp. 28c,
62, 69b, 72, 95b, 135, 150a, 181b). The other drawings are by Funn Budiman.

CONTENTS

FOREWORD

This book traces the architectural development of the smaller house in Britain. That development is traced back as far as it can be: briefly sketching the background of prehistoric dwellings and what the archaeologist has revealed of the houses of the Anglo-Saxons, but describing more fully the story from the time of the earliest standing houses of the twelfth century.

The book is concerned with the development of the ordinary family home, not with great houses. The ordinary family home evolved, however, from manor houses, which are also among the earliest surviving houses of smaller size, so these are part of the book's subject. As manor houses gradually diverge in character from the homes of the yeoman farmer, they cease to be part of the development traced by this book. Similar considerations apply to town houses.

The line between the ordinary family home and the great house becomes easier to see as time goes on. Houses with special features or special elaboration, or which are the individual creations of particular architects, do not belong in an account of the development of the ordinary family home; nor do larger houses: those more than about five windows wide. On Ronald Brunskill's classification, I exclude all Great Houses, cover some Large Houses and concentrate on Small Houses and Cottages. This concentration enables me to discriminate more finely between the successive phases of architectural development than other single-volume histories of the British house.

I can also give a more detailed account than is usual in a book of this kind by concentrating on architectural development. I do not aim to include the social history of the house. On the other hand, unlike many histories of the house, Wales and Scotland are included. Failing to do so means omitting some of the greatest riches of British domestic architecture; it is also highly artificial. There are certainly individual traditions in the two smaller countries, but these are only substantial examples of what occurs in other parts of Britain, and there is much that ignores national boundaries. The important tradition of cruck framing, for instance, extends through England, Scotland and Wales. Tower houses flourished on both sides of the Scottish border, and likewise, styles of timber-framing straddle the border between England and Wales. By the eighteenth century, common styles of domestic architecture were reaching every part of Britain, and the single person with the greatest influence of any on the development of such common styles was the Scot, Robert Adam. It was in Scotland that the finest body of Classical housing was erected.

In writing this book I have drawn on my experience as an Inspector of Historic Buildings at the Department of the Environment, in which capacity I assessed many thousands of houses for listing as worthy of preservation. A general survey such as this, however, inevitably draws in the main on the work of more specialist experts, and I am very conscious of my debt. There have been tremendous advances in the study of ordinary houses in the last generation which I have attempted to summarise in a single narrative. This has not always been an easy task, partly because these specialised studies are often not primarily concerned, as I am, with chronological development.

For the earlier centuries the chronology is indeed still uncertain and controversial, and the extensive work being done, with the assistance of the new techniques of carbon-14 and tree-ring dating, is continually introducing new evidence and new datings, and thus complicates as well as clarifies.

The greatest advances, where knowledge was previously most sketchy, have been in the field of what has come to be termed vernacular architecture. 'Vernacular' denotes the language common to the ordinary people of an area, as opposed to the more sophisticated language of high culture, and it has come to be applied to the traditional, pre-industrial buildings of ordinary people. This book is largely about vernacular houses in this sense, but it also covers the whole stream of ordinary Classical, Victorian and twentieth-century homes now usually regarded as 'polite' rather than vernacular (though designed in a common language), because the design of such houses was ultimately based on treatises and the study of historic exemplars, and increasingly built by industrial methods, not by craftsmanship.

Partly because architectural historians tend to concentrate on great buildings and leading architects there are surprising gaps in the history of ordinary houses. Among the large number of books on Adam, for instance, there is little on his effect on ordinary houses. Local studies and direct analysis of the evidence of photographs, print collections and houses around the country have helped to fill the gaps, but I am less precise than I would like to be on the date when a number of key features were introduced in ordinary houses. I would be grateful to readers who can tell me of earlier dates than I give, for any possible second edition.

Footnotes being out of place in a work of this format, the bibliography must serve as my acknowledgment to all those scholars to whom I am indebted. I would like to express my particular gratitude to Nicholas Cooper, Sarah Pearson, Martin Robertson, Dolly Potter, Ian Gow, Peter Chapman and Francis Kelly for reading sections of the book, and – among many others who have helped in different ways – Christopher Currie, Anthony Quiney, John Walker, Andrew Roberts, J. T. Smith, John Warren, Carole Ryan, David Walker, Charlotte Haslam, David Martin, Peter Child, Bob and Vivien Turner, Cliff Potter, Gerard Daly and my patient editor, Euan Cameron. I am specially grateful also to the staffs of the English and Scottish National Monuments Records, the London Library, Guildhall Library and the RIBA.

1 THE PRIMITIVE HOUSE

Right up to the seventeenth century – and into the eighteenth in large parts of Scotland – the commonest type of house in the countryside was one that was so small and elementary that it is best described as primitive: consisting of only one room, or without windows, or with rough, unplastered interiors open to a flimsy, makeshift roof. Such houses have virtually disappeared and can easily be overlooked altogether in histories of the house. By virtue of their huge numbers, they form the relatively unchanging ground base to the unfolding story of more developed houses.

Prehistoric Houses

The very earliest dwellings in Britain so far revealed by excavation, though certainly not the earliest that existed, are remarkable testimony to the continuity of house-building traditions. They are the Neolithic stone houses at Knap of Howar in the Orkneys, which date from between 3600 and 3100 BC and are preserved up to lintel height. They closely resemble the Black Houses of the north-west fringes of Scotland of some five millennia later that were inhabited into the mid-twentieth century. Like them, they are oblong with rounded ends, the walls being formed of an inner and

Neolithic stone houses, Knap of Howar, Orkney; c.3600/3100 BC (Historic Scotland)

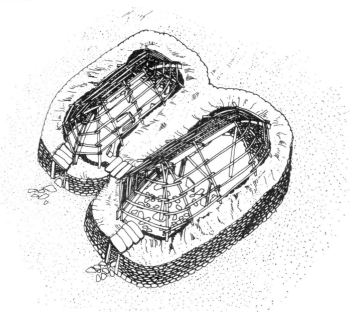

outer skin of stone with infill of turf or rubble, the inner skin being corbelled somewhat inwards to reduce the necessary length of the timbers spanning between wallhead and ridge piece, which is supported by posts at each end. Stone slabs divide the interior into the kitchen and living room. Cooking was on an open hearth, from which the smoke probably percolated through a roof covered in heather or similar material (if later houses are a guide). There is a door but no windows. Butted against the dwelling is a farm building of the same form, an arrangement exactly like that of the Black Houses. Where they and other prehistoric dwellings differ from primitive houses of recent centuries is that they were not the homes of members of the bottom strata of their society but those of its ordinary members, or even its leaders.

Even better preserved are the houses of between 3100 and 2500 BC at Skara Brae, also in the Orkneys, which are generally similar but with squarish rooms and stone furniture, including seats and beds recessed into the walls: this last was another tradition that lasted in Scotland into the twentieth century. They had wooden doors secured by a bar bolt.

At the other end of Britain, in Cornwall, dwellings of similar type have also been located, but from the next major phase of technological development, the Bronze Age (c.2300-c.700 BC). There, a variant was the dry-stone wall backing onto an earth bank. Both types continued through the Iron Age and the Roman period (AD 54-c.410), together with turf houses of similar design, and houses with turf and stone in alternative layers.

Wholly timber houses – so much more perishable than stone dwellings – were no doubt the earliest of all. Prehistoric examples in Britain are of two main types, the conical and the oblong.

The conical house has a long history, which can be traced in Britain at least from the Bronze Age right down to c.100-200 AD, the date of four huts built within a double rampart by Celtic farmers at Rispain Camp in Galloway. Small versions of such huts persisted into modern times, not as permanent homes but for seasonal or specialised use, for example by charcoal burners working in the forests (a reconstructed example of which is at the Weald and Downland Museum, in Sussex).

Anglo-Saxon Houses

The oblong timber house, which also can be traced back to the Bronze Age, and is doubtless much older than that, became the standard dwelling of the Anglo-Saxons. The Roman interlude, which introduced developed Mediterranean house types, seems to have had little or no influence on subsequent developments: brick, for instance, the Romans' chief material for house-building, was only adopted in Britain nearly a thousand years later as a result of quite different influences.

Anglo-Saxon houses were of timber, but differ basically from the subsequent tradition of practically all surviving timber-framed houses in that their posts were earth-fast, or set into the ground, as those of all prehistoric dwellings may be presumed to have been. An earth-fast method of construction gives structures a good initial stability, but also means they have a short life, as the feet of the posts inevitably rot. With the protection of a roof, durability can be much longer than that of a fence post, however. Datable modern earth-fast farm buildings have lasted more than a century.

Larger Anglo-Saxon houses will be discussed in chapter 2. Ordinary houses remained of a primitive nature. They seem to have taken two main forms, both oblong. The superior type was generally some 3.7 to 7.5 metres (12 to 25 feet) long, and about half that in width. The roof, which may have been either hipped (i.e. sloped inwards at the ends) or gabled (i.e. vertical at the ends), was supported either on posts in separate post holes or by posts and planks trenched in the ground in a continuous line (similar to the walls of the Anglo-Saxon church at Greensted in Essex, though they now have plinths). In some cases there are post holes outside the walls, which are thought to have belonged to diagonal shoring or buttressing timbers. Usually there were doorways in the middle of either side and generally the end of the interior was partitioned off, probably for storage, with a separate external door in the gable.

The other type was generally only about 4.5 metres (15 feet) long and was partially dug into the ground; hence it is termed a sunken-floor hut or Grubenhaus. Some of these huts had a single post hole in the middle of each end, suggesting a tent-like roof extending down to the ground from a lengthwise ridge piece. Others had six post holes at each end, suggesting low walls. Others again had

Trenched-plank walls with buttresses: Cowdery's Down, Hampshire; seventh-century (after G. Smith)

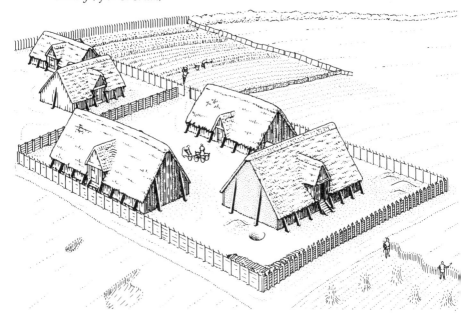

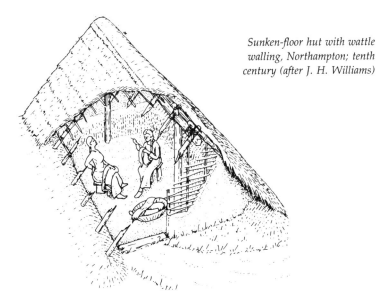

Sunken-floor hut with wattle walling, Northampton; tenth century (after J. H. Williams)

numerous post holes, probably suggesting a raised and boarded floor over a small cellar.

A third type of house, built of wattle alone, without posts, has been found in York, and dated between 900 and 970, during which period York was several times occupied by Scandinavians – Vikings – who also controlled Dublin, where similar 'wicker' structures have been found. They had rounded corners and their hearths suggest that they were domestic. Their remains were only preserved because the sites became waterlogged; they may have been common. Wicker houses recur in Scotland.

Examples of Anglo-Saxon houses with continuously trenched walls have been reconstructed at West Stow, Suffolk, where they were excavated. There is as yet no clear archaeological evidence of any development in ordinary houses during the Anglo-Saxon centuries.

Highland Dwellings and Longhouses

During these centuries, dry-stone dwellings similar to the Neolithic ones of the Orkneys have been excavated in Cornwall, Yorkshire and in the Orkneys and Shetlands (this time built by Scandinavian settlers). At Morgan Porth in Cornwall, dwellings of this type were erected in the tenth and early eleventh centuries. Yellow clay was used between the boulders and rough-hewn rocks of the stone skin. Red clay and shillet (stone fragments) served as infill.

From the ninth century, in the Northern Isles of Scotland, comes the first evidence of longhouses. These are houses combined with byre or stable in a single linear building and a common entrance in the middle for both animals and humans. They were to have a long if patchy history. In Scotland they remained a type of

11

dwelling until modern times. Surviving (upgraded) examples can be seen at Auchindrain, Argyll.

The Continuing Primitive Stratum

All over Britain, primitive dwellings both of timber and of stone and turf continued to be erected, the former at least, it must be supposed, in great numbers. The scanty archaeological evidence is occasionally filled out with documentary evidence. Writing of Wales at the end of the twelfth century, Giraldus Cambrensis describes 'small huts made of boughs of trees twisted together, constructed with little labour and expense, and sufficient to endure through the year'. Houses in the towns must often have been little better. For instance, excavation at 42 St Paul's Street, Aberdeen, has revealed the traces of a thirteenth-century back-street house, probably the home and workshop of a poorer inhabitant. The walls were of wattle, which would have been plastered with mud or dung. The roof was supported by earth-fast posts outside the walls.

Economic advance did lift the standard of primitive houses somewhat at various stages. Probably in the thirteenth century, at a time when more substantial timber-framed houses were improved by the introduction of stone footings, something of the same sort began to happen to some of the humblest homes, at least in areas of England where agriculture reached a certain level of prosperity.

The Hafod and Shieling

One particular type of primitive dwellings calls for mention: the upland hut occupied by pastoral farmers only in the summer, when they took their flocks into the high valleys. In Wales it was termed a hafod and in Scotland a shieling.

In Wales, at the end of the 1770s, Pennant wrote of the interior of a hafod:

> These houses consist of a long low room with a hole at one end to let out the smoke from the fire which is made beneath. Their furniture is very simple: stones are substitutes for stools, and the beds are of hay, ranged along the sides.

Only the platforms on which they were built or traces of walling survive of any of these temporary dwellings, but one at Strata Florida was drawn in the 1880s, shortly before its destruction. This has features we will meet later on: a wicker smoke-hood over the fire, a screen or heck between door and hearth area, and a roof supported by jointed crucks over the middle (as a further drawing shows). The wicker shelf was for hens to nest on.

Black Houses

There are surviving examples of the so-called Black Houses on the Isle of Lewis, and the cognate types elsewhere. They were built of unmortared rubble walls up to six feet thick with a core of turf and rounded corners (though a few, like the restored example at Arnol on Lewis, of as late as *c.*1870, have squared ends). Hipped thatched roofs were supported on slight and rough principal timbers, curved timbers being used to give extra headroom. The more primitive examples were of longhouse type and had an open hearth, the smoke from which found its way through the thatch or out through a hole a little to one side of the fire.

Unlike other primitive houses in Britain, Black Houses usually had additional chambers which, moreover, were sited alongside, rather than at the end of the building. In front was often a combined stable and porch; behind the living room was a store, and behind the byre might lie a barn. To facilitate winnowing in the barn there was commonly an axial arrangement of openings throughout the building. There were no proper windows in earlier, more primitive examples and because the living accommodation was surrounded by other chambers it could only be lit by openings at the base of the thatch, while drainage from its roof was into the thickness of the walls.

In Tiree in the Western Isles dwellings similar to the Black Houses of Lewis were described in 1803. The very thick walls were explained as designed 'to bear the western blast, which sometimes makes dreadful havoc'. The same account adds that 'It is not

Primitive dwelling, Strata Florida, Dyfed (drawn by Worthington Smith, 1888)

Black Houses at Kentangaval, Barra, W. Isles (photographed in the 1890s by Erskine Beveridge; RCAHMS)

always that these poor folk have wooden doors, they then stop the gaps in their huts with thick bundles of heath or straw, tightly tied together'. Sir Arthur Mitchell, writing in 1880, said he had seen thousands of houses similar to the Black Houses of Lewis without even a smoke hole, so that the inside was in a constant cloud of peat-reek and the oozing of the smoke through the roof gave them 'the general appearance of a dung-heap in warm, wet weather'.

As economic conditions improved, Black Houses were progressively improved by the introduction of windows, plastered walls, gable chimneys and partitions, first between people and animals, and then between one room and another.

Primitive Cruck Houses

Black Houses were always a minority type of dwelling, though more durable than most. Far more widespread was the cruck house, which in Scotland was found everywhere except Orkney, Shetland and the Outer Hebrides. Crucks are curved timbers that can be leant against one another in pairs to support the roof directly from the ground, or close to it. (Curved timbers rising from the top of the walls, as in Black Houses, can be termed raised crucks.)

In Scotland and in northern England crucks were widely termed 'siles', and were nearly always rough and slight compared with the relatively high-grade crucks of surviving houses in England and Wales. The ridge piece was called the 'roof tree' and the lesser branches used to underly the thatch were called 'cabers'; but the names varied from one part of Scotland to another, as did the details of construction and roofing material. In contrast to earth-fast Anglo-Saxon houses, the siles of these houses rested on the inner part of the walling or on separate large stones or sets of stones. Often the walling consisted merely of loose stones.

Sometimes there were end crucks – that is, single crucks placed axially – which resulted in rounded ends and roof (a result achieved by raised end crucks in many Black Houses).

An idea of such primitive crucks houses is given by Pennant in his *A Tour of Scotland*. Writing of Deeside in 1759, he describes houses of loose stones, covered with turf, heath, broom or fir branches, 'like so many mole hills'.

Turf and Wattle

As earlier in Cornwall, and no doubt elsewhere, a third way of building simple houses in Scotland was to use turf, or stone and turf in alternate layers. In 1793 'every house' in one part of the parish of Dornoch in the Highlands 'was built of feal [turf] and thatched with divot [turf slice]'. According to George Robertson's *Rural Recollections* of 1829, in the mid-eighteenth-century Lowlands a turf house of this type was commonly 'constructed in all its parts by the gudeman and his servants in a single day, they having previously collected the materials'.

Record of turf houses is also forthcoming for Northumberland. Here, 'earthen' houses were standard till the end of the eighteenth century. Celia Fiennes, writing in 1698, sheds light on several features:

> I was forced to take up in a poor cottage which was open to the thatch and no partitions but hurdles plaister'd . . . noe sleepe could I get, they burning turff and their chimneys are sort of flews or open tunnills that the smoke does annoy the roomes.

Yet another type of house was constructed of wattle, probably quite similar to those of Viking York or thirteenth-century Aberdeen mentioned earlier. Such houses were recorded in Argyll, where they were known as creel or basket houses. On the Hebridean island of Jura, shieling huts were made of a combination of wattle and sods.

The homes of the bulk of the population in England were probably not so different until recent centuries. Dr Guest, in about 1800, described cruck cottages in Berkshire lit only by a hole in the gable, which also let out the smoke. Housman, in his *Topographical Description of Cumberland*, of 1800, wrote:

> 'Most of the ancient houses belonging to the common people in the country are extremely simple, consisting of a kitchen and parlour only; in the former the family sit, eat and do all their household work, and in the latter they sleep and sometimes keep their milk, butter and cheese.'

*Old Leanach Cottage, Culloden, Inverness; a cruck cottage with canopy chimney;
before 1745*

Primitive Chimneyed Houses

One degree less primitive than most of the houses so far discussed
were those possessing chimneys of a kind. Such cottages were
built right down to the early nineteenth century in Scotland. A
chimneyed cruck cottage dating from before 1745 can be seen at
Culloden. This has a hanging lum, or fireplace canopy, one of the
simplest forms of chimney, which seems to have been introduced
in the eighteenth century. Externally, such chimneys were mere
cylindrical tufts in the thatch.

Thatch-tuft chimneys were also to be found on one-roomed
cottages in Wales. One such, at Pont-rhyd-fendigaid in Dyfed, was
still occupied in 1910. As in Scotland, the thatch was held down
by cords. A small window lit the bedroom end, which was
probably divided from the living area by a screen of furniture, as
was likewise often the case in Scotland. Even close to metropolitan
London, a number of drawings show similar rough dwellings as
late as around 1800.

2 THE ERA OF THE OPEN-HALL HOUSE

From Anglo-Saxon times to the sixteenth century, houses that rose above the level of primitive dwelling were normally timber-framed and open-hall, that is to say their main section was of one storey only, consisting of a tall chamber (the hall) open to the roof, with a hearth in the middle of the floor, not in a fireplace under a chimney. The main exceptions to this general pattern were stone-built first-floor halls and some town houses.

In their layout, modest hall houses were like those of the aristocracy, but on a smaller scale with simpler embellishment. How early or widespread they were is still unclear, but small, non-gentry landowners occasionally had hall houses in the thirteenth century and they were numerous in prosperous areas of the country by the end of the fourteenth century.

Certain features were common to open-hall houses throughout the period of their predominance.

The open hearth was usually near the centre of the hall and formed of stone slabs. The rest of the floor would have been of compacted earth in most halls. There were usually no hearths in other rooms (though movable braziers were sometimes used where there was no hearth, at least in towns). In simpler homes the smoke from the open hearth escaped through the doors and windows and percolated through the thatch, which was the commonest roofing material right through the period (though shingles or tiles were also widely used). In houses that were better provided there were sometimes louvres over the hearth or smoke exits at the ends of the roof ridge as gablets (miniature gables).

At one end of the hall would be the table, sometimes with a slight canopy, emulating the halls of the aristocracy. At the other end would be the entrance, in the side wall, usually with another doorway opposite. In better houses the entrance doorways were separated from the hall by a screen or partition. The duplication of doors probably always tended to carry the implications of 'front door' and 'back door', the former being the entry for guests and more formal use, the latter being the entry from farmyard and outbuildings. However, it may partly have had to do with controlling the movement of the smoke according to the direction of the wind.

Not so long ago in western Ireland callers were still expected by the lee door and, in a similar way, in the admittedly severe conditions of the western Highlands in the first years of the nineteenth century it was noted that 'Most commonly every hut has two doors, that when the wind blows hard, the one to windward may be shut, and that to leeward opened' (Mrs S. Murray, *A Companion [to] the Western Highlands*, Vol. II, 1803, p.375-6).

Even in regions of the mildest climate the direction of the wind would have been a consideration in having windows on both sides of the hall, for before the days of glazing it was important for it to be possible to open those on one side to let in the light while keeping shuttered those on the other side to keep out the wind. Not for nothing is the derivation of window 'wind-eye'.

Superior houses might have tracery, but on the evidence of sockets, ordinary houses had rectangular openings with plain square mullions set diamond-wise. Shutters were either flaps hinged from top or bottom or sliding panels. The hall windows were generally double the height of others, either side of the horizontal middle rail if there was one. The evidence suggests little change from the earliest open halls to the sixteenth century.

There were usually smaller rooms at one end of the hall or both, sometimes single-storeyed, but more often two-storeyed. If there were two sets, the rooms at the entrance or 'lower' end of the hall would generally be used as service rooms – for dairy or brewing purposes, food preparation and storage – and the rooms at the 'upper' end would be for private use for the owners, the principal upstair one being called the solar. The two standard service rooms in better-provided houses were the pantry, for food (from the French *pain*, 'bread'), and the buttery, for drink (from 'butt' or 'barrel' – nothing to do with butter). Occasionally these rooms were very low, being used solely for storage. Often in earlier or more modest houses both sets of rooms would be doubled up at one end of the hall.

The rooms at one end or both could be linear with the hall, and under the same roof, divided from it by partitions which in some cases did not rise the full height. Alternatively, in larger or later houses, they could be under separate roofs at right-angles to that of the hall; they are then termed cross-wings. They could project beyond the width of the hall either on one side or both.

The halls of many early hall houses were aisled, like churches – or like larger barns – which remained aisled long after halls. Like parish churches, many hall houses had only one aisle. The object was no doubt partly to bridge the width of the hall without having to use long timbers that were difficult to obtain, but perhaps mainly to emulate royal and aristocratic halls, and even churches. It is important to recognise that symbols, status, dignity and embellishment weighed far more heavily, compared with convenience and comfort, than they do to our utilitarian mentality.

The mention of aisles might suggest that hall houses were very large (as of course the grand ones were), but they could also be small: some halls were no more than about 4.5 metres by 3.7 metres (15 feet by 12 feet).

Crucks and Box Frames

At least from the time of the earliest surviving timber hall houses and until they came to an end, there were two basic types of frame: cruck frame and box frame. Crucks were used both in the primitive

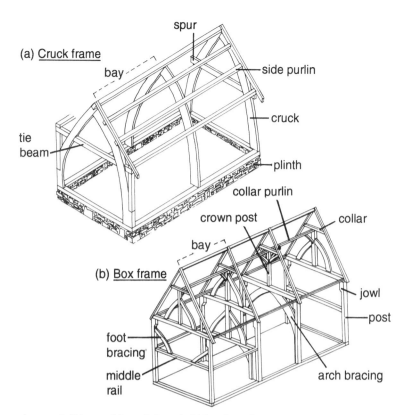

An open-hall house: (a) cruck-framed, (b) box-framed

dwellings discussed in chapter 1 and in hall houses. Box frames, as the name suggests, consisted of a grid of horizontal and vertical timbers jointed together; the roof composed of triangular trusses was structurally separate, merely jointed onto the top. The assembly of the two types differed. Each pair of crucks was first jointed together, with its cross-beam, and the pairs were then reared one by one. By contrast, the posts of box frames tended to be reared individually, the other timbers being added subsequently.

The length between one truss and the next is termed a bay. Houses (and the halls within them) were referred to in medieval and later records by their number of bays, though bays were not necessarily of even length within a house. Trusses normally had a tie beam across the bottom of the triangle (or the equivalent level of crucks). They are then termed 'closed'. Trusses spanning the middle of the hall without obstructive tie-beams are termed 'open'. To add strength and dignity to open trusses, they were sometimes given arch braces between post and collar (the cross-timber near the apex of the truss). This echoed the arches of churches or the grandest halls.

To aid assembly, all the members of each truss were often scored with the same number, usually denoted by a set of knife strokes.

These are known as carpenters' marks. All that can be said about dating from them is that oblong cuts made with a chisel date from the late sixteenth century onwards.

The origin and cultural significance of the two types of framing have been a matter of debate. It has not so far been possible to distinguish archaeologically between the post-holes of the two types, so there is no knowing which is the earlier. It used to be suggested that crucks belonged to the highland parts of Britain and were Celtic, while the box-frame was lowland and Germanic. Certainly crucks were common in eastern Wales, the north of England and Scotland, and rarer towards the eastern seaboard of England, but they are absent from the quintessentially Celtic south-west Wales and west Cornwall (and almost unknown in Ireland), while being common in the east Midlands and extending to the east coast in north Yorkshire and County Durham, within the area of Germanic settlement. Moreover, box-framing is as early in Wales as the earliest surviving crucks there and recently crucks have even been found in East Anglia, where they were thought to be totally absent. Judgement is therefore in abeyance.

Crucks became characteristic of poorer houses, but in the first centuries were also used in substantial and ornate halls. They gave way to box frames as floors were introduced, since their curvature made them unsuitable for upper storeys.

Oak was the commonest wood for timber-framing. It is relatively soft and workable when newly felled, but hardens as the sap dries out, until it is difficult to drive a nail into. That is why it was the practice to use oak for framing while still fresh, without seasoning, even though this meant that it warped later. Provided it is not steeped in water it is exceedingly durable. Elm is more resistant to water and was much used for floorboards, but also for framing. Chestnut, willow and poplar were occasionally also used.

Throughout the open-hall period the usual infill to the inner and outer walls of timber framing was wattle and daub. Wattle generally consisted of hazel or cleft oak woven round staves. Daub was a mixture of clay, dung and chopped straw.

Methods of Dating
It may at first seem surprising that the part of an open-hall house most likely to have survived in recognisable form is the roof. Windows and doors have naturally almost always been replaced, but the wall framing has usually also been greatly altered or encased if not entirely renewed. Examination of the roof is the chief means of dating medieval houses. The previous existence of an open hearth can sometimes be inferred from smoke-blackened timbers in the loft; evidence that the chimney stack has been an insertion may also show that the house was originally open-hall. Occasionally, open-hall houses have subsequently been demoted to barns and can be readily viewed and understood, being usually little altered. In the case of the great majority of those that survive

at all an examination of the loft is the prime requirement.

There are four main methods of dating: by documents (mostly indirectly), by style (mainly of mouldings), by type of plan and structure and by scientific analysis of timber specimens.

The evidence of documents is often available for cathedrals and royal buildings, and from their development, with due allowance for time-lag down the social scale and away from the centres of innovation, a contribution can be made to the dating of lesser houses. For these, documentary evidence is seldom available and anyhow it is rarely possible to match particular surviving houses with those in the documents, which are normally identified solely by owners' names.

Stylistic dating can be achieved by reference to the chronologies of mouldings and the like, that have been built up over a century and a half of the study of churches and greater buildings, with allowance for time-lag in their use in lesser houses. The limitation is that many early houses have no surviving mouldings.

Dating by type of plan and structure is the method based on by far the greatest wealth of data, as large numbers of houses in different parts of the country have been fully recorded, almost all in accounts published since 1950. The starting points, however, must be dates fixed by other methods. A chronological outline began to emerge from the 1950s, but many difficulties remain, not least because many plan types and structural features had long time spans, and overlapped chronologically and geographically.

A specialised method of typological dating on the basis of joints was advanced by Cecil Hewett in the 1960s and 1970s, based on the hypothesis of an evolution from simple to complex and taking as starting points buildings (mainly in Essex) that could be dated by mouldings, documentary hints or analogy with known dates of cathedral roofs. But little in the way of firmly agreed date ranges has resulted. Choice of joint seems to have depended on too many variables, and is therefore only one of many features from which specialists try to form a coherent picture of development. That the lap (or halved) joint tends to be early, and the alternative mortice and tenon tends to be later, seems to be the main useful conclusion.

Two scientific methods of dating timbers have been developed since the Second World War. The first of these is carbon-14 analysis, based on the rate of decay of the radioactive isotope carbon-14 in organic matter. Originated in 1946, the method's application to archaeology was progressively refined until around 1970 it could date medieval timbers to within 40 to 100 years either way, but unfortunately with only a two in three probability of accuracy, in relation to any one sample. The second method is by tree-ring analysis (dendrochronology), which gradually in the 1970s and 1980s replaced carbon-14 analysis by offering considerably greater precision. Its basis is the variability in the growth put on by trees between one year and another, manifested in the breadth of the added ring to be seen in a cross-section of the trunk. Sections of timbers in an ever-older series of overlapping specimens can be matched against one another and a continuous series thus extended into the past.

The use of tree-ring dating in particular, applied in harness with the ever extending work of recording house structures, makes this an exciting time for the history of medieval houses. A firmer sequence emerges year by year, confirming, on the whole, the development already tentatively mapped out from typological analysis. Nevertheless, any account has to be cautious, if only because many of the relevant buildings have not yet been sampled.

THE ANGLO-SAXONS TO THE TWELFTH CENTURY

Anglo-Saxon Halls

Already in Anglo-Saxon times there were open-hall houses. There is a famous analogy in Bede's *History* of 731 between 'man's present life' and the flight of a sparrow 'through the banqueting hall where you sit in winter to dine with your thanes and counsellors. Inside, the comforting fire warms the room; outside rage wintry storms of snow and rain. The sparrow flies in swiftly through one door of the hall, and out through the other.' Halls also feature in the epic poem *Beowulf*, which dates from the tenth century but incorporates much older material.

Halls of this kind are not ordinary houses but are relevant as forerunners of later hall-houses. The aisled plan that seems to have been the norm among the earliest surviving houses of the twelfth and thirteenth centuries was already foreshadowed in the royal palace at Yeavering, Northumberland, dating from the early seventh century. Other great halls followed different patterns, however. King Alfred's hall at Cheddar, of c.875, was not aisled and its side walls were bowed out towards the centre, shiplike, and the roof must have swelled correspondingly. This would seem to have been an archaic feature, perhaps related to seafaring traditions. The ninth-century royal palace at Northampton was of stone, but that is so far unique; it seems safe to assume that lesser halls would all have been timber-framed. The evidence is sparse, but at Goltho in Lincolnshire a series of four successive aisled hall houses beneath a manor house of the twelfth century have been excavated.

Other excavated sites fill out the evidence. Dated to the early twelfth century is a double-aisled hall at Llantrillyd, south Glamorgan, and the manor house at Brome, in Suffolk, belongs to the late twelfth century. The aisled hall achieved its acme of prestige in William II's huge specimen at Westminster of 1097-99, which may have consisted solely of two equal aisles.

What was characteristic at Goltho and elsewhere, including Westminster where the hall probably contained no ancillary rooms, was that the various functions that in later centuries were carried on in one integrated house were scattered around a group of buildings. This approach died out very slowly, a fact which is easily lost to view because ancillary buildings are so much more likely to have been destroyed than the main house. In particular, kitchens, with their fire risk, were for long often separate.

Non-aisled Anglo-Saxon hall-houses also existed, for instance at Chalton in Hampshire. There is no clear dividing line between these and the primitive Anglo-Saxon houses discussed in chapter 1, partly because it is a matter of guesswork how any particular house was roofed and whether its height or finish would place it as a forerunner of later hall-houses.

Twelfth-century Aisled Halls

A very few timber houses attributed to the twelfth century, and therefore probably still of earth-fast construction, have survived in part. This may be explained by the dry conditions enjoyed by the feet of the arcade posts, away from the outer walls, which led to their retention, together with the truss they supported, when those outer walls were rebuilt. A key case is the fairly large Fyfield Hall, Essex, the core of which has been dated on the basis of mouldings to two phases: the earlier twelfth century (or even the late eleventh) and *c.*1240. Supporting the remains of a complete aisled truss of phase two are two arcade posts and full-height

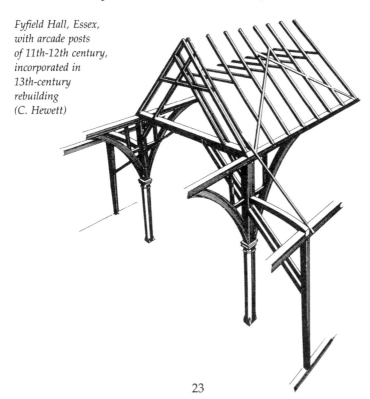

Fyfield Hall, Essex, with arcade posts of 11th-12th century, incorporated in 13th-century rebuilding (C. Hewett)

partitions at the ends of the hall, with planking, from phase one. It has been discovered that the arcade posts extended about 1 metre (3 feet) below ground level. The same explanation may well apply to other cases, where the feet of the posts have not been investigated, such as Burston Manor in Hertfordshire, of which only part of the central truss and some rafters are visible of the original structure. This house can probably be dated by the scalloped capital to no later than 1170-90.

With the survivals of probably twelfth and earlier thirteenth century houses comes the first satisfactory evidence of structure. The features that seem to be common to them are the following: long diagonal passing braces (or lacing ties or parallel rafters) running parallel to the roof slope and extending, wholly or partially, from roof to aisle wall, engaging in turn rafter, collar, tie beam and arcade post; the similar scissor braces, which cross below the apex of the roof; more generally, parallel, duplicated framing members; a tendency to straight braces, rather than the curved ones of later date; dragon ties (diagonal horizontal braces at the outer corners of the frame at eaves level); a nearly square cross-section to the timbers, rather than the oblong of later dates; and joints mainly effected by halving, often of a dovetailed form, and face-lapped, with limited use of the mortice and tenon joint that was gradually to replace the lap joint. In a negative sense, a common feature of these houses is the absence of longitudinal members in their roofs.

From its second phase Fyfield Hall has passing braces in the roof truss and running from the tie beam across the aisles. Some of the arcade braces are rounded almost to the form of semicircular arches, like the arcade of a Romanesque church, or the grandest aisled halls (such as Hereford, c.1160, or Oakham, c.1190).

Another of the aisled halls that may date from c.1180-1200,

Old Court Cottage, Limpsfield, Surrey (perhaps c.1180–1200) (a) capital of aisle post, (b) cross-section showing passing braces (after R. T. Mason)

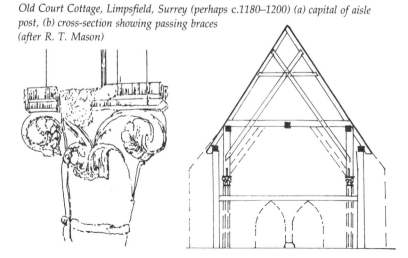

though it has been put as late as *c.*1250, is Old Court Cottage, Limpsfield, Surrey. The early date is again based on the arcade capital; the later date applies if it was backward in imitation of stone capitals in churches. It was the 'court house' from which the Abbot of Battle's Limpsfield manor was administered – one step down from being a full manor house. It has all the structural features mentioned as characteristic of the earliest framed houses. It originally had aisles on each side (removed when new wall-framing was erected), together with a cross-wing, which is probably somewhat later.

Cruck Houses
There is documentary evidence for their existence from shortly before 1200, but no surviving examples as early as that have been so far identified.

First-Floor Stone Houses
There are disputed examples of first-floor halls before the Conquest of 1066. The first that survive upstanding, in large part or fragmentarily, are of the middle or later twelfth century. They are of moderate size and are found both in the country, as manor houses, and in towns, as the homes of wealthy merchants. They are built of stone (and none of them retains its original roof). From the time of the Norman Conquest there had been of course much castle building in stone. The choice of stone for houses, however, stood in contrast not only to the previous centuries but, more strikingly, to the next three centuries as well, when few such houses were built, probably because timber-frame construction markedly improved.

The entrances to ground and first floors were separate, with an external staircase, usually of wood, and doorways near the corner of the building, sometimes in the end wall, more often in the side. The upper room was subdivided, probably at first by a leather curtain, but soon by a wooden partition. It was usually lit by two-light windows. These would have been shuttered; glass was too expensive except for palaces and churches.

By the late twelfth century, or earlier, the first storey was divided by a stone wall into hall and solar, the latter a term of French origin denoting a bedroom, or private room, for the owners of the hall. It usually lay behind the upper end of the hall.

In some of the more prosperous towns, first-floor halls were quite numerous by the end of the twelfth century. Naturally, given the pressures of redevelopment in cities, very few of them have survived, but from archaeological and documentary evidence, it is known that there were thirty or more stone houses in Canterbury, for instance, by the early thirteenth century, some partially timber-built; in Lincoln there were said to be 'a vast number of beautiful Saxon and Norman doorways, constructed in the most finished manner' in 1782. In York, the wall of a first-floor hall, with a typical

Jew's House, Lincoln; reconstructed view; c.1175 (lower windows uncertain); c.1175

window, survives off Stonegate and there is evidence of others. Even in smaller towns like King's Lynn merchants were beginning to build stone houses by 1200.

The most famous of these town houses is the so-called Jew's House in Lincoln, which has been dated to *c.*1170-80 on stylistic grounds. The interior has no surviving features, but the house is valuable for preserving both door and window details. It is surprising that the chimney rises above the door; this feature is not found on the other survivors and it is not known how common it may have been.

The evidence suggests that most first-floor halls had fireplaces, though they cannot have been strictly necessary except where the floor was timber. Moreover, the existence of fireplaces in first-floor halls shows that it was not out of ignorance that they were omitted from ground-floor hall houses.

Another house similar to the Jew's House, and of similar date, exists further up Steep Hill. In Southampton, something is known of four stone houses, two partly upstanding, one excavated and one demolished but recorded. All of them probably had a shop or warehouse on the lower floor. The late twelfth-century house – misnamed Canute's Palace – in Porters Lane followed the general pattern in having a hall and chamber over two rooms of corresponding size; there was an attached warehouse with a room above it. The other three houses seem all to have been double-depth and at right-angles to the street, with hall and chamber alongside one another, each presenting a gable to the street.

Another surviving merchant's house, also late twelfth century, is the Music House in Norwich, where a vaulted ground floor is divided into two rooms, in the usual linear plan, but there is a single big hall upstairs. The existence of very small windows on the ground floor and the larger one above confirms that living quarters were on the first floor and storage and the like on the ground floor. Unlike the other first-floor halls, it has a porch, now altered. It had an internal spiral staircase in the thickness of the wall, at the corner of the house.

The other surviving twelfth-century town house, though considerably altered and restored, is Moyses Hall in Bury St Edmunds, which like the lost Southampton examples, has parallel chambers. On the lower floor one of these is of two spans of groin vaulting, with two columns down the middle.

In the country, an early example of the stone-built first-floor hall is Hemingford Manor, Cambridgeshire, dating from c.1150. Here, the principal surviving internal feature is the fireplace in the side wall, which has a segmental head and flanking shafts with typical Romanesque cushion capitals.

The earliest surviving fireplaces in stone buildings in England are the round-arched fireplaces in castles, but the misnamed King John's House in Southampton also has a segmental arch. By around 1185, the hooded type was introduced (the first known examples are at Conisborough Castle). There is a hooded fireplace, supported on corbels, at Boothby Pagnell, which is reckoned to be of around 1200 (see figure overleaf). This is the best-preserved of all these first-floor houses, though later windows have been inserted. The chimney is extant. Its cylindrical form was probably standard, judging by examples in France and at a couple of English castles and one in Southampton. Hence the inclusion of one on the reconstructed view of the Jew's House.

The plan at Boothby Pagnell, with two rooms on each floor, ground-floor ones vaulted, and external stairs, seems to confirm this layout as standard. Variations revealed by excavation at the manor house at Wharram Percy, East Yorkshire, however, suggest caution. Dated to the last quarter of the twelfth century by its

Boothby Pagnell, c.1200; middle window later (A. F. Kersting)

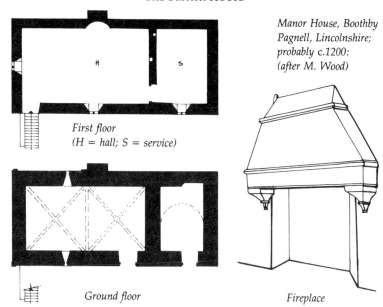

Manor House, Boothby Pagnell, Lincolnshire; probably c.1200: (after M. Wood)

First floor
(H = hall; S = service)

Ground floor

Fireplace

waterleaf mouldings, this dwelling had a deep basement rather than ground-floor chambers, and there was a timber floor over it, supported on massive wooden posts (called samson posts), rather than vaulting. Nevertheless, the forms of door, window and chimney fall into the expected patterns.

Roofing

There is useful evidence at Wharram Percy that, whilst thatch was the main roof covering, tiles were used round the chimney, doubtless to reduce the fire risk. For the same reason, tiles would have been used more in the towns than in the country, though it is clear, if only from later prohibitions, that thatch was still the normal material even in London. Perhaps surprisingly, there is evidence that slates were in use by the twelfth century, if not before, at least along the south coast (brought by sea from Devon, and possibly Cornwall).

There is evidence from a manuscript depiction of around 1000 of flat square boards being used for roofing. Oval shingles (oak tiles) are shown in the Bayeux Tapestry, and even royal buildings were still covered with shingles in the mid-thirteenth century.

Gable finials in the form of knobs, spurs and foliated scrolls also appear in the Bayeux Tapestry. Similar finials are found in the Guthlac Roll of a century later, whilst a lion and a wyvern are shown in a mid-twelfth century drawing of Christchurch Priory, Canterbury; Saltford Manor, of c.1150, has a stone lion. Such ornamental details are among the least likely features of early houses to survive. Any mental picture of them should make allowance for this and other forms of decoration.

THE THIRTEENTH CENTURY

In around 1200 an all-important transition took place in the method of constructing timber-framed buildings. The earth-fast method of setting the posts into the ground was abandoned and instead the frame was raised on padstones or continuous plinths. This change vastly increased the durability of timber houses.

The new method seems to have spread rapidly after the long centuries during which even the grandest timber-framed halls were earth-fast. It is striking that, on the sparse evidence so far available, the first timber-framed manor houses on footings may be hardly earlier than the first of the durable houses of a lower status – bearing in mind that dates on both sides are mostly speculative or approximate. Very likely the plinth or padstone that made lesser houses durable was also what encouraged lords of the manor to adopt timber as an alternative to stone.

In any event, there was, it seems, little difference between small manor houses and houses of somewhat lesser status; indeed it is not always possible to discover whether a particular house was a manor house or not (that is, the home of the lord who owned the whole or part of a village and had jurisdiction over its people). For both, the two leading characteristics continued to be parallel framing members and aisled plans. The change, around 1200, from Romanesque to Gothic, however, meant that superior doors and windows had pointed, not rounded, heads.

Aisled Halls

During the thirteenth century, aisled halls spread over consider-able parts of the prosperous areas of the south-east of England, from East Anglia, through Kent and Sussex to the upper Thames.

Essex is rich in aisled houses; indeed it has been reckoned to have one-fifth of all known aisled halls in England. Suffolk also has a fair number. The earliest so far identified is Purton Green Farmhouse, Stansfield, dated to around 1300 and perhaps never a manor house (see figure overleaf). It shares many of the features of Old Court Cottage (see page 25). Its hall was almost certainly of at least two bays – if so, about ten metres (33 feet) long. The aisles were carried round the lower end and presumptively round the upper end too. Two trusses survive, with two sets of passing-braces in the open, probably central one and indications of the same in the closed one at the lower end of the hall.

In most of these features Purton Green is like aisled halls of similar date, but it is without surviving parallel so far recorded in its range of six arches at the lower end of the hall beneath the closed truss. Three of these seem to have been doorways, two doubtless giving access to the usual service rooms and one leading either to a detached kitchen or, more likely, to stairs (as it does now), since there seems to have been an upper room or loft under the sloping aisle roof, with partitioning towards the hall.

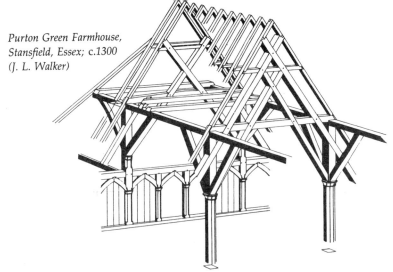

Purton Green Farmhouse,
Stansfield, Essex; c.1300
(J. L. Walker)

In the Vale of the White Horse, Oxfordshire (till 1974 in Berkshire), is a group of early houses which includes the earliest precisely datable surviving wall-framing of a two-storey house so far reported in Europe. This is at Aston Tirrold, at right-angles to a later range, and has been dated to 1282-84 by tree-ring analysis. It is of box-frame construction, with very large panels and braces in the top angles of the box. The lower floor is a semi-basement. The roof has been remodelled, but was originally hipped.

By contrast, at Lime Tree House, Harwell, nothing below the roof survives from the original structure. Christopher Currie's research suggests a date late in the 1240s, while the timbers have been given carbon-14 dates of 1240-60 ±20 years and a dendrochronological date of 1239+. It was a roughly built aisled house, apparently with cantilevered ends, around which the aisles were continued, like Purton Green Farm.

Lime Tree House, Harwell; c.1246
(reconstruction C. Currie)

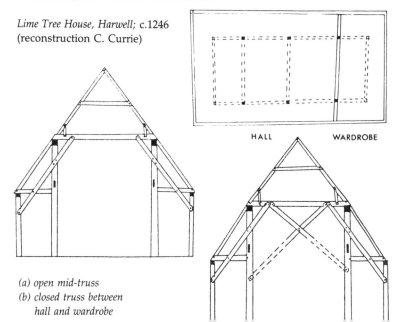

HALL   WARDROBE

(a) *open mid-truss*
(b) *closed truss between*
    hall and wardrobe

Cruck Houses

All the houses so far discussed are box-framed, but the earliest surviving cruck frames also date from the thirteenth century or just after and are found in the Vale of the White Horse. One, re-used at Baker's Close, Radley, is dendro-dated 1277 (−15/+20). Another is 83 The Causeway, which has been dendro-dated 1305. One of the cruck trusses here has doubled collars; another is truncated; a third has evidence of a different kind of duplication, struts between the arch-braces and the cruck blades, a feature otherwise known from the late thirteenth or early fourteenth centuries in Chichester and Worcestershire.

Cruck houses, also probably of the thirteenth century, survive in the West Country too. Pilliven, in Witheridge, Devon, has straight, square-section minor timbers and halved joints, features already noted as indicating a very early date. Wick Farm, Norton St Philip, Somerset has been claimed as of similar date.

Simpler than passing-brace houses, cruck-frame houses were no doubt commoner. Rough crucks of light timbers such as all but the wealthy must have used will scarcely ever have survived. This is confirmed by the fact that all of the several hundred cruck houses that were listed in the manor of Settrington, East Riding, as late as 1599 have all but vanished.

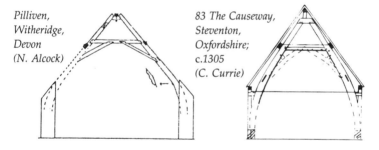

Pilliven,
Witheridge,
Devon
(N. Alcock)

83 The Causeway,
Steventon,
Oxfordshire;
c.1305
(C. Currie)

Stone Ground-Floor Houses

Houses of stone with halls on the ground floor are usually larger than those whose history is being traced in this book. The evolution of such houses steadily diverged from that of middling and smaller houses, but Cogges, in Witney, Oxfordshire, of c.1260-70, is an example of one that is still more or less on a par with the timber-framed houses we have considered. It consisted of an

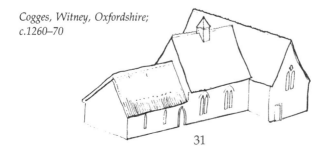

Cogges, Witney, Oxfordshire;
c.1260–70

unaisled hall, with service rooms at the lower end and a cross-wing of private chambers (rebuilt later) at the top end. Two double-light windows with plate tracery survive (one moved) and one of the two opposed doorways. The original roof went when a first floor was added.

First-Floor Halls

A few first-floor halls of non-aristocratic status were still being built in the thirteenth century. One example is West Dean Rectory, Sussex, which was the home of a wealthy clergyman, and has been dated to c.1280 on the style of the windows. Constructed of flint with stone dressings, it has two rooms on each floor, a chimney and adjacent winding staircase at one end and a garderobe in a slight projection at the other. It was more usual for fireplaces to be on the front wall, as in the Jew's House, Lincoln, or on the back wall, as at Boothby Pagnell. The end-wall position may have displaced the high table from the top end of the hall.

Cottages

Excavations now suggest that houses above the level of primitive huts were being erected by better-off peasants by the thirteenth century, and that they too were being improved by the introduction of padstones and plinths. Some even had walls of stone up to the eaves if one partly upstanding excavated case is not unique. This is a cottage from Hangleton, near Brighton, conjecturally reconstructed at the Weald and Downland Museum, which has been dated to the thirteenth century or earlier, without further precision. When excavated in 1952-4, it was found to have walls surviving to a height of 0.9 metres (three feet). It was built of flint, like West Dean Rectory, and had two rooms, a main room with an open hearth and an inner room with an oven.

The form of the roof is unknown, but there was a 8cm (3in) gap at one corner, and it seems likely that this was the position of a post. This suppositious post could have been the last survivor of a complete set of earth-fast posts that were superseded when the more permanent flint walls were built. If that was what happened, the roof can hardly have been supported on crucks, whatever other form it may have taken.

The explanation of what happened is suggested by excavations at West Whelpington, Northumberland. Here there is evidence that houses that began with earth-fast posts later had stone walls inserted under them when the bottoms rotted and were cut off. The same process also looks likely at the excavated sites at Upton in Gloucestershire and Goltho in Lincolnshire.

At Houndtor and Okehampton in Devon similarly constructed houses, but on the longhouse plan, were being built by the late twelfth or early thirteenth centuries. They had two rooms and a loft in the house part. Cornish longhouses – for example, at Trewortha – had similar plans, but stone furniture.

Town Houses

As in the country, stone-built town houses seem to have become rarer, rather than commoner, except among the wealthy. At any rate, there is even less evidence from surviving fabric.

Regulations shed some light. In London, following earlier regulations issued probably at some time after 1191, the banning of thatched roofs was elaborated after a fire in 1212. The list of roofing materials forbidden on new houses suggests what was commonly used at the time in London and elsewhere: reeds, straw, rushes and stubble. Existing roofs of reeds or rushes were to be plastered over. Archaeology confirms that roof tiles were coming into use at this date, not only in London but also in Canterbury and Southampton. Judges' eyres (reports) of 1244-6 and 1276 on London are evidence for the existence of porches, pentices (canopies) and flights of steps down to undercrofts and jetties, about which we shall have more to say.

In Oxford and Southampton there is evidence of galleries at the front of individual houses, over the undercroft, which may indicate a wider occurrence of the arrangement still found at Chester of continuous galleries of this kind, giving pedestrian access to shops at first-floor level.

In Chester, they are known as 'rows'. Beneath them are undercrofts built of large, well-coursed local sandstone. A few have vaults. Most have massive timber beams carried on square chamfered samson posts, corbels in the side walls or upheld by curved braces. On this substructure joists covered with boards

Booth Mansion (eastern section), Watergate Street, Chester; reconstruction of house, c.1280 (after Chester Rows Research Project)

were carried, sometimes, at least, overlain with stone flags on rubble (probably as fire-proofing).

In Watergate Street these timbers give dendrochronology dates variously between 1201 and 1248, so that the Rows that already seem to have overlain them appear to antedate the great fire of 1278 which was probably what facilitated the redevelopment of Chester on a consistent pattern. In places, the thirteenth-century superstructures have partly survived within later work. Some were partly or even wholly of stone. Within the eastern part of the Booth Mansion of 1700 are particularly extensive remains. The undercroft is almost intact. Above it was a small shop and behind that a spacious hall. This had an open hearth, unlike West Dean Rectory or the twelfth-century first floor halls described earlier. Over the shop was the bedchamber of the owners. The roof is conjectural.

In Hertfordshire, at 2 West Street, Ware there is a portion of a town house with many of the features mentioned already. It is a two-bay structure which has been interpreted as a kitchen section of a service cross-wing, the rest of the building having been lost. The central truss has passing braces and there are no longitudinal timbers; there are dragon ties; the timbers are of nearly square section; the joints are side-lapped where after 1300 mortice and tenons would be expected. Along with the house at Aston Tirrold, this survival is precious for retaining original wall-framing, with posts at roughly 65-90cm (2.5-3ft) centres, with straight, mainly foot bracing (i.e. running from the posts to the feet of the panels, as opposed to head bracing, which rises from the posts to the heads of the panels). It is interesting too as a service room with a hearth. Cooking normally appears to have been done either in a separate building or over the hearth of the hall. Service rooms generally give no evidence of having had hearths, though the oven in the inner room at Hangleton is another exception.

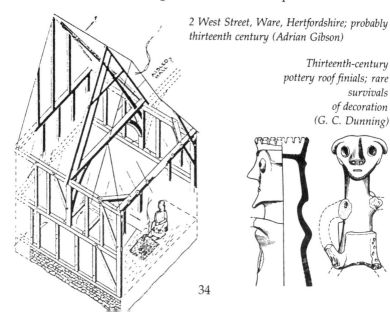

2 West Street, Ware, Hertfordshire; probably thirteenth century (Adrian Gibson)

Thirteenth-century pottery roof finials; rare survivals of decoration (G. C. Dunning)

THE FOURTEENTH CENTURY

In the towns the fourteenth century saw the advent of the three-storey house without open hall; both in town and country, stone houses with ground-floor halls began to spread. The vast majority of middling and smaller houses remained timber-framed, however. These, and the roofs of stone houses, underwent important, interrelated changes in structure (and some related changes to layout) – several of them originating well before 1300.

To improve the structures of timber-framed houses, the longitudinal members known as purlins were introduced and, along with these, new types of truss, most strikingly the crown post truss but also its rival, the king post. There was a corresponding fading of duplicated members and passing braces, though not without a long overlap. Related to these changes was the adoption of a jowl, or thickening, at the heads of posts, to accommodate the multiple joint there (see figure, page 19).

A new feature of a different kind was the jetty, the projection of a storey over the one below, which rapidly gained popularity. Exploiting this feature was a new house type, the so-called Wealden house, which emerged in the middle of the century and was to be much favoured in the next. The aisled hall tended to die away in its path, but persisted elsewhere and indeed was just starting its period of popularity in parts of the north, where middling houses were now for the first time being erected. At the same time, a combination of the new base cruck with the so-called spere truss was developed as a shadow of the fully aisled hall, especially in the West Midlands, where too the first middling houses were being built.

The Purlin

A purlin is any longitudinal roof timber. Ridge purlins were often introduced to give longitudinal stability to roofs, but more important and used more consistently was the side purlin (connecting the trusses at a midway height) and the collar purlin (running along the centre of the roof and connecting the transverse collars of each rafter). Side purlins are unexciting as structural members, but they were to carry all before them, becoming standard features of roofs down to at least 1700.

Side purlins first arrived on the scene around 1275, but it is important to emphasise that they did not quickly lead to the extinction of the previous method of stiffening by duplication. Numerous examples of overlap exist, and passing braces in particular persisted in aisled roofs, to which they were suited. As late as c.1450 (or later) a barn at Nettlestead, Kent, had duplicate bracing to the tie-beam. Roofs without horizontal members also persisted to some extent. Even a house of superior status, Northborough Manor House, Northamptonshire, dated securely in the first half of the fourteenth century, did without them.

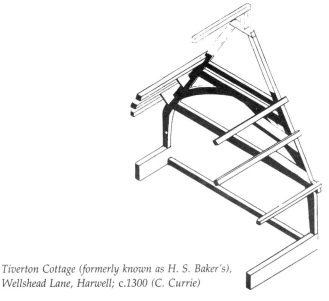

Tiverton Cottage (formerly known as H. S. Baker's),
Wellshead Lane, Harwell; c.1300 (C. Currie)

Side purlins are first known to have been used at Salisbury
Cathedral by 1237. The key early case of their use in a house is
Tiverton Cottage (formerly known as H. S. Baker's), in Wellshead
Lane, Harwell. This also has duplication of collars (the lower one
being arch-braced), and indeed the purlins are doubled. The
timbers concerned have been dated to 1275 ± 30 years by
radiocarbon tests, *c.*1300 by dendrochronology.

The Crown Post and Collar Purlin
The second method of longitudinal stiffening was visually more
exciting. The crown post was a vertical timber rising from the
middle of the tie-beam but stopping short of the apex of the roof,
instead supporting a purlin extending the length of the roof, on
which rested the collars of each truss. The crown post is of
disputed origin, but was first used in churches in England from
*c.*1220. That it was adopted as much for its visual appeal as a
feature of the open roof as for its rather cumbersome structural role
tends to be confirmed by its comparative rarity in barn roofs. Its
verticality and its curved braces, which could radiate in all four
directions or only two, can be seen as a manifestation of Gothic
taste.

The earliest known secular use of the crown post is in two grand
houses: the Old Deanery, Salisbury (between 1259 and 1274) and
Manor Farm, Bourn, Cambridgeshire (after 1266). Both are
examples of overlap, having scissor-braces and passing braces
respectively. By the 1320s the crown post was widespread for
middling houses, though this is more readily apparent in the case
of town houses than it is for houses in the country.

An early dated example is at Lady Row, Goodramgate, in York,
the oldest timber-framed building in the city, dating from 1316
(figure, page 38).

Early rural examples of the crown post are found in the Weald, where Kent, Sussex and Surrey meet. Several are attributed to the first thirty years of the fourteenth century. One can be viewed at the National Trust's Clergy House, in Alfriston, East Sussex, which is still open to the roof, unlike most open-hall houses where roof features are hidden in the loft. This house probably dates from shortly after 1360.

Among middling houses in East Anglia, almost as early as the first examples in the Weald is Edgar's Farm, Stowmarket, probably built in the 1340s. Yet another case of overlap, this combined a crown post over its two-bay hall with aisles and passing-brace trusses. The walling has wide-spaced posts and multiple curved braces.

Edgar's farm, Stowmarket (probably 1340s; re-erected at Stowmarket open-air museum, Suffolk)

King Posts

The great alternative to the crown post roof for box-framed houses was the king post, which rises from the middle of a tie-beam or collar to support a ridge piece. An early example is at Leadenporch House, Deddington, Oxfordshire, dated to *c*.1325. By around 1350 the king post was to be found in larger buildings in the north. Meanwhile it occurred sporadically in the south and reached Wales by the late fourteenth century, at the aisled Hafod, at Llansilin, Clwyd (overleaf), a side purlin house, which is one of the earliest durably built houses of moderate size in Wales. However, the king post failed to catch on to any extent in the south, whilst becoming typical on the Yorkshire uplands for lesser houses, probably because it suited the lower pitches of around 40 degrees that were necessary with the use of stone tiles rather than thatch.

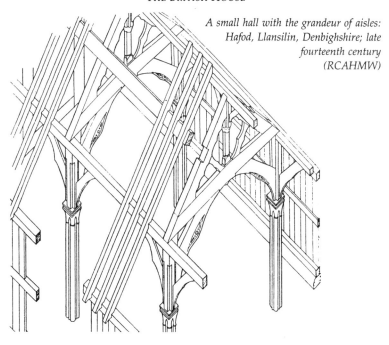

A small hall with the grandeur of aisles: Hafod, Llansilin, Denbighshire; late fourteenth century (RCAHMW)

Lady Row, Goodramgate, York, 1316; showing crown post and jetty (RCHME)

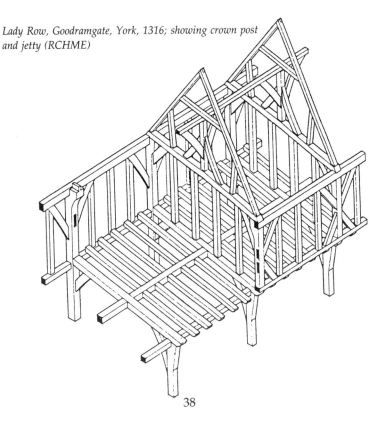

Jetties

The first documentary mention of a jetty is in the judges' eyres on London of 1246, but the first surviving one is at Tiptofts Hall, Wimbish, Essex, in about 1300, though it is especially characteristic of towns and there were no doubt many earlier urban jetties. The jetty had two practical advantages. First, it made the process of fitting together the timbers of a house easier, because the floor joists needed only to be morticed into a beam at one end. Second, it gave a little more space on the upper storey in proportion to the ground occupied: a jetty could project by nearly a metre. This advantage was significant in towns where land was densely occupied. More compelling everywhere was undoubtedly the aesthetic appeal, clear from the fact that houses were often jettied only to the front. Maybe jetties were a status symbol too, emphasising the possession of storeyed parts where others had only a single storey.

The Goodramgate town row of 1316 mentioned above is jettied. Hill House, in High Street, Burford, Oxfordshire is another early example (added to and altered later). The solar wing with a jettied upper storey faces the street.

Internal Jetties and Galleries

Internally the first-floor room at the top end of the hall was sometimes jettied, probably as much to produce an effect similar to the dais canopy in grander houses as to enlarge the upper room. An example from early in the century is 8 Purfleet Street, King's Lynn, which had both ancillary units at the street end of the hall; the section between the shops and the hall was jettied into the latter.

Related to the internal jetty is the side gallery, cantilevered from the wall of the hall and linking the upper rooms at each end, thus saving the need to have two sets of stairs. This tactic was adopted in many different places. An early fourteenth-century example is 58 French Street, Southampton (see figure, page 46).

Wealden Houses

The jetty was a component in the creation of the extremely successful Wealden house type, which seems to have originated around the middle of the century, without aristocratic antecedents. It consisted of a hall with jettied wings at each end. The wings projected to the front (and occasionally to the rear) but there was a single hipped roof of even span over the whole house, resulting in a deep overhang over the central hall section.

The Wealden was the characteristic form the open-hall house took when it first became common not only for lords of the manor but also for wealthy farmers (yeomen) in the south-east of England, so often the area at the forefront of economic growth. Wealden houses were common not only in the area of the Weald from which they take their name, but also through most of Kent

Bayleaf, from Chiddingstone, Kent; c.1400; right-hand end c.1500

and much of Sussex; they occurred occasionally over a much wider area. In Kent some were the homes of peasants, if peasants are defined as people owning less than 20 hectares (50 acres).

The Wealden house remained fashionable for nearly two hundred years, until the 1530s. The hall was usually of two bays and normally had crown posts with moulded bases and capitals.

The Clergy House, Alfriston, previously mentioned for its crown post, is an early example. The section behind the top end of the hall is separate, perhaps for the priest's housekeeper, an unusual arrangement for the date but an example of a division of household – or addition – which was to have many successors. Bayleaf, from Chiddingstone, Kent, is an example restored as far as possible to its original appearance at the Weald and Downland Museum. It is jettied to the front of both wings and to the end of the service wing. It mainly dates from *c*.1400-1405, according to tree-ring analysis, but the service end was added in *c*.1500-1515, replacing a pre-1400 wing. The house is thus an example of so-called 'alternate' development, whereby in successive building campaigns first one section and then another is alternately rebuilt. At the solar end it had a garderobe (or latrine) in a small projecting chamber with a wooden seat over a shaft which led down to a cesspit. This was probably a rare amenity.

Aisled Halls
Unlike the component features of the purlin and the crown post, the Wealden house could not be combined in the same building with the outgoing aisled plan but superseded it outright when it was adopted. The aisled plan nevertheless persisted strongly in some areas and actually spread to others at the yeoman level in the fourteenth century. It was especially favoured in East Anglia.

Edgar's Farm, probably of the 1340s, has already been mentioned. As late as around 1500 an aisled hall was built at Depden Green, Suffolk.

Hafod, at Llansilin, Clwyd, is the only fully aisled house known in Wales.

In the north of England, aisled halls at the level of the manor house had arrived by the beginning of the fourteenth century. The earliest known example is Elland Hall, in West Yorkshire, no longer surviving, which has been dated to around 1300.

Even on the home territory of the Wealden in Sussex and Kent aisled halls were being erected throughout the fourteenth century, and even as late as the 1460s.

Aisle Substitutes

By 1300, several ideas for removing the obstructive aisle posts while retaining the grandeur of the aisled roof were being devised.

One method was to support the aisle truss on a long tie-beam, in what is termed raised-aisle construction. It was being used for manor houses in Essex before 1300, and in the period after the Black Death of 1348-50 reached the modest level of White Cottage, Wacton, Norfolk. This had the service and chamber bays in simple linear extension to the two-bay hall, without cross-wings or jetties – a plan common to many small hall houses in and around East Anglia.

A second method was that of the hammer beam, in which both the aisle posts and the middle part of the tie-beam were eliminated. This system was used in Pilgrim's Hall, Winchester, *c*.1290, but during the fourteenth century it was used only for a few manors and for inns and large houses in Salisbury, such as 9 Queen Street of *c*.1306, the home of a wool merchant. It was also used for some

Left: Hammer-beam roof:
9 Queen Street, Salisbury;
c.1306 (RCHME)

Right: Raised aisle roof:
White Cottage, Wacton,
Norfolk; c.1350+

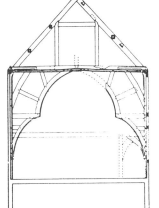

royal buildings, culminating in the new roof for Westminster Hall of 1394-1401. It occurred sporadically in the fifteenth century, and in Wales the rare examples date from between c.1485 and c.1600.

Spere Trusses and Base Crucks

A third method of modifying the aisled hall was by intruding a base cruck in place of the aisle truss in the middle of the hall, while retaining the one at the lower end of the hall, in the form of a so-called spere truss.

Base crucks are a variant on the ordinary full crucks discussed in the previous chapter. They stand on the ground, but reach not to the apex of the roof, but only to collar level, above which rises a subordinate truss. Base crucks made it possible to obtain extra span while avoiding the obstruction of the arcade post of the aisled plan – particularly desirable if the size of the hall was modest. The earliest instance of their adoption seems to have been for alternate trusses in an otherwise aisled barn at Siddington, Gloucestershire, perhaps as early as c.1220.

The spere truss is an aisled truss at the lower end of the hall which is made into a screen by panelling closing the two aisles. One in isolation was at the Bury, at Clavering in Essex, dated to the early or mid-thirteenth century. The earliest case of the combination of base cruck and spere may have been the much-mutilated Chennels Brook Farm, Horsham, Sussex, which has been tentatively dated to the end of the thirteenth century, partly on the basis of a filled-in window that has neat chamfering to the jambs, head and sill and an octagonal central mullion with well-moulded cap and base. This house, however, is an unusual compromise, because it had a single aisle truss between the base cruck truss and the spere truss. At the upper end it had a cross-wing (one end of which was later removed, along with the aisles, the remaining fabric being encased in brick).

In the Yorkshire countryside base crucks were used in what seem to have been among the first durable houses at the level of manor house (or similar status), around 1300.

The combination of base cruck and spere truss came to be especially favoured in the Midlands and the neighbouring parts of Wales.

Chennels Brook Farm, Horsham, Sussex; perhaps end of the thirteenth century (H = hall, A = aisle, S = service); spere walls screen the doors (after R. T. Mason)

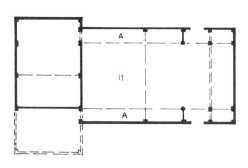

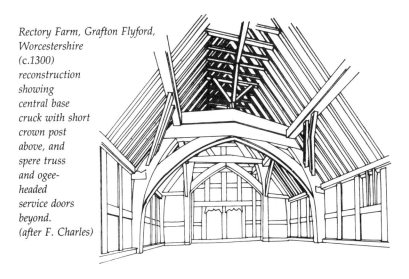

Rectory Farm, Grafton Flyford, Worcestershire (c.1300) reconstruction showing central base cruck with short crown post above, and spere truss and ogee-headed service doors beyond. (after F. Charles)

Ornate Roofs

Particularly associated with the combination of base cruck and spere truss was the ornate roof. From about 1350 the embellishment of roofs with cusped wind-bracing blossomed in the West Midlands, subsequently spreading to smaller houses, and across the Welsh border. (Wind-braces are diagonal timbers between purlins and principal rafters, stiffening the roof. Cusps are the sharp angles between adjoining curves.) This embellishment has been held to reflect the Decorated style, which had burgeoned from the end of the 1290s (though the not dissimilar Perpendicular style arose from around 1330 too, if not before). Hafod is a good example (see figure, page 38), but much less grand houses could boast a treatment not so inferior.

Small Houses

By the end of the century, lesser yeomen were beginning to build hall houses (that is, houses with an open chamber approaching two-storey height). Even the poor widow in Chaucer's 'Nun's Priest's Tale' had a hall. This might have been like the two-bay hall that was the original Crofton Farm, Orpington, Greater London, dated to shortly after the Black Death. The bays here, of unequal size, were separated by a moulded octagonal crown post. There were a large number of small hall houses at this date in East Anglia, including White Cottage, Wacton (page 41).

Wall-Framing

Surviving wall-framing is scarce. Large panels continued to be the norm. Often there were no braces; when present, braces were usually large. In the Weald, braces were now curved, but the braces on Lady Row of 1316 are straight or only slightly curved, though those on other fourteenth-century York buildings are

39 The Causeway, Steventon (mid fourteenth century); cruck-framed hall and box-framed cross-wing

curved. The front of Lady Row has both head and foot bracing, the rear only foot bracing, showing that bracing was at least partly for show. The studs are widely spaced: three per bay. Sometimes upward and downward bracing were combined to produce a St Andrew's Cross, as at 47-9 New Canal, Salisbury, probably of *c.*1330, or the mid-fourteenth century 39 The Causeway, Steventon, Oxfordshire.

Both these last houses retain their bargeboards (diagonal boards applied to gables), the cusped Salisbury ones being the only surviving medieval examples in the city. Other examples are scalloped or traceried.

Stone Houses

Stone had long had greater prestige than timber and now began to gain ground in the construction of smaller houses. This was to be seen in the two main English areas of good building stone, the limestone belt from Dorset through to Northamptonshire and the sandstone area of the north, the Yorkshire manor houses of which have already been mentioned. Its earliest manifestation was perhaps in Oxfordshire, where numerous smaller houses of the fourteenth century survive. Sometimes a transitional combination of stone ground floor and timber upper parts is found. For instance, several houses in Burford have stone doorways evidently reused from such part-masonry predecessors.

Rural First-Floor Hall Houses

One of the few known examples of rural first-floor hall-houses is the remarkably intact Lodge Farm, Pamphill, Dorset, probably dating from the close of the century. It is thought to have been a house with the specialised function of hunting lodge, though the accommodation is conventional.

It is built of ironstone rubble, with limestone dressings, and has a three-bay arch-braced collar truss roof, with ridge piece and side purlins. Open to this roof were a two-bay hall and a solar beyond a massively framed panelled partition (now altered). A winding

Lodge Farm, Pamphill, Dorset (probably late fourteenth century) (RCHME)

stair in the thickness of the front wall, lit from the narrow window, debouched into the hall. At the rear was a latrine turret. A four-centre-headed door survives, together with the hall fireplace (originally probably the only one, the ground floor being used for storage or service rooms and the kitchen being detached).

Town Houses
In the fourteenth century most houses in towns throughout Britain were still timber-framed; but perhaps even more widely than in the previous century, cellars and party walls (at least up to first-floor level) were often of stone, and sometimes so were other elements of the structure. At 8 Purfleet Street, King's Lynn, the outer walls were of stone. In London and elsewhere a fashion lasted through into the fifteenth century for a combination of chalk and flint in a chequerwork pattern. The infill to timber-framing was usually lath or wattle and plaster, but sometimes stone was used – in York, for instance.

Even at the beginning of the century, many houses in London were of three storeys, or two storeys with garrets; this was the case, too, in main streets in some other towns, though in York the surviving 54-60 Stonegate was exceptional in having three storeys early in the century. The top floor nearly everywhere was open to the roof; garrets were added only in the sixteenth century.

Ground-Floor Halls in Towns: By now it begins to be possible to generalise about the planning of houses in towns. The more substantial town houses consisted, like those in the country, of an open hall with two sets of storeyed chambers attached to it. The hall could be aligned to the street, with the chambers behind it, or one storeyed section could face the street and the other lie at the rear end of the hall.

In general, larger houses were parallel to the streets and smaller ones at right-angles; the proportion of the latter tended to increase as towns got more crowded and plots were divided and subdivided. There was, however, much variation between towns. In York, the parallel plan seems to have been standard till around 1400; Stamford was similar. In Oxford, the late thirteenth or early fourteenth-century Tackley's Inn had a series of small shops in front of the parallel hall-and-chamber range.

On the other hand, the right-angled layout was standard in several other towns that have been investigated, such as Southampton, Exeter and King's Lynn. The early fourteenth-century Medieval Merchant's House, at 58 French Street, Southampton, is an example restored for public viewing by English Heritage. Built in c.1290, it was remodelled after 1338. Its hall was on the elevated ground floor, with a shop in front and chamber behind, more shop space in the undivided stone undercroft and chambers front and rear on the upper storey, linked across the hall by the gallery.

A compromise between the basic parallel and right-angled types was to set the hall at right-angles to the street, but to have the chambers forming a cross-wing to the hall parallel to the street. A

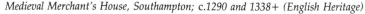

Medieval Merchant's House, Southampton; c.1290 and 1338+ (English Heritage)

narrow couryard alongside the hall was reached usually by a passage running through the side of the front section, which contained shops below and solar above. Such a plan is found in King's Lynn houses. There, the ground floor in the shop section tended to be very tall and sometimes entirely open to the street. Beyond the hall, within the same walls and separated only by a partition, there often lay warehousing or workshops. There were also likely to be other outbuildings such as kitchens in the depth of the plot. An early fourteenth-century example is 8 Purfleet Street. This had both ancillary units at the street end, with the section between the shops and the hall jettied into the latter.

Another variant was to have the hall lengthwise along the street, with a gable-fronted cross-wing alongside, as at 47-9 New Canal, Salisbury. This contained on the ground floor both the screens passage and a carriageway through into the courtyard behind. It includes two rare fourteenth-century windows with trefoiled ogee heads to the lights.

Yet another type was the courtyard house, with ancillary rooms facing the street and the hall at the back of the yard, but this is in the category of mansion.

In London no small or middling fourteenth-century houses survive, but much archaeological and documentary evidence has been marshalled to shed light on domestic architecture. Somewhat grander houses still possessed a ground-floor hall, sometimes stone-built, with a fine roof and no rooms over it. An example is provided by a lease of 1384 which specifies a front range with a ground storey 12 feet (3.7 metres) high, the first floor 10 feet and the third floor 7 feet; behind were to be a hall 40 feet by 23 feet (12 metres by 7 metres), a parlour, kitchen and buttery, all over a cellar 7 feet (2.1 metres) high, designated for storage.

Towards the end of the century the introduction in the towns of a new type of room was an indication of growing wealth and desire for privacy: the parlour, a place for conversation (related to the French *parler*, to speak). Chaucer writes of a 'parlour' in his *Troilus and Criseyde* of c.1374. In London it was a reception room, not used for sleeping in and usually on the ground floor.

Urban Kitchens and Chimneys: Kitchens were still often in separate buildings, even in the case of modest houses like the range of five built shortly before 1390 in Abchurch Lane, London, where the kitchens were in a continuous range across the backs of two tiny yards (divided by a wall), according to a plan of 1612. Number 8 Purfleet Street, King's Lynn also seems to have had a detached kitchen. As chimneys were increasingly introduced, however, separate kitchens probably became less frequent. As early as 1308, a London skinner planned to build a chimneyed room onto his hall house, with a larder next to it and a solar above.

In London, chimneys were supposed to be built in masonry, but tiles and flat bricks, which were beginning to be exported from

Flanders, were alternatives. In 1370 a range of eighteen shops on the corner of Godliman Street and Knightrider Street each had a chimney, all paired except for those at the ends. One stimulus to the building of chimneys was the gradual spread of the burning of coal from industry to houses during the fourteenth century.

Chimneys also enabled kitchens to be moved upstairs. By 1400 in London the kitchen was often next to the hall on the first floor, with adjoining service rooms that seem to have been little more than cupboards. Shops were often let separately from the house above and behind.

Upstairs Halls in Towns: So now, in London, the hall was generally a first-floor room, often directly over the shop, as mentioned in a building contract of 1310 and a will of 1328. In these cases the hall began to merge with the solar, which might be used as a workshop, instanced in a legal case of 1300.

In a smaller city like Exeter, house types were not so very different. The middling house without open hall, and usually gable-fronted, was established well before 1300 and was very common by the later fifteenth century. These houses were of two or three storeys, with one large or two small rooms on each floor. Often they had a cellar, which was frequently only partially below ground. The ground floor was generally open to the street. A chimney stack was situated in the rear or side wall.

Tenement Ranges: Rows of smaller houses were now common, at least in larger towns. An early surviving example is Lady Row, Goodramgate, in York, dating from 1316, already cited for its crown posts and its jetty. It was built as a range of tenements eleven bays long and two storeys high. The tenements were of one bay each, except for one or possibly two double-bay tenements. The ground-floor room in the single-bay houses is 5 metres by 4 metres (16 feet by 13 feet). There were no chimneys, so heating must have been by braziers, and cooked food must have been obtained from shops with hearths or ovens.

Four similar rows were built elsewhere in York within a generation. At one of these – St Martin's Row, Coney Street – louvres are specified in the contract of 1335.

Another example of integrated development is Middle Row, Watling Street, Dunstable, dated by means of dendrochronology to as early as c.1310-20. This has a back-to-back plan, foreshadowing the nineteenth century. Consisting of two ranges of four houses, all gable-fronted, it took advantage of an island site. It may have been a rare arrangement.

Poorer Urban Housing: In London small houses had no hall, only a shop and a kitchen, and many shops had only one storey over them, and might have only two rooms in all. As in the country, evidence of yet poorer housing has hardly survived, but in Lower

Brook Street, Winchester, a row of single-room houses with mud walls has been excavated; they had a hearth in one corner and a sleeping area screened off in another.

Staircases in Towns: The evidence for staircases in towns is sparse. In London, only larger houses seem to have had newel stairs of wood or stone; documentary sources suggest that others had to make do with ladders: from which people fell to their deaths from time to time, even though ropes were often provided. However, London can scarcely have been worse provided than other towns, where stairs seem not to have been limited to larger houses. In Exeter, for instance, middling houses had stairs in a rear corner, usually in the form of open steps. Only humbler houses were reduced to ladders. As in London, grander houses had winding stairs. The modest Dunstable range previously mentioned also had staircases; unusually, we know the position: against the party wall at the backs of the houses.

Urban Sanitation, Drainage and Water Supply: In London, cesspits, previously made of timber, tended by the fourteenth century to be stone-built. With space at a greater premium, privies were more frequently indoors, often in or off the solar and usually served by a chute in the party wall, lined with boards. A house mentioned in 1360 had two privies; perhaps this was common.

Rainwater drains often ran through houses, especially through the kitchen, but downpipes do not seem to have been used; gulleys betwen roof spans, lined with lead, wood or possibly shaped tiles, simply led water to spouts.

By 1350, a number of houses in London seem to have been connected with the city's piped water supply, which mainly served the public conduits from which most people took their water in pails, though some houses had cisterns to store rainwater and many had their own wells.

Details, Urban and Rural
Throughout the earlier fourteenth century, doorheads were usually still two-centred, as at Humphreys, Lindfield, Sussex, which has been dated to the first third of the century. The ogee (double curve) was an alternative brought in with the Decorated style. From the mid-1380s, however, starting at the grander level, the four-centred arch began to come in with the spread of the Perpendicular style. There was a good deal of overlap and at Exeter, for instance, doorways might be either two-centred or four-centred, the latter being considered more impressive.

Occasionally, timber houses had windows that rose above the standard diagonal bars to the luxury of traceried heads, as at 9 Queen Street, Salisbury, of c.1306 (see page 41) or The Lodge, Pamphill, of c.1390 (page 45). Rarely, panelwork across the top end of the hall was similarly treated, as at Humphreys. Rather more often, the dais beam was given decorative carving, or at least a moulding – a hollow at Bayleaf for instance.

Outside London, where tiles were now standard, thatch was generally still the normal roof covering, though tiles were also widespread in Kent, and in some places local supplies of stone flags were available for some of the more substantial houses.

Ceiling beams were sometimes moulded, though in the Weald, prosperous though the area was, this was not the custom. Exeter shows the variety of materials that could be employed: in the 1390s one house had partitioning and wainscoting of oak, elm, poplar and deal from Riga. In London boarding was now commonly of deal. For wall coverings, painted cloths were introduced, at least in grander houses, by the fourteenth century.

THE FIFTEENTH CENTURY

The fifteenth century was not one of startling changes in domestic architecture. In tune with the Decorated and Perpendicular styles in church architecture, however, timber-framed houses were modified in this century by the rise of decorative wall-framing, especially close-studding, and the related blossoming of the ornate roof interior and of the Wealden house. The century was also notable for the spread of large numbers of well-built farmhouses to the south-west and some areas of the north.

The Expansion in Devon

This century is the first to which surviving houses in Devon below the level of manor can be securely ascribed. Smoke-blackening of remnants of original thatch show many existing farmhouses to have started as open halls, even though they have since been altered in almost every respect. Since dating is difficult, some may be pre-fifteenth century. Certainly fifteenth-century roofs survive in large numbers. What was characteristic of Devon was that the walls were usually of cob and that the rooms were often divided from one another by screens which were only slightly higher than the doorheads.

Down to the eighteenth century, cob was the usual walling material in Devon and the neighbouring parts of Somerset and Dorset, except on and around Exmoor, where granite was readily available. Cob was made of clay or sand subsoil, usually with an admixture of straw or dung, and laid in layers above a stone plinth. It was protected from the weather by lime render or wash.

The screen partitions in Devon usually served to form a through-passage between the opposed doorways of the hall. They also usually divided off an unheated inner room at the top end of the hall and an unheated service room below the passage. Sometimes the partitions were not head-height but extended up to the roof.

Devon roofs were generally of cruck construction, most com-

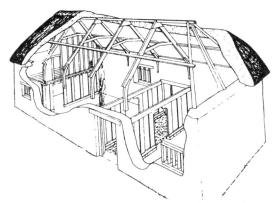

A typical fifteenth-century Devon farmhouse, with head-height plank and muntin partitions, internal jetty and jointed-cruck roof (Brian Blakeway)

monly the jointed type, though full crucks were also frequent. A jointed cruck is one formed of a wall-post and a principal rafter, joined at eaves level.

In Devon, jointed crucks sometimes rise, not from ground level but close to eaves level, thus constituting a raised cruck. The wall-post is then merely a short stump. A standard Devon feature was the end-cruck, supporting each end of the roof ridge and giving the roof a hipped form.

Cornwall

Cob was sometimes used in Cornwall, especially for upper floors, but by the fifteenth century, if not before, granite or slate were the normal material for houses. An early representative house is the Old Post Office at Tintagel, which was probably built as a small manor house (and became a Post Office in the nineteenth century). It is of classic open-hall plan, with the chamber at the left-hand end and service room at the right-hand end, but the opposed doors were not merely screened from the hall, there was a solid wall creating a separate through-passage.

The house had a fireplace rather than an open hearth though former indications of smoke-blackening could point to an originally open hearth. Having a fireplace at this date was a sign of superior status; so was its 'lateral' position (i.e. on the *side* of the hall). It is the shouldered jambs supporting the massive slate lintel which help to suggest an early fifteenth-century date for the house. The chamber also had a fireplace, but the service room was originally unheated. The hall is extended forward into a bay next to the chimney in a West Country fashion. The two-storey bay next to it,

Tintagel Old Post Office, Cornwall, early fifteenth century

lighting the chamber, and the room over it, is a Tudor addition. At the back of the house is a winding stair in a turret. The roof, bearing its heavy burden of slate slabs, consists of raised crucks with cambered collars. Crucks, however, were rare in Cornwall. The timbers, like the massive walls, are rough; Cornwall was not a wealthy area.

Smoke Bays, Smoke Hoods and Northern Aisled Halls

Prohibitions show that poorer houses in towns often had timber chimneys. Rural houses began in the late fifteenth century to have a spacious variant on this: a smoke bay. The hall was floored over except for a short bay at the end, in which the smoke still rose to escape through the roof in the normal way. In the early sixteenth century many houses in the south seem to have been built with them and they became common in the midlands.

The smoke hood of the north was similar, but sloped inwards to a gable chimney. It was adopted to the exclusion of the open hearth by the lesser gentry and yeomen at least from the time they began to build durably in the mid-fifteenth century.

There is evidence of smoke hoods in the aisled halls built in the Halifax area, probably near the end of the fifteenth century, by yeomen prosperous from sheep and textiles. Aisled halls thus spread to this new class from the gentry just when they were dying out in the south. Some were double-aisled, but the majority were single-aisled (and easier to light). The aisles were probably used for service functions, leaving free the room at the lower end of the hall for textile work or storage. Generally they were partitioned off, and had a cross-wing at the lower end. The roofs were usually king-post. Many had a dais canopy. All seem to have had a cross-passage beyond the smoke hood, which was to be the standard northern plan.

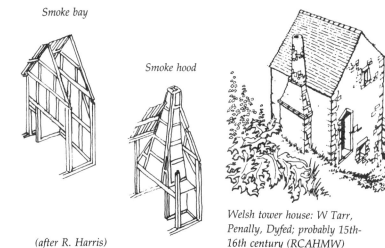

Smoke bay

Smoke hood

(after R. Harris)

Welsh tower house: W Tarr, Penally, Dyfed; probably 15th-16th century (RCAHMW)

Roof Types

Crucks were the dominant roof type in eastern Wales between the Black Death and around 1570. Plas Ucha, Llangar, Gwynnedd, of 1400, and of mixed cruck and box-frame structure, is a splendid example of the ornate carpentry lavished on houses of quite small size during this period. In England, by the mid-fifteenth century, crucks were being given up by the upper classes but were still spreading among the middling. Raised crucks were being adopted for the halls of lesser people by the later fifteenth century.

For box frame houses the crown post continued to be popular, and was standard in fifteenth-century Wealden houses and in York.

After around 1400 the king post roof became a predominantly northern type, among vernacular houses almost wholly so.

Wall Framing

Large framing continued to be the commonest type before the mid-fifteenth century, and had the widest distribution. A complete absence of bracing occurs at Tiptofts, in Wimbush, Essex, c.1300, but this is the only certain example. By contrast, St Andrew's Cross bracing was widespread, being found for instance at York, in Essex and in Hampshire. Angle bracing was now the standard treatment, either in the form of head (or arch) bracing, at the head of the panel, or of foot (or tension) bracing, at the foot of the panel (or occasionally both together). Footbracing was commoner in the south-east and East Anglia, and in towns, headbracing elsewhere. Multiple diagonal (or herringbone) bracing also occurred (see figure overleaf).

Square framing (also known as small framing) was introduced in the fifteenth century, spreading from the west. It was to become standard except in East Anglia (see figure, page 73). It generally consisted of two panels to each storey (or three up to the eaves).

Close studding spread in the fifteenth century. It is likely that it originated in the properous south-east, and certainly it became most widespread there. Prodigal in its use of timber, it was very much a feature of display and never spread to houses of modest character. A very early example is The 'Medieval Merchant's House', Southampton, as remodelled after 1338. An early rural case is Durham House, Great Bardfield, Essex, dated to the late fourteenth century, where it is combined with St Andrew's Cross and parallel bracing. By 1497 an Italian traveller, Andreas Franciscus, wrote that 'very many mansions' in London were close-studded.

Close studding was particularly popular in East Anglia, where there are notable examples from the end of the fifteenth century at Lavenham. Little Hall there, which has a typical East Anglian layout of solar cross-wing and service rooms in line at the other end, has a combination of herringbone bracing and close-studding (see overleaf). It was not much favoured in middle southern England (Wessex) and in the west it had a mixed reception. It was

Little Hall, Lavenham, Suffolk; the left-hand gable-fronted cross-wing was probably built before 1400; the rest is late fifteenth century

extremely rare on cruck framing. In Exeter in late fifteenth-century houses it appears in a modified form, with wider intervals than elsewhere. At the small manor house of Lower Brockhampton, Herefordshire, it is applied rather half-heartedly to parts of the frontage. It is used on the Wealden houses of Coventry and York, as well as most of those of the south.

The decorative rather than structural role of close studding is shown by the fact that it was often applied on the front of houses alone. This is confirmed by the way in which in the Weald it often consisted merely of boards, not true studs, and bracing was concealed behind it.

Stone-built First-Floor Halls

Examples of first-floor halls are even rarer than in the fourteenth century. An example is at Neadon, Manaton, Devon, and dates from as late as the end of the fifteenth century. It had a windowless ground floor and a first floor probably originally divided into hall and solar, with its own entrance. Surviving are a fireplace, garderobe and a small timber cinquefoil window. There are examples in south-west and north-east Wales (see figure, page 52). On the borders of England and Scotland a descendant of the first-floor hall house was the pele-house, very similar to the house at Manaton. Elsewhere in Scotland the type has an afterlife in the many houses where the staircase reached the first storey externally.

Details

Ceilings in rare cases were boarded, as they were in grander houses, having a gridwork of strip mouldings with mouldings at the intersections (for example, the late fifteenth-century Garrads House, Water Street, Lavenham, Suffolk). The main beams here are still unenclosed and these beams would often have moulded chamfers (see figure, page 63).

Panelled partitions took the form of overlapping planks or plank and muntin which also could have mouldings (see figure page 51). Panelling on the walls gradually extended from the level of royal palaces in the thirteenth century until in the country it reached the level of parsonages. Typical of the late fifteenth century were doorways which had three and four centred heads cut out of the solid wood, with sunk spandrels and moulded frame.

Town Houses

Plan Types: In York, houses at right-angles to the street only seem to have begun to be built in the fifteenth century, and never seem to have been the majority; they were usually three bays deep (9-12 metres, 30-40 feet). York houses were sometimes built as pairs, with twin gables, with one large room on each floor. Three-storey houses parallel to the street were very common. Houses were now always jettied to the front and sometimes to the rear.

A London contract of 1410 gives an idea of a modest house in the capital at that date: a shop on the ground floor; hall, larder and kitchen on the first floor; principal chamber, retiring room and privy on the second floor. A Bristol contract of 1472 was similar. Butcher's Row in Shrewsbury also had halls and living accommodation upstairs. At the end of the century, however, a Canterbury block of four houses specified shop, store, hall and kitchen on the ground floor; and a chamber reached by a stair from the hall on the upper floor.

The late fifteenth-century house in Exeter that used to be 16 Edmund Street, but has been moved, had a shop and kitchen in a ground floor area no more than 3 metres by 4.2 metres (10 feet by 14 feet); a hall on the first floor; two chambers on the second floor

16 Frog Street (ex-16 Edmund Street), Exeter (c.1500; windows later)

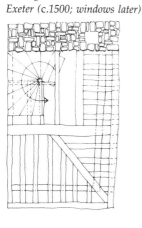

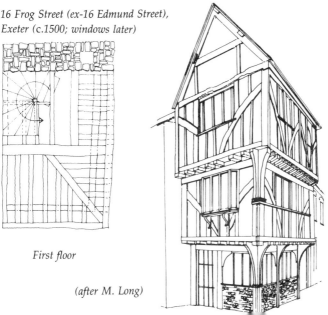

First floor

(after M. Long)

Spon Street, Coventry, a Wealden range in the town (c.1450)

and a cockloft in the gable. A row of similar small houses in Church Street, Tewkesbury has been restored and one unit reconstructed and opened as a tiny museum. Part of the ground floor is open to the roof and contains an open hearth (i.e. forms a smoke bay); over the rest is a chamber and a garret.

Open halls, already beginning to disappear in the cities in the previous century, were now on the wane in quite small towns, like Burford in Oxfordshire. Here the majority of smaller houses were now tall and narrow, with a back and front room on each floor: for instance London House, which followed the common pattern in having a stone-built ground floor and timber-framed rooms above.

Wealden Houses: The Wealden house was adapted to town use in the fifteenth century in many different places. From the south-east it spread as far as York, Stratford and Yeovil. It was perhaps most suited to hall houses at right-angles to the front range, as may be seen in Goodramgate in York, which has a cross-wing facing the street. At Spon Street, Coventry, it is used lengthwise, however. Here, several houses have been restored to something like their medieval appearance. In the area round the Weald, where the type was most popular, it is found in quite small towns. The longest Wealden range of all is at Battle, dating from 1460/77.

Scotland

Little is known about ordinary-sized houses in Scotland at this date. In the countryside there were almost certainly no houses of a standard between primitive dwellings and the tower houses of the lairds. In the town, even the houses of the wealthy were still only of two storeys at the end of the fifteenth century, the ground storey being used for storage and commercial purposes, like the first-floor hall houses of earlier periods in England.

3 THE STOREYED, CHIMNEYED HOUSE

It was in the sixteenth and seventeenth centuries that the open hearth gave way to the chimneyed fireplace and the open hall house was replaced by a house that was two-storeyed throughout. The new chimneys were often brick, and in the seventeenth century the use of brick also became widespread for complete houses of ordinary size. In the same century, window glass became normal for most houses.

These were great improvements; moreover, this was the period when, over most parts of England, durable houses were put up for the first time. This great wave of building was christened, by W. G. Hoskins, the 'Great Rebuilding'. Since he wrote, it has inevitably been shown that the rebuilding was not quite so dramatic as he had suggested and occurred in different parts at more dispersed periods; but it remains important to note that the great mass of houses to be seen was not the result of an even development over the centuries, but was largely produced in surges of economic growth (and no doubt, too, surges of mutual emulation between neighbours), with the focus of architectural activity moving from one area of another as the decades passed.

In the south-east, a great rebuilding had already taken place in the fifteenth century, in the form especially of the huge numbers of Wealden houses, but around 1500 there was another surge, largely consisting of the remodelling and casing of the existing stock; this accelerated after 1570 and continued till 1700.

For most of England, however, it was only from the later sixteenth century onwards that a 'great rebuilding' began. W. G. Hoskins based his thesis especially on the Midlands, where the rebuilding took place between 1570 and 1680. In Devonshire there was intensified building activity from around 1575. In the Lancashire Pennines, substantial numbers of yeomen houses were built from the early seventeenth century onwards. By the early eighteenth century the wave of building had largely accomplished its work; progress on the Yorkshire side of the Pennines and in the Vale of York was similar. In the Lake District, rebuilding took off not long after 1600 and lasted till nearly the middle of the eighteenth century; it is striking that the large majority of surviving farmhouses fall within those limits. In large parts of the north, however, the wave of rebuilding was from 1660 onwards. In the East Riding it surged only after 1770 and in Northumberland it had barely begun at the end of the eighteenth century.

In Wales, the Great Rebuilding spread from east to west, beginning around 1485 and reaching Cardiganshire only in the nineteenth century. Scotland's Great Rebuilding also took place later, towards the end of the eighteenth century and the early nineteenth.

1500-1575

This period saw the introduction of chimneys and the flooring over of open halls in most ordinary houses. The two developments almost always went hand in hand, because now that smoke no longer needed to escape through the roof, there was every reason to gain an extra room over the hall. Moreover, status lay now not with an ornate open roof, but with a conspicuous new chimney or an ornate fireplace. Along with the introduction of chimneys and the flooring over of halls went the widespread adoption of the through-passage plan and of horizontal mullioned windows.

Introduction of the Chimney

Chimneys were common in towns long before 1500; from the beginning of the sixteenth century they proliferated in the country too, following the example of the houses of the aristocracy. The yeomen farmers of the south-east led the way, as ever. A contract for a house in Kent of 1500 specified two fireplaces back to back under one chimney (and an upper storey throughout). Some houses were built with chimneys but still had an open hall. Generally, however, flooring over was introduced simultaneously.

In the Weald there were no chimneys in framed houses before 1500. The earliest were entirely of timber except for the stone fireback and perhaps a few courses of brick at the top; on average one fifth of the area of the house was taken up by the new feature. Generally, chimneys were of brick, but west Cambridgeshire was one area where clunch (chalk blocks) was often used in timber-framed houses.

Chimneys spread westwards fairly rapidly. They reached Wales in around 1560; an early example in Staffordshire of a brick stack dates likewise from 1560. The combination of four flues in one stack began in London in around 1550. It spread as far as Wales only at the end of the seventeenth century.

The Through-Passage Plan

At first, chimneys were inserted in many different positions: at the top end of the hall, on a side wall (termed 'lateral'), midway between the opposed doors at the low end of the hall – or backing onto the space between the doors, which was thus fixed as a through-passage. It was this last 'hearth-passage plan' that became dominant everywhere except the south-east, where it had first been adopted but now disappeared with the end of the open hall which prompted its use elsewhere. It was natural that chimneys were generally inserted at the lower ends of halls, so that the cooking could be done away from the owners at the table at the high end, and presumably conservatism that the traditional opposed doors of the open hall were usually retained.

Three areas were resistant to the hearth-passage plan. In the south-east the back to back fireplace plan (specified in the contract of 1500) became standard from *c.*1550. In East Anglia, the chimney was sometimes placed away from the passage in small houses, and in three-unit houses there was never a passage at the back of the chimney because there was a fireplace in that position heating the second room, there being no structural advantage in the second chimney being located at the gable in a timber-framed house. The third area that went its own way was Cornwall, and the south-west to a limited extent. There, a position on the front wall was preferred.

In the Severn Vale, the through-passage plan became rare by 1630. About half the cases there were conversions rather than new houses. By the late sixteenth century, most yeomen houses in the area had two fireplaces, and many had a heated parlour too, sited at the top end of the hall. Below the passage there was a service room or kitchen, which had a fireplace or was given one later. Lateral chimneys, aping the usual position in the houses of the aristocracy, were occasionally adopted, either in the front or the rear wall. This seems to have been the favoured position in the first yeomen houses of which we have knowledge in the Lancashire Pennines, both for chimneys and the alternative smoke-hoods. Around Halifax, however, both were positioned axially.

Wales
Chimney insertion began in the mid-fifteenth century in grand houses in Wales and in the mid-sixteenth century in smaller houses; in grand houses the chimney was positioned on a side wall, in smaller houses three main plan types emerged when chimneys and upper floors began to be inserted. The first type has the chimney at the gable, usually with the stair winding up beside it and a through-passage away from the gable. It is common in Snowdonia, and the former Pembrokeshire. Y Garreg from Waunfawr, near Caernarfon, of *c.*1570 has been re-erected at St Fagan's open-air museum. The second type has a lateral chimney heating the main room, and a through-passage away from it, with

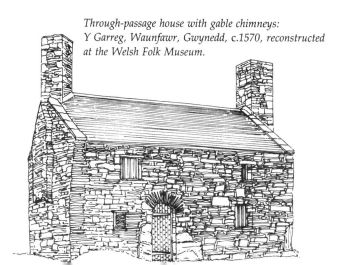

Through-passage house with gable chimneys:
Y Garreg, Waunfawr, Gwynedd, c.1570, reconstructed
at the Welsh Folk Museum.

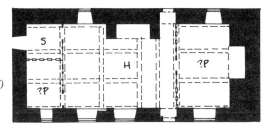

Through-passage, lateral-chimney house; Plasneywydd, Llanfair Talhaearn, Clwyd; 1585 (P = parlour; after RCAHMW)

either the service rooms or a parlour below the through-passage (if there is a third unit). The earliest dated storeyed lateral-chimney house seems to be of 1571 (and the latest, 1722). The third type has the chimney backing on the through-passage in the English manner, again with service rooms below the passage or at the top end of the house. This type is much commoner in the south than the north. The earliest dated example is of 1589, in Denbighshire. It is extremely rare in Caernarvonshire and Pembrokeshire, and unknown in Anglesey. A fourth type is a minor one. It has the entry in the gable, either next to the chimney or with the chimney in the opposite gable. It is confined to two-unit and one-unit houses in south-east Wales.

Aisled Halls
The earlier pattern of aisled hall in the Halifax area was still common in the mid-sixteenth century, and possibly even later, when open-hall houses of all types were dying out.

The Horizontal Window
With the flooring over of the open hall, the proportions of the main room in the house were transformed, in a manner conducive to horizontal rather than vertical windows. This was especially the case with stone-built houses, which were given long windows with wooden or stone mullions.

In the Severn Vale one unglazed window, dating from the sixteenth century or earlier, survives to show the most widespread type for stone houses. It has square-set wooden mullions, chamfered, with step stops. Stone mullions were just beginning to appear in non-gentry houses in this area in the sixteenth century, with hollow chamfers; a king mullion and four-centred arches, generally a dating feature for the sixteenth century, were occasionally set over windows. Transoms (horizontal bars) also became popular in the sixteenth century. In Gwent and the nearby parts of Herefordshire, wooden windows with diamond-set mullions were standard for farmhouses between 1550 and c.1610 in combination with rubble walls. These windows were still unglazed. In the Weald even quite small houses had window mouldings in the sixteenth century; there was also an increase in the number of lights and in the overall size of windows. In the Lancashire

Pennines, windows were often deeply recessed and in the important rooms usually had arched lights.

The Enlargement of Yeomen Houses
The south-east led not only in the introduction of chimneys but also in terms of size. Three-cell houses there were widespread; elsewhere in the south and west they were rare before 1600 and two-cell houses were standard. No open halls seem to have been built in the Severn Vale after 1550. Many in an arc from Devon to Warwickshire were single-cell. Beyond that, it is perhaps too easy to assume that the lack of surviving smaller houses indicates that, among the non-gentry, primitive dwellings were universal outside the towns. In the north, multiple storeys were only common in smaller houses after 1660. Storeyed houses arrived in the East Riding of Yorkshire only in the early eighteenth century and in Northumberland only in the late eighteenth century. In the relatively prosperous Vale of York, however, documentary evidence shows that a fair number of well-built two-storey houses were put up before the end of the sixteenth century.

On the Lancashire Pennines members of the lesser gentry were building stone houses by the mid-sixteenth century; probably some yeoman did too, though probably not with mortar.

Crucks
Crucks seemed to have ceased to be common in Wales just after the mid-sixteenth century, while by contrast they became common in the north of England only in the seventeenth and eighteenth centuries.

Box Frames
The flooring over of the hall could be advertised externally by running the jetties of end-sections right across the front. In the earlier sixteenth century this 'continuous jetty' is found in many

Continuous jetty at Tudor House, King Street, Margate; c.1525 (Tudor House Museum)

superior smaller houses across the south, especially in towns and villages. Often the jetty was now faced with a moulded board. The roofs of such houses were usually crown-post still. From the mid-sixteenth century, however, the jetty began to decline in popularity. In Wales the box frame was only becoming common as the sixteenth century began.

Roofs

With the introduction of upper chambers over the hall, crown posts and king posts alike became obstructive; ceasing to be visible from the hall, they also lost their ornamental function. Instead, therefore, the side purlin method of longitudinal stiffening was gradually standard from the early sixteenth century onwards. Two different systems were favoured. In cruck and former king post

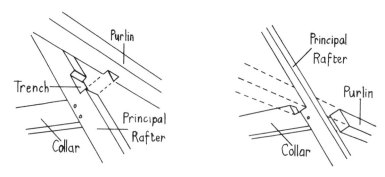

Side purlin: (a) laid in or trenched, (b) clasped, (after R. Harris)

areas, the purlins tended to be laid onto or into the outside of the principal timbers, whereas in former crown post areas the purlins tended to be clasped between the collars and principals or tenoned ('butted') into principals. In the Midlands both systems were used.

In the Weald, the introduction of garrets was an additional reason for the abandoment of crown posts, which took place around 1540. After a brief period of queen post trusses, cross-ties above the level of the tie beam were discontinued and the framed-rafter butt-purlin roof reigned till 1700, if not longer.

Wall-framing

Large framing became rare everywhere from around 1550, though examples occur into the eighteenth century. In the Weald close-studding continued up to the end of the century. Meanwhile, mainly in the west (and not at all in the north-east) close-studding with a middle rail became common from around 1500. Ogee (or wavy) braces were an alternative, favoured, for instance, in London and the Weald from the mid sixteenth century and briefly in York towards the end of the century (see figure, page 69).

Stone Houses

In the sixteenth century the building of stone houses spread from the gentry to yeomen farmers, first in Devon and Gloucestershire; but it remained rare. At the end of the century, stone was even sporadically used in Sussex and neighbouring areas. In the Vale of Severn, however, stone seems always to have been used. Almost all houses were of rubble, either limestone or sandstone, and earth mortar was used throughout the century. Brick was used for chimneys, however.

Similarly, in the upland areas of western Wales and the Lake District, it is an open question whether timber houses preceded the surviving ones, all of stone, from the sixteenth and seventeenth centuries.

Doors

Everywhere four-centred arches continued for doorways. In Gwent and the nearby parts of Herefordshire, for instance, they were standard for doorways of farmhouses between 1550 and c.1610. In the Weald the depressed four-centred arch persisted as late as 1630, but became ever flatter.

Interiors

In the Weald, lapped boarding and muntin and plank (or post and panel) partitions became widespread at the top end of the hall (the dais partition). On the hall side lapped boarding was occasionally given shallow moulding, and the posts of post and panel partitions were chamfered and often moulded; the panels were moulded sometimes. In Wales, Devon and other areas, plank and muntin partitions were standard through the sixteenth century. In Wales guilloche-moulded partitions can be fairly closely dated between 1570 and 1591. In the Severn Vale partitions were of stud and lath and plaster, the studs usually being concealed and panels not being used.

Now that halls were floored over, ceiling beams become more important. Ornamental chamfers become important for a century and more. No very clear evolution of chamfers is found, but the Severn Vale is representative. There, in the sixteenth century, ceiling beams had deep chamfers of five inches or more; these sometimes had a plain run-out (at all dates); straight and diagonal stops are generally sixteenth-century; other varieties can also be seventeenth-century, except a straight bar stop, which is only found in the seventeenth century. Mouldings were not common, but two houses have a series of hollows and convex mouldings.

Stop chamfers:
(a) moulded,
(b) run-out with bar,
(c) lamb's tongue
(A. Quiney)

In richer areas like the south-east and East Anglia such multiple-moulded beams were common in the best farmhouses. Often in such houses joists remained very large, closely spaced and square or flat. In Wales in the later sixteenth century, and elsewhere also in superior farmhouses, counterchanged joists were favoured: that is, joists at right-angles to the beams, with lesser joists crosswise to these, and sometimes yet smaller ones crosswise to these.

From early in the sixteenth century, walls at least sometimes had painted decoration. The main types in the Weald, in the approximate order of their use, were: black letter texts; pictorial decoration; imitation of wooden panelling or carving, and repetitive pattern. Naturally, very little survives, but there is a rare example of a complete plank and muntin partition at Cross Farm, Westhay, Somerset, which has been dated to the second half of the sixteenth century. By the same period it was an established practice in some areas to apply painted cloth to walls: a professional at this craft died in 1578 in Essex, and in the East Midlands even a labourer with little land had painted cloths by around 1596. Wallpaper (with stencilled decoration), is first recorded in 1509; it was no doubt slow to spread from the homes of the rich. Direct stencilling onto wall surfaces may have advanced more rapidly.

Most floors continued to be of earth, but in East Anglia, clay tiles (pamments) were introduced in the sixteenth century. In upper rooms boards might be loose and regarded as movable furnishing, as is shown by a 1597 will from Essex, which says that 'boards and planks in the garrets and upper chambers . . . nailed and unnailed [are to] to remain in the house'. Boards were sometimes laid parallel to the joists and even rebated between them so that the joists acted as alternate floorboards. Elm was the usual timber employed. Instead of boards, improbably, plaster was sometimes used, laid on laths, reeds or straw, especially in the East Midlands.

Fireplaces

By the sixteenth century, middling houses in stone-built areas had stone surrounds to fireplaces with a four-centred arch and chamfer. A scroll and hollow was the commonest moulding. Other houses had heavy wooden lintels, usually not chamfered. With the abandonment of open hearths, there was a need for an alternative means of curing bacon. In Somerset, parts of Devon, and Dorset, bacon-smoking chambers were often made beside fireplaces, drawing smoke from the fire and returning it to the flue above the chamber. Over one hundred survive.

Staircases

Ladders were superseded by stairs in the sixteenth century in relatively advanced areas, such as the Severn Vale. They were of both the winder and newel types, some constructed of stone with wooden risers and treads, others entirely of wood. In that area, in through-passage plans, the stairs were almost always placed in the rear wall of the hall, next to the door from the passage, but in other plans they could be almost anywhere – often in the end wall, next to the fireplace. In Gwent and the nearby parts of Herefordshire a winding staircase was standard from around 1550.

Stairs have very frequently been resited and sixteenth-century arrangements have to be inferred from a filled opening in the floor joists, the layout of partitions or sometimes from mid-height windows that originally lit staircases. In the Lancashire Pennines, such evidence indicates that by the late sixteenth century stairs were usually next to the parlour, though occasionally in the parlour wing or even perhaps rising from a lobby giving access to both parlour and service room. In smaller, two-cell houses the stair position is seldom identifiable; most probably these made do with ladders well into the seventeenth century.

The north: the sphere of the smoke-hood

In the north the through-passage plan, though in a few areas it faded in the seventeenth century, in general persisted right through to the eighteenth century; but it did so against a rather different background from that in the south. The north was not just economically behind the south, but in a different tradition in one important respect: non-gentry houses having a smoke hood rather than an open hearth. At Carlton Husthwaite, in the Vale of York, is the earliest surviving example. It consists of a converging structure of plastered timbers, supported in front of the hearth on a cross-beam (a bressumer), which funnels the smoke up to a chimney resting on corbels projecting from the back wall. There was therefore not the same need to switch to a full chimney, a change which was only made much later.

The backwardness of the north can be exaggerated. In the Vale of York timber was still one third the cost of stone in the early sixteenth century, though steadily rising, so it is unsurprising if non-gentry houses were timber-framed (such houses have survived hardly at all).

Longhouses

What must be regarded as a particular form of the through-passage plan was the developed longhouse of Devon, which had a byre on one side of the through-passage and the dwelling on the other, now built in good mortared masonry and with a full partition or wall between them. The earliest are later fifteenth-century, but are clearly in a continuous tradition with the thirteenth-century longhouses of Houndtor. The shippons (byres) now usually have a separate door, as for instance at Sanders, Lettaford (see figure overleaf), and sometimes no door from the cross-passage. Frequently in the sixteenth century, upper rooms were made by flooring over each end of the hall, often with internal jetties, as at Sanders. Chimneys, usually lateral, were added when they were wholly floored in the sixteenth or seventeenth century. These

Devon longhouse: Sanders, Lettaford; 16th century and later (Landmark Trust)

longhouses were almost all on Dartmoor. A few were still being built in the eighteenth century.

Because of their inevitable rebuilding or modification, long-houses are difficult to recognise with certainty, but they extended beyond Devon – to Dorset, for instance, where an example probably of around 1600 has been found – and at least sporadically to the Severn Vale (indicated by signs of 'alternate development', by very wide through-passages, very long lower ends and positioning of the service rooms at the top ends of houses). They were also widespread in Wales and the north, but surviving examples are later (see below).

Pele-houses

In a narrow strip running twenty miles on either side of the Scottish border a first-floor hall house of defensive nature was built in some numbers between the mid-sixteenth and the mid-seventeenth century. It arose because of the cross-border raiders of the time, and as a stronghold for raiders themselves. Often termed a bastle (a name best restricted to larger tower-houses), the

Glassonby, Cumbria; 16th century pele

pele-house was generally about 6 metres by 11 metres (20 feet by 36 feet), with stone walls some 1.2 metres (4 feet) thick. The ground-floor chamber for livestock had a vaulted or heavily beamed ceiling, narrow vent slits and a narrow entrance with slots for drawbars. The first floor usually also consisted of a single room, with one or two small windows and a fire hood. A small hole allowed ladder access from the ground floor, but the main entry was by an external ladder to the first-floor doorway. Security improved after the suppression of raiding after 1600, but a few non-defensive peles were still being built over fifty years later.

Scottish Towns

Although still thatched, towns in Scotland were beginning to be stone-built. In Elgin, for instance, there was a marked shift to stone, which became the dominant material in the sixteenth century. Timber framing was still used even for substantial houses, however. In fact the only known fully timber house surviving to the mid-twentieth century was the Earl of Kinnoull's 'ludging' in Perth, of around 1600. The available evidence is limited to stone houses.

Somewhat as in England, the grander houses were set lengthwise to the street and the humbler houses were at right-angles, presenting crow-stepped gables. The expansion of towns tended to be effected by building on the gardens behind the existing houses. Thus, closes were formed, reached by a pend (or through-passage), which might have a lockable gate. This can be seen to have happened at St Andrews, Stirling and Montrose, for instance.

On the lengthwise houses, miniature gables crowned the dormers, some of which were two-storey. In more substantial houses a stone stair tower was often the chief feature of the exterior, projecting from one corner and having corbelled jetties and its own crow-stepped gable. It sometimes rose one or more storeys above the house.

In Edinburgh, no sixteenth-century house survives in anything like its original state, but a bird's-eye-view map of 1544 shows that the largest houses rose to only two storeys and garrets, and the majority were thatched, though pantiles (as still to be seen at Culross, in Fife) were no doubt gaining ground. Property records reveal that typical houses had shops, stables or cellars on the ground floor, a hall and a chamber on the first floor, and a garret in the roof. Some had a wooden gallery in front, others had one at the rear. The space beneath the gallery might be open or boarded-in as part of the ground-floor accommodation. Tenements in Glasgow were similar.

The structure behind the wooden galleries was masonry, and according to a probably over-simplified account given by Maitland, the eighteenth-century historian, in 1508 Edinburgh town council permitted owners to advance their frontages by seven feet (2.2 metres) provided that for the purpose they bought timber from a stock the council had acquired.

Rather than being supported on posts, some galleries were cantilevered. An example was Mary of Guise's House, now destroyed.

John Knox's House is the one surviving house in Edinburgh in which wooden galleries may still be seen, though considerably altered. Its core dates from the early or mid-sixteenth century (and, if a tradition first recorded in 1784 is to be trusted, is the house Knox occupied from 1560 to 1569). The original structure is marked by the crow-stepped gables that rise above the later encasing features. Facing the street are the much-restored galleries, originally perhaps open and now fitted with later sash windows. The forestair is a replacement. The splayed corner and return front are extensions datable to between 1556 and 1573, by the owners' initials. The window, with its pilasters and crowning urns, shows the kind of Classical detailing by then current in Scotland.

The internal plan is confused, but essentially consists of a front room and a back room on each floor, with newel staircases at front and back. Among sixteenth-century fittings are a large mantelpiece with a quirked edge-roll and sections of panelling, one dated 1561.

John Knox House, Edinburgh, early or mid 16th century; corner and left-hand front between 1556 and 1573; later sash windows and restorations

THE VERNACULAR CLIMAX: *c.1575-c.1642* AND BEYOND

This was a period of great richness and variety in domestic architecture, even leaving aside the rise of the fully Classical house, which will be considered in the next chapter along with the closely associated rise of the brick house. In nearly every part of Britain there was now considerable building activity, in many regional styles. Construction flourished in three different materials: timber-framing, cob and stone.

During these years a great leap forward in the comfort and convenience of ordinary houses took place nearly everywhere, second only to the introduction of chimneys and the flooring over of halls. The key change was the rapid spread of glazing, but among other advances was the growing replacement of ladders by framed or spiral staircases. Because glass had become 'so plentiful and within a little so cheap', as William Harrison put it in 1577 in his *Description of England*, dormers and bay windows as well as long rows of mullioned lights were feasible.

An array of windows, especially on timber-framed houses, played a great part in the external display that was so characteristic of the period – echoing the exuberance of the plays of Shakespeare (written *c.*1590-1612). Ornamental framing was equally important. In stone, display took the form of ornate doorheads and other carved detail. In both stone and timber, further elements of display were porch wings, chimneys and façade gables (see below).

Classical detail became widespread, a small but significant example being the ovolo (quarter-circle) moulding, to be found on both wooden and stone window mullions and in many other contexts. Finials, pendants and brackets were also given Classical forms.

In planning, the key innovation was the introduction of the lobby entry, though the through-passage entry held its own over a large proportion of the country

Classical consoles and egg-and-dart: 68-9 High Street, Bewdley, Worcs.

Ornamental framing: Bishop Percy's House, Bridgnorth, Shropshire; 1580

69

Glazing

The glazing of windows became well-nigh universal during the seventeenth century. It is significant of its more widespread use that in 1599 a court ruled that glazing was a fixture integral to a property, contrary to earlier practice; it recognised that now 'without glass it is no perfect house'.

Though glazing was still exceptional in the Weald in 1600, it reached the homes of all but the poorest there by 1650. In Cambridgeshire, smaller houses were also being glazed by the middle of the century, whilst in Wales glass began to appear in fairly small houses by around 1590. In Exeter glazing was common by the end of the sixteenth century, though some houses were still installing it in 1639. Progress in other areas was slower.

In England and Wales glazing was contained in wrought-iron casements, produced by the local blacksmith and introduced around 1600. Diamond panes were usual till the mid-seventeenth century, when rectangular panes began to supersede them - though even a good house in Yorkshire could still be given diamond panes in 1687.

Dormers and windows in gable ends of garrets were just beginning to appear towards the end of the sixteenth century – in the Weald, for instance – to light rooms created to provide accommodation for farmhands and servants. A rare dating for dormers in Wales, but in a large house, is that of Plas Newydd, Cefn Meiriadog, Clwyd, of 1583.

Gables and Porches

Perhaps because of the prestige of town houses, long gable-fronted for lack of space, rural houses too often came to present an array of gables. Sometimes, as in East Anglia, they occurred naturally from cross-wings, projecting or otherwise; but along the Limestone Belt gables were often set around the attic dormers, flush with the face of the house and extending down to the eaves line. Such façade gables, as they have been termed, were sometimes continuous across the frontage.

Porches must also have been favoured partly for adding to the array of gables. Storeyed porches were especially characteristic of the period. They began to be popular among the lesser gentry in the 1560s in the West Midlands, spreading to the level of parsonages by the 1580s. To some degree, they spread to almost all parts of England and Wales. They persisted through to the end of the seventeenth century.

The Ovolo Moulding

This is a useful dating feature, found on window mullions, door frames, fireplaces, ceiling beams and newel posts, but its timespan varied according to area and the simpler splay was always much commoner (and the cavetto and reserved chamfers were also used). In the Weald the ovolo became almost universal as early as

Ovolo-moulded window: 309 Badminton Road, Mayshill, Westerleigh, Avon; 1642

the mid-sixteenth century. In East Anglia it began to be used in around 1650. In the south-west it was favoured from c.1580 and went out as early as c.1630. In the Cotswolds, on the other hand, it flourished from 1615 to 1675. In Somerset and Wiltshire it is found from beginning to end of the seventeenth century. In North Avon dated examples are fairly continuous from 1594 (the earliest dated house) to 1698. In the Banbury region dated examples start in 1615, are frequent in the 1650s and cease in 1694. In Stamford the ovolo's heyday is the early seventeenth century, but it lingers right into the eighteenth century for basement windows. In Gwent, 1625-75 is the ovolo period.

Indicative of all the more developed areas of the North, the ovolo appeared first in the Lancashire Pennines possibly in the early 1590s, certainly by the 1620s.

Lobby-entry Plans

The earliest known lobby-entry house dates from 1536, in Nottinghamshire (see overleaf), but the plan only became prevalent among non-gentry houses at the end of the sixteenth century. It naturally arose when a chimney was inserted midway along the through-passage of an open-hall house. The earliest known example of such an insertion is of 1571, in Surrey. The plan was taken up for new houses perhaps partly as labourers began to be distinct from the family on farms and thus separate entrances to hall and parlour came to be favoured. By the beginning of the seventeenth century, lobby entries were almost standard in the south-east.

Another advantage of placing the chimney in the cross-passage, or where the cross-passage would previously have been, was that it could provide two fireplaces, one for the hall and one for the parlour. This implied a position for the parlour at what would have been the lower end of the hall, previously the less common position. Otherwise, however, the layout of rooms in lobby-entry houses remained at first unchanged, with a subdivided service room at the opposite end of the hall. Occasionally, change was

71

even slighter, with only one fireplace, and an unheated parlour, or the parlour was retained at the 'upper' end of the hall by having a second chimney at the gable end. Another variation, probably datable to the second half of the seventeenth century, was for the parlour to have its own external door.

Like so many other housing innovations, the lobby-entry house seems to have spread outwards from the more prosperous south to the rest of the country, but even in timbered East Anglia there were still as many houses of through-passage plan. In the West Midlands, the lobby entry was applied to a T-shaped plan from early in the seventeenth century, with the chimney in the middle, and parlour and service rooms forming one range and the hall extending at right-angles.

(a) Typical lobby-entry plan; (b) urban equivalent, also common c.1550–1680

An L-shaped plan was also widely adopted across the south in the first forty years of the seventeenth century, whether by extending an existing building to provide an extra parlour or service room or by building a wholly new house. In East Anglia cross-wings continued to be favoured, usually projecting at the rear only. By contrast, in the East Midlands, houses with single cross-wings were rare.

The Limestone Belt was resistant to the lobby entry, partly because the chimneys in stone houses were most economically incorporated in the gables. In the south-west and the north the lobby entry only appeared rarely, probably largely because in these areas farmers were not socially divided from their labourers in the seventeenth century. This is suggested by the fact that even when northern houses had a lobby entry, access to the parlour was usually not from the lobby but from the hall, the family privacy that the lobby entry afforded being thus foregone.

In Wales, the lobby-entry plan was widespread in eastern areas, especially in the Severn valley and into the central region. It was adopted mainly for timber-framed houses, but to a lesser extent for stone houses too. There are no dated examples before 1600; on the other hand, cases occur as late as 1722 and 1736. An example from the mid-borders, at Carno, has a porch wing characteristic of both sides of the border, and a rear wing housing not only a staircase, as was now frequent, but a kitchen. This room was increasingly included in prosperous farmhouses to remove cooking from the main living room (or bring it into the house from its detached building). There was a taste in Wales for the overall cruciform plan that resulted at Plasauduon and there are similar examples in stone.

Plasauduon, Carno, Powys; probably c.1640

Decorative Framing

Display on timber-framing houses took two main forms: decorative framing, which was particularly favoured in the west, and elaboration of window arrangements, which had its focus in the southeast but was to be found in towns over a much wider area. Multiple gables added to the effect of both types of display, especially in the towns.

Decorative framing arose naturally out of the square panelling tradition of the West Midlands and eastern Wales, and was widespread there; but it was concentrated particularly in Cheshire and south Lancashire, where square panelling had now spread. There is a wide scatter of early examples, however: Yorkshire 1574, Somerset 1578, Shropshire 1580, Kent 1593. The square panels (now often quite small, prompting the term 'close panelling') were filled with various types of pattern. The commonest was that of circles and lozenges formed by short curved braces, set concave and convex respectively. This type occurred widely, but particularly over a broad area around the West Midlands. Wavy braces, known in the previous period, were found in many areas, whereas thick cusped braces forming stars, quatrefoils and so forth were a north-western speciality, used in rows of strong gridwork (not unlike the stone panelwork of Perpendicular churches). Parallel bracing and herringbone patterns were used less tightly, and often in larger panels. They are to be found over a wide area, but not in the south-east. An early example that combines many of these patterns is Bishop Percy's House, Bridgnorth (figure, page 69).

In more modest houses and away from the heartland of decorative framing the panels and their braces were larger, fewer and less repetitive. Decorative bracing was often combined with close-studding or restricted to gables. One prominent example is the rather large Old House, Hereford, dated 1621. Another is the late sixteenth-century Hall's Croft, Stratford-on-Avon. The far end of this house was added in the early seventeenth century. Both houses have close-studding lower down. The Old House is double jettied, Hall's Croft is jettied only above the ground floor.

Decorative panelling was not much seen on smaller houses even in its heartland. These generally contented themselves with the practical corner braces, which were now straight. In general, decorative panelling went on till fashion shifted to the fully Classical or to the Artisan Classicism of the middle and late seventeenth century. In Warwickshire, it faded after 1625; in Cheshire it persisted, with increasing Classical detail, into the 1670s.

Close-studding continued to have its main seat in and around East Anglia, and was the favourite panelling in the south-east, but even in the West Midlands there were some almost wholly close-studded buildings (for instance the String of Horses from Shrewsbury at the Avoncroft Museum, originally two houses of 1576).

Display Fenestration

The main area for display fenestration was Sussex and the surrounding counties. As so often, this area made an early start. Farmhouses began to include such windows in the second half of the sixteenth century, at the time when glazing spread to such houses. The parlour also replaced the hall as the principal room at this time, so it was here that the best windows were placed.

Projecting windows, not deep enough to be called oriels, were an early form of display. They were supported by either brackets or a cove. They were often fitted snugly under jettied gables, themselves a new form of display, adopted in and around East Sussex from about 1590 (the last in the east High Weald being c.1700). By a natural extension of the idea, they could be extended down to the ground as a bay window.

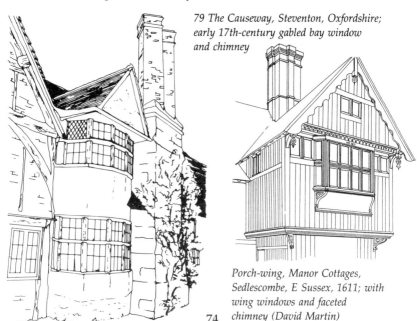

79 The Causeway, Steventon, Oxfordshire; early 17th-century gabled bay window and chimney

Porch-wing, Manor Cottages, Sedlescombe, E Sussex, 1611; with wing windows and faceted chimney (David Martin)

74

A second development, from *c.*1565, was that of so-called flanking windows, then termed clerestory windows and perhaps best called wing windows. These were smaller windows on each side of the main windows, the tops being at a common height but the bases only halfway down the main window. Wing windows were standard features by 1600.

A third development, in larger houses, was that of the frieze window, in which the wing windows joined up between the main windows to form a continuous band, occasionally even continuing round the corner to the adjacent front. There were precedents of a kind in Sussex, but the feature really started about 1560. In a few cases the main windows were omitted so that an even, horizontal strip resulted.

Display fenestration faded in around 1640 in the south-east. Elsewhere it was less prevalent, except in towns, but bay windows and modest projecting windows were widespread. Sometimes bay windows were polygonal and therefore angled back beneath their gabled heads (see figure opposite).

Other Trends in Timber-Framed Areas

While jetties were still spreading in certain contexts, unjettied houses began to be popular around 1560 for rural houses in the south-east and East Anglia and were standard by 1600; in Essex they entirely replaced jettied houses in the seventeenth century, partly because the lavish use of timber necessitated by the latter was no longer feasible. Perhaps somewhat in compensation, decorated porches were popular in East Anglia, though less so in the south-east.

At the western end of timber-framing, in the through-passage area of Herefordshire, in addition to porch-wings a feature was often made of projecting lateral chimneys. Lateral stairs were also fairly common there in the early seventeenth century.

As the price of timber rose, there was increasing use of stone for farmhouses across southern England, often for the lower parts of chimneys or in combination with bands of flint. In small areas of Berkshire and Cambridgeshire houses were built in clunch.

Cob and Granite, and the South-West

Clay mixed with straw, and other similar combinations, took different names in different parts of the country, but cob, its name in the south-west of England, serves as the best generic term. It was probably used almost everywhere at one time. Most of the surviving examples are seventeenth-century (or later), however.

There were two main methods of building in cob: laying it in layers or building it from pre-formed bats or lumps. The layer method (or the similar use of shuttering made from boards) seems to have been the usual one in the seventeenth century, certainly in Devon. East of the Limestone Belt, clay bat or lump was later to be preferred, but perhaps no earlier than 1801, when a Scottish method of the 1790s was introduced to Cambridgeshire. Blocks were made somewhat larger than bricks.

In Lincolnshire, mud was the main alternative to slight and poor-quality framing for small houses in the seventeenth century and beyond. An example, possibly dating from the early seventeenth century, may be seen at Church Farm Museum, Skegness. A similar, if later, house may be visited on the opposite coast of Britain, at Penrhos, Dyfed. In Cumbria and probably in the East Riding of Yorkshire, alternate layers of mud and chopped straw were combined with modest crucks. On the Solway Plain north of the Lake District, it is recorded that the whole community would turn out in cooperative spirit and build a mud house in a single day, ending with a party.

Cob houses were mostly built by the poor, but at least in Devon, East Anglia and Northamptonshire they were lived in even by the well-to-do. As late as 1777 in the East Riding two curates' houses had mud walls – but one was also mud-floored and both were amongst the worst parsonages in the country.

Devon is the classic area for cob, probably because of the suitability of the clays and slatey aggregate (or shillet) with which they were mixed. Building in cob was a standard method of construction from the fourteenth into the nineteenth century. Though stone was often used in combination with cob for display features like chimneys, only on Dartmoor was the local granite a serious rival for the external walling of rural houses until the rise of brick in the eighteenth century.

In the south-west, the through-passage was very much the norm, and front chimneys were found all over Devon, Cornwall and north Somerset; they began towards the end of the sixteenth century and persisted for a hundred years thereafter.

In late sixteenth- and seventeenth-century Devon, old houses tended to be modernised and extended rather than new ones built. A farmhouse excavated at Middlemoor, Sowton, showed eleven major remodellings between the early sixteenth century and the early eighteenth century. Farmhouses often developed a considerable complexity and numerous rooms.

Expansion was most commonly by outshuts (that is, extensions under the roof slope), but often also by wings built on at right-angles. Occasionally the hall was enlarged frontally (the room above being correspondingly extended). Separate access to upper rooms was achieved by having several staircases – three or even more. Two-storey porches were often included or added.

Surviving door and window detail is not much to be found in seventeenth-century rural Devon, as this detail was mostly wooden and has almost always disappeared. A very few mullion and transom windows survive, rather more single windows (usually with ovolo mouldings). Where granite was used, however, there is often heavy roll-moulding round the doors and the spandrels are often lugged and carved with stylised foliage.

Similar granite doorways are characteristic of Cornwall, where roll mouldings were also applied to fireplaces, sometimes with a central peak and sometimes forming a more conventional four-centred arch. Flat lintels were standard, with or without chamfers.

The Limestone Belt

The shift from timber-framed building to stone continued along the Limestone Belt. In Lacock, Wiltshire, the transition has been dated at *c.*1600. In north Northamptonshire, rubble was used to build small houses from the late sixteenth century, without dressings and with gables only sometimes coped. During the seventeenth century there was a great deal of house-building in stone all along the belt from Dorset to Lincolnshire.

Throughout the Limestone Belt plans were predominantly linear. In Dorset, the hearth of the main room had always been in the gable, but during the seventeenth century the second hearth also moved to the gable. Three-room houses often had the unheated room in the middle of the house, an unusual arrangement nationally, but frequent also in north Avon and other parts of the Limestone Belt.

Banded flint and squared rubble (and the alternative checkered pattern) were common in adjoining areas of Dorset, Hampshire and Wiltshire at this period. Limestone banded with ironstone is found in west Dorset and at the other end of the Limestone Belt, in Northamptonshire and Leicestershire.

In Avon and Gloucestershire, dormer windows in façade gables are much more prevalent. These often have moulded copings. At the feet of the gable there were generally kneelers (moulded terminal projections). In Burford, 162 High Street (figure overleaf) has ball finials crowning the gables, which are characteristic of the later seventeenth century, when they are also found on staircase newel posts. Even diminutive one-and-a-half-storey two-cell Cotswold cottages often had a single façade gable, as may be seen at the well-known Arlington Row, Bibury, Gloucestershire. Bay windows too were very much a Cotswolds feature. Those with gables corbelled out over their canted sides are especially to be found to the east, in Stamford, Lincolnshire, for instance.

At the Avon end of the Cotswolds, bay windows were rare but porch wings were almost standard. Usually steeply angled to match the slope of the façade gables above, and placed over the central entry, they produce a strongly symmetrical result. They died away only in the eighteenth century.

Further north in Northamptonshire and into Lincolnshire, façade gables were also infrequent. Isaac Newton's birthplace, Woolsthorpe Manor, is representative of a prosperous yeoman's farmhouse in this area (figure overleaf). It is a more substantial version of the four-square front of Dorset houses, being three-unit, with parlour at the higher end, doorway giving onto the hall and kitchen at the lower end, and staircase originally in a rear turret.

Woolsthorpe Manor, Lincolnshire; probably shortly after 1623 (the small 'fire window' on right lights main hearth)

Cotswold façade-gable house: 162 High Street, Burford; probably late 17th century

Like many houses in the Banbury region, Woolsthorpe has windows in the gables. The mullions are ovolo-moulded, but instead of the drip moulds of the Burford limestone house illustrated above, it has Classical cornices. In a consistent pattern, the cornice mouldings are of the same ogee (or cyma) profile as the gable kneelers, and similar cornices not only cap the chimneys (as was standard for good houses over the Limestone Belt), but also form the shelves over the fireplaces, which have four-centre-headed openings. Both fireplaces and chimneys are of standard Limestone Belt types (see figure, page 87).

Dated examples of different mullion mouldings have been assembled for more than one limestone area. The key runs are as follows. Banbury region: splayed 1574-1750 (mostly 1654-75), cavetto 1574-1636 (but only three examples); Cotswolds: splays (much the commonest) 1575-1750 and beyond, cavettos 1570-1618 and 1675-91 (with a sharp break between); North Avon: splays 1594-1720 (but never common), cavetto 1654-1718. Humbler houses and less prosperous areas of the Limestone Belt, such as Northamptonshire, had mostly plain gable mouldings and wooden window lintels.

The North and the Hearth-passage Plan

In the north the earliest storeying-over of halls dates only from the 1570s, it would seem, so it coincided with the glazing revolution that was largely separate in the south. On top of those changes was the change from timber-framing to stone building. A document of 1594 suggests that only then did smaller houses in the Vale of York combine cruck-framing with stone end walls.

Throughout the north, the dominant plan was that of the hearth-passage and its variant the heck entry. The smoke-hood, being adequately adaptable to storeyed houses, continued to be standard below the level of the upper gentry.

The hearth-passage plan arises naturally both from the open-hall tradition and from that of the longhouse (which seems from excavated examples in the north to have been continuous through to the seventeenth century). In both cases there was a through-passage at the lower end of the hall or main room.

On the hearth side of the passage lay the hall – in northern farmhouses termed the housebody or firehouse. A typical smaller house of North Yorkshire at Ryedale Folk Museum shows the arrangement. The partition between the entry and the hearth was

Stangend, a cruck longhouse from Danby, N Yorkshire, re-erected at Ryedale Museum, Hutton-le-Hole; 17th century; showing carved post at front of heck supporting smoke hood

called the heck. Built on to the hearth side was a bench or settle. Standard carved decoration was present on the corner post (known, but perhaps only since the nineteenth century, as the witch post). Lighting the vital area under the smoke-hood was the small fire window.

In North Yorkshire as in many parts of the north, including the Lake District, the fire was fuelled by peat, burning on a hearth that was only slightly raised. There were two methods of suspending pots over the fire. One was from a rannel bauk (known as a rannel baulk in the Lakes), which was a piece of wood that rolled on two transverse beams spanning the inside of the fire-hood at first-floor level. The other was from a crane hinged from the back of the hearth, usually of iron, from which reckons (adjustable hangers, called ratten crooks in the Lakes) could be suspended.

In north-east Yorkshire the majority of farmhouses of before 1700 are single-storey and usually cruck-built – in both respects like Stangend, which has rubble walls except for the close-studded gable. The earliest surviving storeyed houses in the area probably date from around 1680-90 and did not become the norm till the latter part of the eighteenth century.

Longhouses in the North

Stangend was what may be regarded as a hearth-passage house of a specialised kind (maybe the original kind): it is a longhouse, with the byre on the lower side of the passage. In the seventeenth century, longhouses were to be found in several areas of the North. They frequently had only one hearth. Occasionally in North Yorkshire this was still an open one (and there was therefore no fire window). The inner room there was generally a parlour, but sometimes a dairy. Alternatively, the service room was sometimes set between hall and parlour. By the later seventeenth century there was usually a bedroom over the inner room and the byre was walled off from the passage. Stairs were now commonly included, sometimes with their own window, and were often sited in the inner room, which ceased to be a bedroom. Occasionally there was also a window in the middle of the gable. In North Yorkshire longhouses were not necessarily inferior to other plans as a type. Most were of two full storeys and these often had a good staircase in a rear turret. By 1700, however, the true longhouse was obsolete in the area, though an arrangement identical except for separate access remained common.

Modest longhouses have been identified too in the Lancashire Fylde district. These add to the examples of unbaked earth construction, being built around a kind of wattle, and called clat and clay. They are not so different from the wattle houses of tenth-century York or the wicker houses of Scotland (see pages 11, 12, 15 and 128–9). Chimneys were often added at a later date.

Northern Three-unit Houses

In the normal hearth-passage farmhouse on both sides of the

Pennines the service room took the place of the byre, producing a full three-cell layout. The top end of the range could be substantial. Peel House near Halifax has the early date 1598 carved on it. The kitchen, in a rear wing behind the housebody originally with a smoke-hood, was a lavish extra at this date, when the yeoman's cooking would normally have been done in the housebody. Display extended to porch-wing, façade gable and round-arched windows – the last characteristic of superior northern houses (or of best rooms) of around 1600.

Heck-entry Two-cell Houses

If there was neither byre nor service to be sited below the hearth-passage, the passage itself could be dispensed with, leaving the entry in the gable or in the front wall facing the heck. If a third room was subsequently added, another hearth was often put back to back with the existing one, with its own heck. This created a northern version of the lobby entry.

End-stack, Central-entry Houses

This plan developed for the same reasons as in the Limestone Belt and Wales, because it suited stone houses of two cells. An early, well-detailed Yorkshire example dates from 1619.

On the Lancashire side of the Pennines too, new houses were increasingly built with a central entry, the earliest dated example being Burwains in Briercliffe, of 1642. The entry was likewise still often directly into the housebody. Foulds House, Padiham, of 1677, is an example. Unusually, an inventory that can be related to this house survives. In addition to the housebody (on the left), it had in the right-hand side of the house (later rebuilt) the parlour, with milkhouse and 'shop' behind it. The shop was a textile workshop.

Foulds House, Padiham, Lancashire, 1677

Outshuts and Rear Wings

When the single aisle of Yorkshire tradition was partitioned off, it formed an additional room under the roofspace, which was useful for service functions. The same room is termed an outshut (or pentice) when built as a separate room in a new house, as naturally developed out of the Yorkshire tradition. Outshuts also became widespread in Lancashire, facilitated by the arrival of glazing and the end of the need for windows on both sides of the main rooms. In the early seventeenth century there might be parlour cross-wings to give extra space, but they then tended to be superseded by an outshot, which sometimes grew to one and a half storeys. Alternatively, a wing of one or two storeys could be added behind the housebody, as at Peel House.

In the second half of the seventeenth century, probably after a cessation of building during the Civil War, houses in Lancashire grew taller, occasionally rising to two storeys plus attics.

Lake District Houses

The heck entry plan was standard in the Lake District, the variation being mainly in the outshut. Some farmhouses were probably once longhouses. At Wall End, Deepdale, the byre is still extant and at Beckstones Farm, Patterdale, the byre was converted to a room below the passage (known in the Lakes as the downhouse) by insertion of a chimney. The strength of an earlier longhouse tradition may be shown by the way in which byres and barns continued regularly to be built as linear continuations of the house, occasionally with a through-passage between them (without an entry to either). Also frequent was the practice of building a second farmhouse in line with an existing one, no doubt to accommodate widows or separate branches of a family that split a farm.

Minus the byre, Beckstones Farm has one of the most standard Lake District plans. At the upper end of the firehouse were the buttery and parlour, divided by plank-and-muntin partitions (see page 51). The parlour was at the front, the buttery on the cooler

Glencoyne Farm, Ullswater,
Cumbria; 1629

rear side of the house, while the stairs were sited in an outshut projection. Within this type, stairs varied from the tightest spiral in a semicircular turret to more spacious ellipses or even a dogleg arrangement (probably only after 1700).

Less common among extant houses is the simplest type of plan, which is probably also the earliest, including as it does the cruck-built houses (perhaps even late sixteenth-century). In this type the stairs did not project but were sited either in the firehouse area or the area of the buttery.

More developed than the Beckstones Farm type were the houses that had a buttery as well as the stairs in a rear outshot, making possible a full-depth parlour. The stairs in such houses were more often dogleg; dated examples are from the end of the seventeenth century and the beginning of the eighteenth.

A wholly different layout in a minority of farmhouses had the entry in the front of the house, with the stairs next to the heck. This suited small houses, in which there was sometimes insufficient space to subdivide buttery from parlour.

The downhouse, already mentioned, was an extra room added by the more prosperous farmers, probably mainly a brewhouse. It was usually, it seems, built onto existing houses, rather than original. Sometimes it had separate access from the outside and occasionally was detached altogether or of one storey only. Often, it was built with its hearth back to back with that of the firehouse, and its heck continuous with the existing one, the entry being switched through 90 degrees to face the hecks. Alternatively a hearth passage ran between the firehouse and the downhouse, and the chimney for the latter was in the gable away from the passage. This used to be regarded as a classic Lakeland plan, but at least in the central parts of Cumbria it is in fact uncommon, though it is exemplified in Glencoyne Farm, Ullswater. Here the firehouse is to the left of the hearth passage with its door at each end and the fire window is matched by a balancing small window away from the hearth of the downhouse.

In the Lake District, the smoke-hood was either made of timber and plaster (rarely surviving today, but to be found at High Birk House, Little Langdale), or of stone (which has less often been replaced). The chimneys over timber smoke-hoods were supported on corbels projecting from the gable wall, which at least sometimes were also of timber.

At the lower end of the firehouse in the Lake District, it was usual to have a plank-and-muntin partition with which was incorporated an oak press cupboard between the two doors (see overleaf). The cupboard generally had double doors below and a more recessed section, also with doors, above. The frieze of fluting was a frequent form of decoration in this period, to be found on panelling and overmantels, for instance. The earliest recorded date on a Lakeland built-in cupboard is 1628, the two latest are both 1735. After that date cupboards were plain.

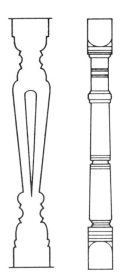

Glenside, Troutbeck, Cumbria: cupboard dated 1634

Early 17th-century balusters:
(a) pierced splat (flat), (b) bobbin

These cupboards were particularly the object of display in the Lakes, where there were not many other outlets, but built-in furniture is known elsewhere. Many areas, including North Avon and the Lake District, had fireplace spice cupboards with finely carved doors.

In small houses in the Lake District, the lack of easily worked stone meant that most seventeenth-century windows were of wood. Those that survive usually have simple splays. As in many parts of the north, with the replacement of thatch by stone slates – probably from the late seventeenth century onwards – roofs were renewed at a lower pitch and upper storey walls correspondingly raised.

Doorways and Fireplaces

The North showed most imagination in the design of doorways, with many forms, especially curvilinear and recessed-panel ones. Yorkshire was particularly rich, but even the Lake District had its share. Fireplace lintels were sometimes similar (see overleaf). Windows, too, were given strikingly shaped heads, again especially in Yorkshire, where the stepped variety is called a West Riding window, the central light being taller than the side ones.

Yorkshire doorways (E. Ambler, 1913)

84

Rarer are round-arched doorways of almost Romanesque heaviness, in the north dating from the early seventeenth century and in the granite areas of the south-west persisting into the eighteenth century. Coiled kneelers and stops were typical of Cornwall.

In Wales, too, the seventeenth century was a period of ornate doorheads, particularly in the south-east; but these were mainly internal. All were of timber. The earliest dated example is of 1599 and probably the last is of 1711.

Common to all areas were doorways and fireplaces with either straight or four-centred heads. The straight heads, either wood or stone, could be chamfered, the four-centred heads could have carved spandrels, and could also be simplified to a flat triangle. Fireplaces where cooking was done often had very wide cambered stone arches, a profile also given to many smaller fireplaces in the north.

In stone areas, hood moulds were placed over doors, though less frequently than over windows, and the more florid had decorative returns such as the lozenge type widespread between 1610 and 1685 or so. Often, especially later in the century, hood moulds were continuous across the frontage, foreshadowing the plat (flat) bands of classical usage. A line of jutting stones served in Lakeland.

Chimneys

The most widespread use of brick remained the building of chimneys. Diagonal chimney shafts were a characteristic feature of the early and middle seventeenth century. They were often of great size, even on medium houses: no doubt the purpose was to display a prestige feature. The house in Steventon referred to above (see pages 74–5) is a good example. The next, overlapping stage integrated the shafts in a single stack. In the Limestone Belt the chimney was usually topped with a flat entablature. Brick stacks were often of stepped cross-section (see figure, page 74) or had the arched panels found on so many features (see page 87).

Pargeting

Most surviving examples of pargeting, external decorative plasterwork, are seventeenth-century or later. It seems to have flourished first and most extensively in East Anglia, where the dwindling supply of timber (and lack of good stone) first led to a slight and simple framing that was best covered. It is significant that in the Weald, where timber supplies held up better, pargeting was used only from c.1600; no doubt local taste played a part too.

Pargeting is perishable, however, and it was more widespread than the better-known survivals suggest. Eighteenth- and early nineteenth-century prints and drawings show that it was a feature of both York and London. There is evidence of it from as far as Devon in one direction and Lancashire in the other.

It could be incised or relief. The incised kind, probably earlier

Pargeting: (a) incised (Suffolk), (b) relief (Little Moorfields, London; J. T. Smith, 1814)

and always commoner, was produced by pronged or combed instruments, which made simple, usually geometric patterns, often within an overall grid of panels. Relief decoration, which produced the more striking results, was modelled by hand or impressed from moulds. It ranged from motifs such as fleurs-de-lis, Tudor roses and animals to all-over foliage or even strapwork (geometric patterns of bands turned in curves and right-angles, with scrolly terminations, as if cut from leather; see figure opposite).

Plasterwork and Wall Decoration
When the plastering of ceilings began, in the late sixteenth century, joists and floorboards in non-gentry houses were still exposed to the room below, and till the mid-seventeenth century the plaster was applied direct to them. The plastering of ceilings below the joists in the modern fashion gradually extended to ordinary houses from around 1600 (in Wales from the mid-seventeenth century). In advance of modern practice, chaff or chopped straw was used in both ceilings and partitions for sound insulation.

Along with other forms of display, decorative plasterwork flourished during this period, and sometimes was a feature of quite modest houses. The art flourished particularly widely in Devon.

Plasterwork overmantels were to be found in many parts of the country, sometimes with similar motifs to those on ceilings, sometimes with the royal arms or other heraldry, often with dates and owners' initials. Causeway Farm, Windermere, for instance, has a rustic vine-trail enclosing initials and the date 1658.

In general, styles were national – even shared by Scotland, where ribwork designs may be viewed at Provost Skene's House, Aberdeen, for example.

(a) Strapwork wall painting,
Calico House, Newnham, Kent;
(b) enriched ribwork ceiling,
4 S. Quay, Great Yarmouth,
Norfolk (both early 17th century)

Under the pressure of Classical restraint, decorative plaster-work, like other forms of display, died back from ordinary homes in the first half of the eighteenth century.

Even more widespread than plasterwork in the seventeenth century, were painted wall decoration and wall cloths. The scanty survivals are reminders that the stark black and white of historic timber-framed interiors today are very unlike their original appearance. Both timbers and walls were painted.

Panelling

Framed panelling developed out of vertical planking at the beginning of the sixteenth century. At first it was tall and narrow, but gradually it became only slightly taller than wide, and so termed 'small square', with pardonable inexactitude. Almost universally, it was of oak. Wainscot, as early plain panelling is often called, was probably originally a suitable type of oak.

Small square panelling with typical matching door, E. Riddlesden Hall, W. Yorks
(1648)

Panelling earlier than the mid-seventeenth century is now rare below manor house level, but much must have disappeared. That it reached middling people earlier than is often supposed is suggested by the bequest in 1581 by an Essex shoemaker to his widow of his tenement during her life, 'provided she shall not remove any of the wainscot nor the glass'.

The framing of small square panelling was generally given a simple scribed moulding. At first this was applied only to the short verticals (termed stiles) which extended between the continuous horizontals (termed rails). It was subsequently also applied to the rails, but died away short of the straight 'mason's' joint with the stiles. Only in the mid-seventeenth century did the diagonal 'mitre' joint, which allowed mouldings to run right round the panels, spread from grander houses to middling ones. In slightly superior work fluted pilasters masked the joins between the movable sections of four to six panels' width. In considerably grander work the panels were moulded in linenfold and other patterns. In ordinary houses, panelling seems usually to have been painted in the seventeenth century.

Staircases and Floors

The framed staircase was widespread by the middle of the seventeenth century except in areas of the north and Wales. In the south-east, open-well staircases were being built by the early 1590s. In East Anglia open-well or dogleg staircases in projecting wings were usual by c.1630. By c.1600 in North Avon there was a true newel stair (that is, one winding round a newel post extending through several storeys). Balustrading, at first limited to the top of the spiral, began at the same date (see figures, page 84). Both in North Avon and in the Cotswolds stair turrets also start to occur before the outbreak of the Civil War in 1642, though sometimes with the old form of winding flight. Turrets persisted till around 1720, sometimes combined with other rooms. Conversely, stairs were sometimes included in porch wings. In lobby-entry territory, a winding stair was sometimes sited between the lobby and hearth.

Joists tended to become slighter after 1600, and be laid on edge, gradually narrowing towards the modern oblong section. Ground floors were usually flagged. Upper storeys now had nailed boarding, except in the East Midlands, and in some other parts, where upper floors were often still plastered, giving a surprisingly durable surface. Woolsthorpe Manor, Lincolnshire, is an instance.

Town Housing

In the main streets of London, houses of four storeys were usual from around 1600. Larger houses were one or two rooms wide and three rooms deep. Smaller houses were still of one room on each floor (commonly consisting of a chamber on each of the two floors between the kitchen and the garret). By 1660, all London houses had window curtains. Many had lead cisterns for water storage.

In many towns shopping streets and marketplaces were arcaded. The Buttermarket, Dartmouth, is a rare survival. Its 'grotesque' carved brackets and guilloche (plaited) ornament to the panel frames is typical of the classical detail on early seventeenth-century town buildings.

End-to-end windows were often found on high street houses. The Bear and Billet, Chester, and the even more extensively glazed and rectangular Bessie Surtees House, Newcastle, also exemplify the persistence of the timber-framed tradition beyond 1642, away from the South.

Town Houses in Scotland
The town houses of Scotland now began to rise dramatically in height, exploiting the strength of masonry, and presumably emulating the high-rise castles of the Scottish nobility. In Edinburgh some seventeenth-century tenements (or 'lands') were twice as high as the tallest post-Fire London houses. They contained flats of only two rooms, even for merchants. They had tall, narrow windows, stair turrets, stepped gables and a mass of chimneys. John Taylor, in his *Peniles Pilgrimage* of 1618, said that the buildings in Canongate were 'all of squared stone, five, six, and seven stories high, and many by-lanes and closes on each side of the way, wherein are gentlemen's houses, much fairer than the buildings in the high street'.

Crow-stepped gables continued; they only died out for cottages in the early nineteenth century. The main rooms, still on the first floor, were reached by forestairs in ordinary houses and turret staircases in richer ones, as at 103 High Street, Elgin of 1634; Kellieludging, High Street, Pittenweem, Fife, probably a little later; and the Study, Culross (figure overleaf). In all these there is a small room at the top, reached by an additional turret corbelled out from the main one. Even houses of no great pretension sometimes had a turret if they were sited on a corner. At ground level the same approach produced undercuttings and chamfered corners to make the most of limited sites on narrow streets.

Unlike in England, casement windows were never popular in Scotland. The usual urban type by the seventeenth century was vertical, divided horizontally by a wooden transom, with shutters below and glazing above (which was leaded direct at first, but later framed in wood with astragals).

From the beginning of the seventeenth century, quarried stone was beginning to be used in addition to field stone and timber was being displaced. By around 1650, the use of quarried stone had spread to Dunblane and Montrose, although of Glasgow it was recorded at the same period that 'the houses are only of wood, ornamented with carving'; by the end of the century Kirkcudbright was said to be entirely of stone. Many houses, however, retained a timber frontage, supported on posts or cantilevered.

In 1674, an Act in Council banned both timber fronts and timber

Gladstone's Land, Edinburgh; between 1617 and 1620

The Study, Culross, Fife; 1633

forestairs in Edinburgh. Stone arches replaced the timber posts. This transformation was evidently in progress some decades earlier, for it seems to have been applied to Gladstone's Land in Lawnmarket between 1617 and 1620. The wooden galleries that would have faced such a building were taken down and the new masonry front was erected 6.9 metres (23 feet) in front of the existing masonry core, and an open arcade and forestair were formed on the ground floor. The crow-stepped gables had carved finials and the skewputts (kneelers) at their base were carved with the initials and device of the Gladstones who carried out the remodelling. The building was six storeys high, with an interior notable for its ceiling painting.

Gladstone's Land is the only surviving example in Edinburgh of the arcading that was common in many Scottish towns at this period as in England. Another good example is 7 High Street, Elgin, later Braco's Banking House, with a triple arcade. It is dated 1694 on the left hand of the two carved dormer gables.

The ornament on these masonry houses was fairly restricted. The dormers had crow-stepped gables or carved finials and sometimes mouldings, while the doorway nearly always had a roll moulding around it.

In 1679, in Edinburgh, a renewed prohibition of thatch required that it should be replaced with lead, slates or tiles within one year.

Slates were used on the richer houses. Red pantiles spread through-out central and eastern Scotland during the seventeenth century. Their use can be seen at Culross, in Fife. Here there are a number of surviving two and three-storey late sixteenth- and seventeenth-century houses. They are of harled rubble with yellow sandstone dressings. Many have ornate dormer window carvings, trade symbols, date stones and inscriptions. They generally have forestairs.

Rural Houses in Scotland
There were just beginning to be houses of middling size outside the burghs. An example is the two-and-a-half-storey rubble-built Old Manse, at Larbert, Stirlingshire, dated 1635. This has a linear layout, with the stairs behind the off-centre door, the parlour at one end and the kitchen at the other. It has a cavetto-moulded eaves, ogival skewputts, chamfered window-arrises and a bead mould to the door. The fireplaces have roll-and-hollow mouldings.

Most people continued to live in cruck houses except, it would appear, in Orkney, Shetland and the Outer Hebrides. Crucks were usually supplied by the laird, lesser timbers and the cladding by the tenant. Because of the scarcity of timber, crucks tended to be slight and often reused. Instead of oak or ash, many people had to make do with crucks of fir, which were not durable.

Clay provided an alternative structure, mentioned back as far as 1586, and with a distribution over the south-east and in Sutherland and Ross. Rounded stones (known as bools) were set in the surface of the clay, sometimes in herring-bone patterns.

If most rural houses in Scotland were very modest, there is evidence that middling people were enjoying rising housing standards. Lime mortar, which made possible load-bearing walls, was in use in Fife as early as 1625 for larger tenant houses, though in most places this was a development of the last forty years of the century. Crucks went out as load-bearing stone walls and second storeys came in. A-frame trusses took their place.

On rubble, there was some use of harling (the Scottish term for a rough external render) even in the sixteenth century, but it seems to have been limited to eastern parts, the north-west coast and the Outer Hebrides, while the use of lime wash, applied direct to the rubble walls, became widespread in the West.

Thatch continued to be the normal roof covering in the country, with heather and turf (or turf overlaid with thatch) still used for humbler dwellings. Early prints are evidence that cottages with large external chimneys were common in Lothian. Most farm-houses probably took the form of single-storey, narrow long-houses. The usual plan was that of the but and ben, that is, an outer room (used as a kitchen) and an inner room (used for sleeping and storage). Larger farmhouses had three rooms, smaller farmhouses only one. Generally there was no upper storey, though the Orkney houses had partial upper floors, as too did the homes of some Lowland leaseholders.

4 THE CLASSICAL HOUSE

Symmetry, vertical windows and the use of Classical mouldings: these were the essentials of the Classical house during its reign from the mid-seventeenth until the mid-nineteenth century. In other respects the Classical house varied greatly. The Classical orders (that is, columns or pilasters supporting an entablature) were often applied to doorways and fireplaces, but only sometimes to house fronts; Classical panelling only ruled till the 1760s, and only in town houses and rather dignified houses in the country; sash windows, which we think of as so characteristic of the Classical house, only came in around 1680; even the horizontal eaves were absent from many otherwise Classical houses till around 1720.

The period of the Classical house may be conveniently divided into five phases: (1) that of the vertical but still casement window and contending styles of façade, lasting till around 1680; (2) that from *c.*1680 to *c.*1730, marked by the introduction of the sash window and an inclination to a Baroque verticality and modelling of the façade; (3) the Palladian phase, marked by plainer fronts and panelling and the rise of the unified terrace, 1720-65; (4) the Adam phase, of 1760-1800, marked by the end of panelling, by the front door set within an arch and by a new decorative vocabulary; and (5) the Regency phase, of 1795-1835, typical features of which are overall stucco, verandas and continuous balconies.

Farmhouses and cottages are somewhat less likely to possess some of the key features by which stylistic evolution is charted in the town. What the arrival of the Classical house chiefly meant for such houses was the adoption of a symmetrical front and the double-depth plan that went with it for all but the smallest houses. This did not happen until around 1680, so it has its place in the account of the second phase, not the first.

Lincoln's Inn Fields, London; 1638/42, only partly built (W. Hollar, British Museum)

THE CROSS-WINDOW AND CONTENDING STYLES, 1615-80

It is easy, but mistaken, to think of the smaller seventeenth-century Classical house as being much like that of the eighteenth century, as the appearance of most surviving houses tempts one to do. More particularly, it is a mistake to suppose that Inigo Jones set the predominant pattern of design for the rest of the seventeenth century, as the theoretical appeal of Jonesian design and its endorsement by the eighteenth-century Palladians easily beguile one into supposing.

The Rise of Brick

The background to the rise of the fully Classical house as it developed in Britain was the adoption of brick in place of timber-framing. Brick had long been used for palaces and the greatest houses, as well as for chimneys, plinths and infill for ordinary houses. Wholly brick houses were being erected for the gentry from the second decade of the seventeenth century. Exceptionally, in King's Lynn, the first houses completely of brick are as early as the late sixteenth century. Great Yarmouth followed in 1636-8. Other East coast towns were rebuilt in brick and flint before 1640; thereafter in brick alone. In Lincolnshire, a house in Freiston dated 1613, is a bench mark for the progress of brick there. However, it was in London that brick took hold earliest for the general run of houses. As early as 1605, James I had issued a proclamation that houses should be built of brick or stone rather than timber. This was soon modified to allow houses to be timber in side lanes, and, in any event, such proclamations tended to be ignored, but clearly the tide was advancing.

Until 1630, English bond, which had courses of stretchers (lengthwise bricks) alternating with courses of headers, was always used when any regular bond was adopted. Henceforth Flemish bond, which had alternating stretchers and headers in every course, gradually gained a dominance which it held till the Gothic Revival.

Whereas timber-framing encouraged long horizontal windows, brick construction called for vertical ones. In that respect the new material was well adapted to the Classical style. On the other hand, the dominant taste at the beginning of the seventeenth century was for the kinds of exuberant display described in the last chapter, which was almost the antithesis of the Classical style. It is not surprising therefore that alongside the houses more or less in the manner of Jones's restrained Italian-derived Classicism there ran a less restrained, less pure style: Artisan Classicism.

The Jonesian Impact

Inigo Jones did indeed introduce fully Classical architecture into Britain more or less single-handedly from the later 1610s onwards. Although he was very much a court architect and his work at first stood in isolation, his influence must have encouraged the spread of Classical design to ordinary houses. Specifically, this meant the adoption of the vertical cross-window, which won early and widespread favour and, more generally, it meant the application of the temple-front scheme for house fronts, the acceptance of which was at first more limited.

The adoption of the cross-window was the culmination of a gradual development from the predominantly horizontal mullion-and-transom window to the vertical window derived from Renaissance Italy and fundamental to the proportional balance of the Classical façade. Following the example of Somerset House back in 1557, at the grandest level of domestic architecture, the grid of mullions and transoms was progressively simplified in the early seventeenth century. Secondary transoms were eliminated and the single one that remained was placed higher in the frame. The central king-mullion was slimmed to the same cross-section. The mouldings disappeared, leaving a square section.

James I's proclamation of 1619, directed at Londoners, gave a boost to the vertical window. Among its requirement was: 'the lights of the windows of every whole storey, to be of more height than breadth, to the end that the rooms may receive air for health, and that there may be sufficient pier of brick between the windows for strength: And likewise the windows of every half storey to be made square every way, or near thereabouts'. This was followed in 1620 by the requirement that the piers between windows should be not less than half their width.

Jones's main contribution was the introduction to England of the temple-front scheme for houses. Derived ultimately from the design of Greek temples, the scheme was developed from the works of ancient Rome during the Italian Renaissance. The ground floor corresponded to the platform or base of the temple, while the windows of the first floor (and the second if there was one) were regularly disposed between the half-columns or pilasters of the order, above which ran the entablature (the set of horizontal mouldings consisting of architrave, frieze and cornice). Just as the ground floor 'platform' of course had windows, so an extra 'attic' storey could be added above the entablature. Dormers could be added in the roof slope.

Jones applied the scheme in various ways in his buildings, the most relevant to ordinary houses being Covent Garden. Built in 1631-7, this is important as the first regular square in Britain. Its 3½-storey façades set no direct pattern, however, for the order was reduced almost to a set of strips and the ground floor consisted of tall open arcades, an arrangement that was to remain exceptional, though it had its counterparts far from London, as we have seen.

However, Covent Garden did show in a general way how the giant-order temple-front scheme could be applied to ranges of houses, and others quickly took up the formula in London (a giant order is one rising through several storeys). From 1638, the

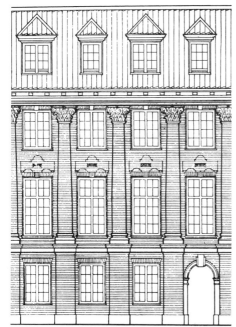

Stair,
51 Lincoln's Inn Fields (1638/42)

Great Queen Street, London;
1638; reconstruction (J. Summerson)

developer William Newton made use of it in Great Queen Street and on the adjacent north and west sides of Lincoln's Inn Fields, selling some sites and building others himself, but in each scheme achieving at least an approximately uniform design. Both sets of houses were of brick and displayed a long series of pilasters, Corinthian and Ionic respectively.

In the Great Queen Street range, probably designed by Peter Mills, the pilasters were sometimes paired between houses. It also had raised panels between the storeys and doors under keyed arches. The Lincoln's Inn Fields houses (figure, page 92) had balustraded balconies cantilevered at first-floor level, decorative bands midway up the pilasters and finials to the dormers. The doorways were straight-headed, apparently with plain surrounds; some had double doors, some toplights. They had front gardens, still a rare feature at that time, which were enclosed by brick walls and piers, apparently with wooden gates.

Although all the houses in both schemes have been destroyed, various records survive. These include the plan of 51 Lincoln's Inn Fields. It had two fireplaces in the party wall but the other two back to back in the middle of the house. The main staircase was of the dogleg type and ran to the mid-rear, but the secondary one was winding and in the middle of the house, lit by a tiny yard shared with the adjoining house, an arrangement that seems to have been common for middling houses in the following decades. Unlike some of the other features of these houses the balustrade of the top flight, now in the Museum of London, is close to

Jonesian models. It is worth going into some detail concerning these houses because they provide rare evidence of the characteristics of the first generation of Classical houses.

Artisan Classicism

It was a brand of Classicism at the opposite extreme to Jonesian purity that was the main alternative to the giant-order houses previously described. This has been dubbed Artisan Mannerism, but the latter half of the label misleadingly suggests a relationship with the highly sophisticated, late stage of the Renaissance in Italy, in the sixteenth century. Though the English artisans of the seventeenth century drew on north European pattern books (themselves bastardising Italian motifs), they departed from Renaissance purity out of ignorance rather than sophistication. They favoured shaped gables, dwarf orders of stubby pilasters and tripartite windows, together with sunk or raised panels and other busy embellishment. The style can be seen as a translation into brick of the spirit of early seventeenth-century timber-framing. Not much of the style has survived subsequent disfavour, but one of the first examples is from the very time Jones was beginning to introduce Italian purity – a house in Holborn, known from a drawing of 1619, which had a curved gable surmounted by a pediment (termed a Dutch gable). Outside London, the style is largely confined to the level of the manor house.

Artisan classicism in brick: 66 Crooms Hill, Greenwich (c.1635)

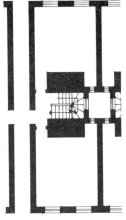

Newington Green, London (1658) a giant pilaster range with Artisan panels (after GLC)

From the Civil War to the Restoration

The war seems to have brought building to a halt nearly everywhere in England. Nevertheless, knowledge of isolated examples allows a tentative picture of the period between 1642 and the Restoration of 1660.

In the first place, other houses with giant-order fronts are known to have been built in the London area. A row of 1658 survives at Newington Green, then outside London.

The Newington range is precious not only as a rare survival but also for providing more evidence of house plans, this time for a more ordinary kind of house than the substantial two-staircase houses in Lincoln's Inn Fields. The only staircase here, instead of being a winder tucked into a convenient corner, was of the dogleg type that was to be standard in town houses for the next 250 years. It had an open well and was situated in the middle of the house, between the front and back rooms. It is once again lit by a tiny yard shared with the next house, which also has small windows to both rooms.

A provincial house front of equal rarity fills out the picture in a quite different style. This is at 9 Southgate Street, Gloucester. As a development of Artisan Classicism (see figure overleaf), it was probably more typical of the mid-seventeenth century.

Contending Styles of the Restoration

The variety of Classical house front that seems to have prevailed in the 1640s and 1650s continued to do so on the restoration of the monarchy in 1660. This is not readily apparent, because little ordinary town building of the twenty years or so after 1660

9 Southgate Street, Gloucester (probably 1650), still with strapwork panels (RCHME)

survives. Probably, just those houses or features that were most characteristic of Restoration taste were those singled out for demolition in the subsequent Georgian period as being old-fashioned. The crucial evidence is consequently as much from engravings as from surviving houses.

The stylistic range extended from Flemish windows, shaped gables and floating pediments, through giant orders of different kinds and superimposed orders to simpler fronts which nonetheless still often exhibited a variety of features peculiar to the period.

Shaped Gables and Floating Pediments
By the later seventeenth century, the tradition of shaped gables was being adapted to the vertical window. In East Anglia it

Fenchurch Street, London (B. Cole, 1756; Guildhall Library, Corporation of London)

continued till the end of the century. Oriels with Flemish-pattern lights also flourished there; Sparrowe's House, Ipswich, of c.1670, is a famous example. In York, shaped gables continued to grace the rear elevations of houses down to around 1720.

The shaped gable style related to the mild kind of Artisan Classicism characterised by pediments floating above doors and windows, examples of which can still be glimpsed in towns in different corners of the country: for instance at 15 Mealcheapen Street, Worcester, a house in Lady Peckitt's Yard, York, and one in High Street, Exeter. Full-blown Artisan houses are found in brick-built areas. Wilberforce House, Hull, of c.1660, is a handsome example, with banded giant pilasters innocent of entablature. Similar, but rarer for being in stone, is Bockenfield Farm, Northumberland, of c.1675.

Gable fronts of the straight-sided type remained common in towns into the eighteenth century, even in up-to-date London, as is shown in a view of Fenchurch Street, among others, whilst a panorama of as late as 1714 shows that most houses in Bath were still gable-fronted even then. A pair of such houses in Green Street survive; they date from after 1716.

Restoration Enrichment

Whether or not they were gable-topped, many houses in high streets were lavishly detailed in the manner of the 1650 Gloucester house. Superimposed orders, one to each storey, such as on the house in the right-hand middle of the Fenchurch Street view, seem

26 and 28 High Street, Totnes, Devon (later seventeenth century)

to have been at least as common as giant orders. Giant pilasters themselves were apt to be placed not in even sequence between each window in the Jonesian manner, but either flanking a central, richly framed window, or at two-bay intervals, as at 26 High Street, Totnes.

The pilasters often had plaster ornament, for the pargeting tradition was still alive (see figure, page 86). Very little of such pargeting survives, but some hint of what there was can be seen at 28 High Street, Totnes, as well as houses in Guildford and Maidstone. They have imitation rusticated ashlar, a common type of pargeting – in Guildford incongruously applied to timber-framed projecting windows, supported on brackets in the early seventeenth-century manner. Both the houses in Totnes are also timber framed.

Post-Fire London

In the City of London, there was an immense amount of house-building after the Great Fire of 1666. This was governed by the Act for the Rebuilding of The City of London of 1667, far the most detailed and effective legislation of its kind so far. The exteriors of all buildings had to be of brick (or stone), except that, 'for the conveniency of shops', the front of the ground floor could be of substantial oak. Regulations were imposed according to four 'sorts' of house, graded according to the size of street which they fronted. The first sort were those fronting 'by-lanes', which were permitted to be of two storeys (not counting cellar or garret). The second sort were those fronting 'streets and lanes of note', which were permitted three storeys. The third sort were those fronting 'principal' streets, permitted four storeys. The fourth sort were 'mansions' not fronting any of these categories of street, which were also limited to four storeys. The Act set dimensions of brickwork and timbers for each sort (except for the fourth sort, where discretion was allowed).

Downpipes were required for the first time. This requirement, like the prohibition of projecting signs, does not seem always to have been complied with, but in general the Act was fairly rigorously enforced. Indeed, its provisions were so well accepted that building contracts frequently simply provided for the erection of a house of the relevant 'sort' according to the Act, leaving only fittings and details to be specified. Roofs of the lower three sorts of houses were to be uniform, and the surveyors appointed under the Act were to give directions to ensure the fascias of shops were at an even height; there were also practical arrangements to encourage homogeneous ranges through shared party walls. A substantial advance was thus made towards the standardisation of house-building arrived at by the beginning of the eighteenth century.

Pentices and Balconies

Some of the Act's provisions illustrate the ways in which Restoration houses still differed from those of the eighteenth century, notwithstanding the trend towards standardisation. For instance, it dealt with pentices and balconies over the ground floor, which were permitted in 'principal streets'. Pentices, or shopfront canopies, may be seen in the Fenchurch Street view (which appears to have been accepted as a principal street for this purpose, though not for balconies). Pentices had to be roofed in lead, slate or tile and plastered on the underside. Naturally enough, they were to be found elsewhere than London: surviving examples may be seen in Severnside, Bewdley, Worcestershire and, in three tiers, on Tudor House, Exeter.

Balconies were evidently popular and perhaps had been since the end of the sixteenth century, when one featured prominently, after all, in *Romeo and Juliet*. Treswell recorded many on timber-framed houses in 1612, often formed by setting back the garret. Smythson drew one on a Dutch-gabled house in Holborn in 1619. They were not the sort of structure to survive well, however. By the twentieth century there was no sign of those originally on the Lincoln's Inn Fields houses. Post-Fire balconies had railings rather than balustrades. Under the Act, they were allowed to project four feet, and were of varying length. Views of the City show them in profusion in principal streets.

Once again, for surviving examples one must turn to provincial towns that have missed wholesale rebuilding. Number 1 St Peter's

Stocks Market, City of London (Sutton Nicholls, 1728; British Museum)

Street, St Albans, has one; so do the Cupola House, Bury St Edmunds (dated 1693), and the Swan Hotel, Harleston, Norfolk. There are no less than three in Guildford High Street, though only one on a house, and that quite a grand one; another is at Shipston on Stour. One used to bridge advanced cross-wings of a house in Evesham High Street, and another fronted a 6-bay Artisan house in Exeter. Evidence of similar balconies exists at Robertsbridge, Sussex, and Bewdley, Worcestershire, and no doubt elsewhere.

That balconies were for use, and not merely for ornament, is confirmed by the parallel vogue for the roof terrace, more than occasionally to be observed in London views. Two, if not three, types are shown in the Stocks Market view. The Manor House, Park Vista, Greenwich, has one to this day.

Roof terraces often lay behind an eaves balustrade. In contrast to subsequent practice until the 1820s, eaves balustrading was a standard treatment, emulating a feature of many of the big mansions of the period and possibly accepted as fulfilling the requirement of the 1667 Act for an eaves parapet at least one brick thick. It seems to have been less a feature of other cities, though a drawing of Bath by Thomas Johnson shows it in plenty on houses round the King's and Queen's Baths in 1672.

Other Restoration Features

Well-marked bands between storeys were standard features in this phase of the Classical house. It seems probable that builders were more influenced by the centuries-long tradition of the jettied house, with its strong demarcation of each storey, than by any notional temple front.

There were other features fairly remote from any Jonesian type of house. Raised or sunk panels interposed between windows, were sometimes to be found (as in the nearest house in the Fenchurch Street view or in another house surviving in Totnes High Street). Decorative motifs might be arranged over the bands, such as the widely sundered halves of a swan-neck pediment. Windows often had key-blocks. Round-arched heads, a Restoration feature used by May at Windsor in 1672, are occasionally to be found, as in two of the houses in the Stocks Market. In otherwise Classical houses, windows were not always of vertical proportions.

Plainer Houses

Houses away from the main streets in London seem to have been plainer and closer to the eighteenth-century pattern, though there was hardly any hint of the temple-front scheme. In particular, each storey tended to be of nearly equal height. This was also the case in Bath right down to the 1720s. Under the 1667 City of London Act, houses of the first, smallest sort were to have both ground and first storeys of 9 feet (2.8 metres), with a garret above. Similarly, houses of the second, middle sort, were to have both these storeys of an equal 10 feet (3 metres) height. Only in the third sort of house was the first floor, at 10 feet 6 inches, to be higher by 6 inches (15 centimetres) than the ground floor. The third full storey of the second category of houses was to be 9 feet; the fourth full storey allowed in third category houses was to be 8 feet 6 inches (2.6 metres).

Probably typical of smaller London houses were those built from the 1670s onwards, mainly west of the City, by the speculator Nicholas Barbon, who had spent his student years in Holland. They had bands over each storey, running across the heads of the keystones, as do some of the houses seen in the main City streets. One of 1675, in Essex Street, had blind half-windows, as characteristic as the open half-windows of his Red Lion Square. Another pointer to future practice was the basement, which was just beginning to be more than a cellar, but with windows only just peeping above the ground, as yet without a front area.

Some at least of the larger houses built in London after the fire of 1666 seem also to have been plain. One example was 34 Great

Tower Street (destroyed in the Blitz), which interestingly presents an almost continuous band of windows on the ground floor, with panelling beneath and short pilasters between. Evidently advantage was being taken of the provision of the 1667 Act allowing timber fronting of the ground floor to incorporate what was presumably a still-favoured pre-Classical feature.

It is noteworthy that the first of the pattern books which guided builders down to the nineteenth century – Moxon's *Mechanick Exercises* – gave instruction on the erection of a wholly timber-framed house, and none for a brick one, even though it was published in London ten years after the 1667 Act (albeit without all its intended contents). Probably, like many later pattern books, it reflected past rather than current practice.

Outside London

By around 1680, when the next stylistic phase was opening in London, the Classical house was still only in the early stages of spreading to the rest of the country, except at the level of the mansion and in city high streets. Not surprisingly, reasonably complete survivals tend to be substantial houses.

One such is of 1674, at Stamford, in Lincolnshire. Number 19 St George's Square is stone-built, our first example of the Classical house in this material. It has quoins, a regular feature of the period, as London illustrations show. The roof has two banks of dormers, again a feature of this phase. Both dormers and roof are hipped, and the latter has a bellcast or upturn. Equally typical are

19 St George's Square, Stamford, Lincolnshire (1674)

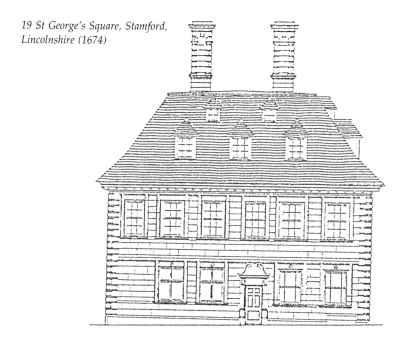

the chimneys, each of which unites several flues in a square stack, with cornice, though the rusticated arches are unusually grand. (More routine chimneys of the period are to be seen in the London views.)

Noteworthy are the ribs joining the ground-floor windows to the band between the storeys, which may not have been so unusual as they now seem. They have a parallel on the right-hand house in the Stocks Market view. The bandwork becomes a grid over the rear elevation. The central window of the front may originally have had an elaborated surround, as many did at this date.

Doorways

Probably the commonest doorcase for more dignified houses of this phase was that crowned by a broken pediment with scrolled terminations. These could be of two patterns: segmental or swan-neck, like that of 19 St George's Square. In either case an urn or similar motif might be enclosed in the break. Centrepiece windows were often given surrounds of the same kind. An alternative dignified doorcase was the arch with keystones and impost blocks of Great Queen Street.

Pedimented hoods on brackets were introduced on the door-ways of larger houses around the mid-1650s and subsequently spread to smaller houses. Commoner, even on quite substantial houses, were the arched hoods of Red Lion Square or the Fenchurch Street pentices. So, too, was the cornice on brackets. A variant did without the brackets.

Some doorways were plainer still, having only a simple moulding around them, hardly different from the windows, as seems to have been the case with some of the Lincoln's Inn Fields houses. After the Restoration, the favoured moulding for such doorways was bolection, to be found, for instance, on houses in Stamford smaller than the St George's Square house.

Another feature whose frequency at this period is difficult to gauge is the toplight to front doors (often termed a fanlight, regardless of its shape). Many doors of this and the following

Doorway with arched hood and toplight (or glazed top panels): Red House, High Street, Sevenoaks; 1686 (after J. Harris, History of Kent, *1719)*

Profile of bolection moulding on panelling – also found on door surrounds and fireplaces

phase rise the full height of the doorcase opening, as does the ten-panel door shown on page 113, though some of these had glazing in the top panels. Many others have clearly been cut down later to insert toplights. However, there is enough evidence that this fairly obvious means of lighting otherwise dark hall passageways was at least sometimes adopted. Three toplights with leaded glazing are shown in the view of the Stocks Market. Significantly, toplights were also sometimes known as transom lights, since a number of surviving examples show that the toplight was ranged level with the tops of the flanking windows and was divided in two to match the upper parts of the windows (see figure, previous page).

Eaves

The commonest eaves treatment to houses of any pretension was a modillion cornice, often paired and often strongly projecting. Somewhat enriched is that at St George's Square, Stamford. Apart from a cove, which was probably commoner in the country than the town (and is seen at 28 Totnes High Street), the other widespread type was a multiple moulding (see figure, page 98).

Railings

Before the introduction of the front basement area, there was not so much occasion for railings, and front gardens were often enclosed by wooden palings; but there were sometimes front steps that needed railings. A drawing of the White House, Bedern, York, shows railings of the same pattern as on balconies, which have alternating straight and twisted posts and ball finials at intervals and on angle posts. The railings round the statue in the Stocks Market have spike finials (likewise found round church monuments), which would also have been used on boundary railings. Spear and dart finials are also known. Scroll decoration which sometimes graced balconies would have been found on other types of railings too.

Interiors

When it comes to the interior of houses of this phase there is a good deal of overlap with previous and subsequent periods.

The feature that characterised the Classical town house and houses of some substance in the country, not only in the seventeenth century but until 1760 and beyond, was panelling of Classical mouldings for hallway, staircase and main rooms. Unmoulded panelling was used for the humbler parts of houses, such as the basement and attic flights or staircases.

From the middle of the seventeenth century and through to the end of the succeeding Baroque phase, bolection moulding was applied to the panelling on the walls in the best rooms, and also to the most important doors, either masking the butt joins between panels or fitted around raised and fielded panels. On a reduced scale, it featured on door and fireplace surrounds. A typical

19 St George's Square, Stamford, Lincolnshire; 1674 (RCHME)

arrangement of bolection panelling at this date is to be seen in a ground-floor room of the Stamford house of 1674.

The mantelpiece here is still like those in the semi-Classical houses of the early seventeenth century. The simpler mantelpieces with bolection moulding tended to have no shelf, or a small shelf formed by a length of cornice above the fireplace surround. Fireplaces that did have a shelf sometimes had an overmantel framed by short pilasters.

Internal doors were commonly two-panel, like the one in the Stamford room, but three-panel and six-panel doors were also standard. The butterfly hinges were also common, as were L-shaped hinges on larger doors. Equally characteristic of later seventeenth-century ironwork were cock's-head latch plates (another example of chronological overlap, as they originated in the sixteenth century but persisted into the eighteenth).

The plasterwork in the Stamford room, echoing the panelling, is representative of a substantial house. The decorative plasterwork of the previous era had faded out, though the beam still stands fully proud of the ceiling. A cornice was standard, however, even if there was no panelling.

There were several standard kinds of stair balustrading, as with so much else in this transitional period. Both the splat baluster and the turned-bobbin baluster of the early seventeenth century remained common (the Stamford house has splat balusters). On the other hand, the change to a fully Classical bulbous profile for turned balusters was introduced at the same time as the first Classical façades, at first waisted as at the *c.*1640 Lincoln's Inn Fields houses. Spiral balusters date back at least to Dawtrey Mansion, Petworth, if that is correctly dated 1652. Both spiral and bulbous types were to continue well into the eighteenth century.

Plans

In London, the arrival of the Classical house was largely marked by changes in the façade and the panelling of the interior rather than by changes in layout. Symmetry of the frontage and a double-depth had already been established. In lesser towns it was rather the reverse. A key change was the adoption of the double-depth, symmetrical layout all but exemplified in 19 St George's Square, Stamford.

Staircases still tended to be tucked into corners in very modest houses, and were generally semi-winding. In London, stairs in houses of ordinary size were dogleg in plan and up to around 1680 were almost always sited like those of the row at Newington Green, between the front and back rooms, sometimes lit from a minute light-well. Alongside the stair there was regularly a closet. As late as 1686, 17 Kensington Square, near London, had a small light-well.

This square is an example of the popularity of this type of layout in the wake of Covent Garden and Lincoln's Inn Fields and of the intensely urban architectural values of the time, since it was built in open country exactly as if it was in the middle of London.

SASH WINDOWS AND THE BAROQUE INCLINATION: *c.*1680-1730

It is difficult now to appreciate the decisive change produced by the introduction of sash windows, because most of the cross-windows of the previous period were speedily replaced by sashes (and hardly any of the residue have survived to our time). The new verticality of feature and sculptural modelling of the façade at about the same time, which can be called Baroque, also make it sensible to recognise the thirty years or so from around 1680 as a phase distinct from that of the mid-seventeenth century.

There were significant continuities, however, including features of the previous phase that already had a Baroque flavour, such as the façade centrepiece, the swan-neck pediment and the spiral baluster. But much domestic architecture was barely touched by the Baroque tendency, especially in the country.

On the other hand, for the village street and the farmhouse, 1680 or thereabouts was an even more important turning point than in the urban centres. For that was the approximate date of the combination of symmetrical front and double depth plan, which together may be said to define the Classical house in the countryside.

Sash Windows

The French had vertically sliding windows by the middle of the seventeenth century (held open with pins), but it was the British who invented the true sash window with pulleys and counter-weights, in about 1670. It was in use at Whitehall and at St. James's Palace by 1672. The Lauderdales chose it for Ham House in 1672-3 and for houses of theirs in Scotland in the same years. Reference in an advertisement in the *London Gazette* in 1688 to the many shops from which sash window glass could be bought showed how rapidly it became fashionable in the capital. In Bath, just beginning to be a fashionable resort, sash windows were said to have been introduced 'a year or two' after 1694.

In her record of travels in the late 1690s, Celia Fiennes's frequent references to the introduction of the new window type show it was widespread in a great many parts of England by then. In the northern countryside, however, it came considerably later in the century.

Casements continued to be used for cottages in the country right into the nineteenth century and for some of the humblest town housing for almost as long, but sashes were otherwise eventually all-conquering. By 1773, they were even found by Dr Johnson in the Hebrides, to his surprise, though the tradition of the vertical window was much older in Scotland than in England.

At first, the glazing bars of sashes were often as much as 3 centimetres by 3 centimetres (1 inch by 1 inch); they were to get steadily slimmer as the eighteenth century advanced. Until well into the eighteenth century the upper sash was often fixed.

The earliest sashes were four or even five panes wide, as on the elevation of a brick house added to the 1703 edition of Moxon (which still has a plain gable above the cornice). The three-pane-wide sash that was to be standard until the nineteenth century probably came in with the narrower proportions, an aspect of the Baroque inclination that only gained sway in the new century. Narrow sashes had the practical advantage that they were easier to raise and lower.

The Baroque Tendency

The Baroque was a fashion in house design corresponding to the phase in grander architecture that was Britain's closest approach to the Baroque style of the Continent. It is exemplified in the late work of Wren and that of Talman, Vanbrugh, Hawksmoor and Archer. In the design of smaller houses the Baroque chiefly meant greater verticality. This phase used to be known as 'Queen Anne', but the dates of that reign – 1705-14 – do not match the time span of the phase and the queen herself did little to change taste.

Verticality was stressed by several innovations, some encouraged by the London Building Acts of 1707 and 1709 (which amended and augmented the Act of 1667). Instead of an eaves cornice (or balustrade), a parapet tended to be set at the foot of the roof-slope. This was required by the 1707 Act, as a protection against fire; but the Act only applied in the cities of London and Westminster, and parapets obstructed the outlook from attic dormers, so the eaves roof continued to be widely preferred, especially in the country, right through to the end of the Classical house.

Windows were a principal element in the new verticality. Not only did they tend to be narrower, but they were also often linked together vertically. This was sometimes done by a forward break in the brickwork, as in Hanover Square, London, of c.1715-20. More frequently, it was achieved by using bricks of a different colour (usually a brighter red) in vertical lines. A similar effect was sometimes produced by mouldings such as aprons below the windows or panels in the parapet over the top windows. Often, a combination of these features was adopted, as in Albury Street, London, of 1706-17 by Thomas Lucas.

Under the 1709 Act, instead of being set flush with the wall surface, windows had to be recessed at least four inches as a fire safety measure – which produced a more three-dimensional, sculptural effect. It should be noted, however, that even in London builders were failing to conform as late as the 1720s, and outside the Act's area of application flush windows naturally lasted longer still. (See figures on pages 111 and 115).

Three other points about windows in this phase should be made. First, the heads were often segmental rather than flat (see figures, pages 111 and 112). Second, narrow windows were common, often alongside front doors or as blind openings to complete the bay system or decorate a blank section of walling (and very seldom a later blocking under pressure of the Window Tax of 1697, as often supposed). This was one aspect of the Baroque inclination that was already present, as we have seen. Third, moulded and cut brickwork was also favoured. Sometimes a roll-moulding was given to the window opening. Sometimes the head of the window was given a slender scallop.

Although there may have been few curves to the British version of the Baroque, there was one rounded feature: the bull's eye or medallion window. It came relatively early and was never very common, but is found in many different parts of the country, often used to illuminate small rooms. In North Avon, for instance, it is found between around 1670 and 1710.

A feature that was both vertical and a sculptural enrichment characteristic of Baroque swagger was the centrepiece embellishment which linked the doorway to the windows above. This was

Albury Street, Deptford, London (c.1709). The windows are linked vertically, the doorhood brackets hand-carved to individual designs (fanlight is later)

often applied to slightly grand double-fronted houses (see figure, page 112). The whole centre bay might be broken forward and perhaps be crowned by a pediment at cornice level, as in a house in St James's Street South, Bath (which still had a pair of gables inscribed below its parapet). Many clothiers' houses in West Country towns such as Trowbridge and Bradford-on-Avon were of this type. Below the first floor there might be a section of balustrading or carved decoration. Occasionally the centrepiece was framed by giant pilasters as, for instance, on houses in Prince Street, Bristol of *c.*1725, probably by John Strahan.

The giant order extending right across the façade appealed to Baroque taste, even in quite modest places like Burford. Giant pilasters framing the frontage at each end were even more common. Sometimes, in more naïve designs, there were superimposed framing orders, as in Queen Square, Bristol, of 1709-11.

The Queen Square houses also have keystones carved into grotesque masks; other well-known examples are houses at Queen

Giant pilasters framing the front: Donegal House, Bore Street, Lichfield (1730)

Anne's Gate, London, of 1700-05. Both sets are individually hand-carved, a characteristic of the Baroque phase. As the eighteenth century advanced, ornament generally became more uniform and mechanical.

Doorcases and Railings

The most striking artistry was displayed on the brackets of doorcases, even on smaller, otherwise simple houses, such as those in Albury Street, Deptford (see page 111). The carving here challenges comparison with that of the Grinling Gibbons school in churches and country houses, of which it should be seen as an offshoot. (The neglect and destruction of many of the Albury Street houses is a national scandal.)

The doorcases of the Baroque phase tended to be tall, flanked usually by fluted Corinthian pilasters and crowned by a heavy projecting canopy, usually flat and supported by carved brackets, as in Albury Street. Brackets often supported a deeper hood, which gave some protection from the rain. A characteristic elaboration of this type sported a scalloped shell within the canopy. A very early example was at 34 Soho Square, London, built by 1680.

The still-popular swan-neck broken pediment of the previous

Great James Street, London; 1720; early fan; typical doorcase

Maze Hill, Greenwich (c.1730); railings typical to c.1760

phase was now usually set over the standard fluted pilasters. It was included in William Salmon's *Palladio Londoniensis* as late as 1734. Fluted pilasters also commonly supported the popular ramped architrave, the segmental pediment that was favoured from the 1680s to *c.*1720 (especially *c.*1700-15), and the Doric entablature with triglyphed frieze, as at Maze Hill.

A distinctly Baroque type of doorcase, that only emerged towards the end of the Baroque phase and persisted well after it, was the so-called Gibbs Surround. This consisted of an architrave punctuated by large blocks. It spread slowly. Originated (or rather re-introduced from Italy) by the London-based Scot, James Gibbs, by 1722, it only seems to have reached Bristol in 1762 (see figure, page 121).

From the 1690s the bars in decorative railings were often curved and sharply angled; foliage ornament was sometimes added to the curls of the previous period. Little urns crowned the stanchions.

Toplights

Moxon shows a toplight in his elevation; others are shown in Sutton Nicholls's views of the mid-1720s. The earliest known surviving true fanlights, in the sense that they are radially patterned, seem to date from no earlier than *c.*1720, but since this shape naturally arises when a top light is fitted in a round-headed doorway, it is likely that earlier fans have simply not survived. The earliest variety of radial fan to have survived is probably the waggon wheel, found in Bedford Row, for instance, *c.*1723. The alternative type, fretted from a solid board, is datable to *c.*1725 at Marble Hill, Twickenham, and familiar at 10 Downing Street.

Albury Street, London; c.1709 (after GLC)

Plan Types and Interiors

From around 1680 the central closet and occasional central light-well disappeared from London houses and a rear closet wing became common instead. As part of the same change, the staircase was now commonly set in the position that became increasingly standard: at the back of the hall passage, lit from the rear. Chimneys were also removed from the middle of the house, now usually being placed in the party wall. Diagonally set fireplaces were common, especially in back rooms.

Indoors, bolection moulding remained characteristic, especially on panelling in the best rooms, but also round doors and fireplaces. An alternative fireplace surround was of flush stone or marble slabs with fielded panels (standard in Bath, for instance, into the 1730s, even the 1740s). This type was often ramped over the centre, like the doorcase described above. A mantel shelf was beginning to be more frequent, but it was very slight and positioned separately higher up.

On stairs, the closed string (see figure, page 95) slowly yielded to the open string with slimmer balusters set two or three to a tread. More lavish staircases usually had balusters of spiral form. This was a favourite Baroque motif, but persisted through to the mid-eighteenth century. It was also often used for the grander flights of a staircase when turned balusters on closed strings were used for flights leading to attic or basement.

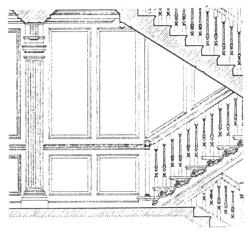

Typical of both Baroque and Palladian: open-string stair with slender balusters and carved tread-ends; 41 Gerrard Street, London; probably c.1730 (Survey of London)

Rural Houses

In the countryside, Classical house design naturally was slow to arrive, simple in its application and indistinct in stylistic phases. The key shift, which took place over large parts of Britain around 1700, was the adoption of a symmetrical frontage. The consequent central entry was associated with the placing of the chimneys at the gable ends and the staircase at the back of the front passage. A corollary of these changes was the adoption of the double depth plan for all houses larger than cottages, the service rooms being set behind the hall and parlour instead of being strung out on either side of them or in cross-wings.

When the double depth plan is not simultaneous with the symmetrical front, it tends to come first. There are late seventeenth-century examples in Dorset, Surrey and Lancashire, for instance. In Yorkshire, because of its aisle and outshut tradition, the double depth plan came early, well ahead of the symmetrical front and even further in advance of the vertical window. Bank House, Luddenden is of 1650.

There are symmetrical farmhouses of the late seventeenth century in Kent, Dorset and Devon. By the turn of the century there are others known in Wiltshire, Somerset, Middlesex and Essex. Midland counties came later.

By contrast, in the South, the double depth house with symmetrical front had reached the level of cottages early in the eighteenth century. Timber cottages continued in many areas, with slight timbers and raking braces. In the southeast they tended to be clad in plaster, tiles or weatherboarding.

In Wales, the earliest double depth house seems to be a grand one of 1582. A farmhouse double depth by virtue of a rear outshut is Tynewydd, Llansanffraid, Montgomery, of 1639. The fully double depth plan with symmetrical front and gable chimneys reached farmhouse level only much later.

On the North Yorkshire moors, an example of a farmhouse with symmetrical front and gable chimneys occurred in the later seventeenth century (still with fire windows – one at each end – and mullions), but for some time it remained an isolated case in

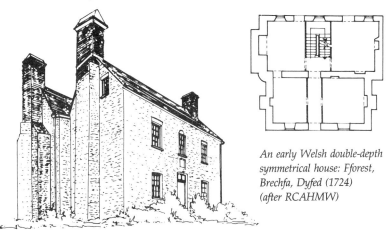

An early Welsh double-depth symmetrical house: Fforest, Brechfa, Dyfed (1724) (after RCAHMW)

that area. There, turned balusters only superseded splat ones in the mid-eighteenth century. Similarly, a small mantelshelf supported on a section of moulding, in the early eighteenth-century manner, persisted till at least 1780 (at which date a crude pulvinated frieze is also found).

The Lake District was still further behind. By the late seventeenth century, horizontal windows became obsolete but gave way to square ones with Yorkshire (horizontally sliding) sashes, named after their main seat. The double depth plan only came in around 1770, the continuous outshut being prevalent from c.1730 to c.1820. The front door only gradually took up an exactly central position and at first continued to open directly into the living room. Crow-stepped gables were common in the eighteenth century.

Brick for smaller houses continued to spread, especially in parts of Kent, Lancashire and the East Midlands. Decorative features included toothed bands arched over lower windows, toothed cornices and shaped gables. A feature that was more rural than urban was the use, at least from around 1700, of blue-grey bricks to provide patterned effects on house fronts. It became a popular feature in the Weald, and persisted into the nineteenth century.

Scotland

From a different background, smaller houses in Scotland also arrived at the Classical formula around 1700. An early case is the house Tobias Bauchop built for himself in Alloa in 1695. It has chamfered quoins, moulded eaves and plain coped gables. The door and windows had lugged architraves and cornices. More modest and typical was Key House, Falkland, Fife, dated 1713 over the door. In elevation very similar to English symmetrical, gable-chimneyed houses, it differs in being only one room deep and having the characteristic Scottish crow-stepped gables. The type was soon to be found widely in Scotland, at first reaching no further than lesser lairds, but in due course inhabited by prosperous farmers too. Even in Shetland by c.1730 an all but symmetrical example occurs. Many of these houses had thatched roofs, and glazing only on the ground floor.

Single-storey houses remained common as they did only in certain parts of England and Wales. Typical was a doorway with a bolection moulding and a cornice or pediment, often incorporating a pulvinated frieze and surmounted by a stone panel. The window surrounds (often chamfered in the early part of the century) were back-set, as were the quoins – that is to say, they were advanced from the general surface of the masonry to allow for the harling. The eaves was moulded, usually with an ogee, occasionally with a bell-cast. Inside, such houses had a central staircase, and most likely bolection-moulded fireplaces. Sometimes these had moulded corbels.

The great majority of houses in the country had no Classical pretensions.

A 'land' of c.1700, with shaped gable: 15 East Shore, Pittenweem, Fife

In the big towns, the land was becoming an increasingly standard form of housing. In Edinburgh, ever taller lands were being built. Milne's Court, of 1690, by James Mylne of the dynasty of masons and architects of that name, rises six storeys plus a garret on the rear. In 1698 the Dean of Guild (who exercised building controls till 1975) laid down a limit of five storeys. Like most other lands, Milne's Court has a plain elevation, but the entrance has a split pediment not so different from those of London houses of the same time, and inside it has a scale and platt (dogleg) staircase in a compartment off the passage between front and back doors. The chimneys were largely along the roof ridge.

The interior of Milne's Court has been much altered. According to Maitland, writing in 1753, shops could be located in cellars or upper storeys as well as on the ground floor and 'persons of distinction' were willing to take flats higher, even above the fourth floor. In the early eighteenth century, flats of six or seven rooms were not uncommon. The principal rooms had panelling, usually of pine from Memel. Ceilings by c.1690 were plastered, but not embellished. Fireplaces were usually bolection-moulded or had circled corners and an impost and keystone carved on the centre. In either case marble was often used.

In Scotland it was in this period that the Baroque feature of the shaped gable enjoyed a vogue. The earliest date for one is 1668, and notable surviving Edinburgh examples are the adjoining lands that make up 312-28 Canongate, dating from 1726 and 1752. The gables here crown façade dormers containing paired sash windows as large as those on lower floors. More commonly, shaped gables are combined with what were becoming a characteristic Scottish feature: wallhead chimneys (that is, chimneys rising from the eaves). The shaped gable died out in the middle of the century.

THE PALLADIAN PREDOMINANCE, c.1730-60

The onset of Palladianism had its main effect on the world of high taste and country mansions. As far as ordinary domestic architecture was concerned, in many respects the middle third of the century, when the Palladians were dominant, was a period of continuity with the previous period. There were, however, two significant kinds of change. The first can most readily be described negatively as the fading of the Baroque tendency, many elements of which had anyway affected only a proportion of houses. Around 1730, or somewhat later in some places, verticality diminished, red-brick banding and decoration and individual features became less variegated and boldly scaled. Specifically, cambered window heads and bolection mouldings became obsolete. The second change was earlier and more positive: the refinement by the Palladians of the implied-order town house and their development of the unified terrace.

As early as around 1714, long before the inclination towards the Baroque faded from ordinary houses, a sharp reaction against the style began in the world of grand, architect-designed work. Among the factors involved in this change in taste was the political one of the transition to the Hanoverian dynasty, when Queen Anne, the last Stuart, was succeeded by George I in 1714 (hence the traditional label of Early Georgian for this phase). The Tories were out of power for two generations, and the dominant Whigs espoused a more restrained, less sculptural style, based on selected aspects of the work of Palladio and Inigo Jones.

The Implied-Order Façade

As early as 1718-23 the arch-Palladian Colen Campbell (the first of many Scotsmen to dominate the English architectural scene in the eighteenth century) arrived at the conception of the implied-order façade. Following the Jonesian model, this treated the ground floor as the platform of a temple front and the two floors above as the zone of the order, with the entablature above that – but omitted the columns or pilasters of the order, retaining only a band, to indicate the foot of the order, and the cornice from the top of the entablature, to indicate its crown.

This scheme was applied by Campbell, apparently for the first time, to a row of four substantial houses, numbers 31-34 Old Burlington Street, London. Only partly surviving, these houses have a first-floor sill band marking the base of the implied giant order and a tall parapet above the cornice. In this design Campbell took the temple-front pattern an important step forward by not having a band, breaking the implied order, between the two upper storeys.

Opposite: (a) 31–4 Old Burlington Street, London; 1718–23, by Colen Campbell (Survey of London), (b) Cumberland Row, York; 1746 (RCHME).

Standard Brick Town Houses

Most houses in London and elsewhere continued to follow the pattern of a band between each floor or unbroken elevation with more or less equal window sizes on each floor. However, the pattern of window openings tended to change in the mid-1730s as the Baroque tendency died away: they were wider than previously and more widely spaced.

Whereas in London and the surrounding area the Palladian dominance meant the extinction of keystones from the windows, in other areas of brick building, and among the brick housing that was beginning to go up in towns even in otherwise stone-built areas, keyblocks and stone lintels were often a conspicuous feature of brick house fronts. Away from London and the rule of its Building Acts, parapets were also less normal. Number 5 Church Street, Tewkesbury, and Cumberland Row, York, of 1746, exemplify both differences. The latter also has a type of recessed doorway different from standard London patterns. Modillioned or dentilled cornices were much commoner than in London, where parapets were commonly finished off with a plain stone capping. As the period advanced there was a tendency for modillions to become smaller and less often paired, and frequently now with dentillation below.

Even modest two-storey houses could achieve considerable Classical dignity now. At Ribchester in the Lancashire Fylde district, for instance, a brick pair of 1745 has moulded architraves to the openings (with cornices to the doors), a band between the storeys, quoins and a moulded cornice.

The Palace Front Terrace

From the slight beginnings of the unified terrace in the early years of the eighteenth century the full grandeur of the palace front treatment was quickly developed by the Palladians. In 1725, Campbell published a very ambitious design for Grosvenor Square in London. It followed Lincoln's Inn Fields (and Leoni's range in Burlington Gardens, of 1721, which otherwise had very little sequel) in having a continuous giant order front with arched and rusticated ground floor and crowning balustrade.

As built, the square had only fragments of unified treatment, but one was suggestive. A group of houses on the north side, though off-centre, was designed with a columnar pedimented temple front over an arched, rusticated ground floor applied to the large house and flanking houses with a matching Palladian implied-order treatment. In other words, this range of houses was designed as if it was a single palace, similar to the country-house façades the Palladians had been building. Already in 1707-14 Henry Aldrich had applied the same formula to a college quadrangle at Christ Church, Oxford (Peckwater Quad).

A full palace front was achieved shortly afterwards, not in London but in the rising resort of Bath. Here in Queen Square in 1729-36 John Wood erected something not much less magnificent than Campbell's project for the metropolis. Faced in ashlar, the range on one side had a commanding pediment over the five central bays, an end-to-end giant order of columns and pilasters and pedimented first-floor windows. Explicitly designed like a palace front, the Queen Square's façade scheme was in 1740 applied to a terrace in Bath: Grand Parade. In other towns more modest unified terraces proliferated. Even a small place like Darlington had a pedimented terrace, built in brick, as early as 1733.

Queen Square, Bath (1729–36, by John Wood the elder)

Limestone elaboration: 66–7 High Street
St Martins, Stamford (probably later
1730s, fanlight c.1770)

Stone-Built Towns

As Queen Square illustrates, in the wealthier part of the stone-building parts of Britain – the Limestone Belt and the Lowland cities of Scotland – the Classical vocabulary, far from being simplified in comparison with London, was more elaborate. Stone was better adapted to such elaboration than brick. Architraves around windows, often lugged (that is, extruded at the top on each side) were characteristic. Over the windows (on somewhat grander houses), pediments might be set or cornice hoods – in Bath the two treatments were often alternated across house fronts from *c.*1755 and through the 1760s.

In the Cotswolds, façades were not quite so richly articulated. In Burford, for instance, Englefield in the High Street has two flat bands and no surrounds to the windows except flat architraves to the central ones – only keystones. In Bradford-on-Avon façades are a little more complicated, with more pediments and sill brackets. A local characteristic, met occasionally in the area from Burford to Bath, but otherwise more often found in the north, is the bipartite window, probably encouraged by the Window Tax, which counted windows separated by no more than 12 inches as being single.

In the north, there was a tendency to greater simplicity, partly because in many places the more dignified houses were built in brick. Nevertheless, the Ribchester range in brick had many stone equivalents. Except on substantial houses, window surrounds and mullions were often unmoulded, though the kneelers that remained widespread provided an ornamental element now almost obsolete in the south. Modest houses frequently had plain chamfers to the doorways and windows more horizontal than vertical. Middling houses with sash windows often compromised with the horizontal tradition by adopting the bipartite type.

Materials and Construction
Welsh slates were beginning to be used more widely. For the most part, tiles were the standard covering in brick areas, though pantiles were an alternative; stone tiles remained in use in the stone areas, including Bath (where Cornish slates were used, for front slopes).

For roof trusses, Salmon's *Palladio Londoniensis* of 1734 recommends a queen-post truss of about 35° pitch for pantiles or slate and a king-post truss of 45° pitch for plain tiles, both strengthened with short raking struts. This was probably representative of good practice. Most houses required a roof of more than one span. To accommodate attics, mansard roofs were also common.

Under an Act of Parliament of 1729, 8¾ inches by 4 inches by 2½ inches was set as the size for bricks within 15 miles of London; this was widely followed elsewhere. Flemish bond was the commonest, but header bond was also used.

Floorboards tended to get narrower, towards (8-10 inches) 20-25 centimetres, and by the middle of the century were as likely to be of pine as elm. In the main rooms the edges were often stained and polished to frame a carpet or painted canvas floorcloth. Stone tiles were sometimes laid over joists in hallways; the commonest pattern had small, darker squares set diagonally at the corners of the larger tiles.

Urban Plans
The closet wing tended to fade away. In Bath, for instance, Queen Square had them but they seem to have become rare after 1740. Instead, larger houses in Bath were often given polygonal or bowed staircase projections at the rear, already a feature of Queen Square in 1730. From around 1754, the time of John Wood I's houses in the Circus, it was instead rear rooms which were extended in this way, thus varying their shapes.

Staircases in terraced housing were normally at the rear, but a position at the front of the house or between front and rear rooms continued as occasional alternatives. Chimneys were also usually in the party walls, though cases occur of the older position between front and back room, as in Cumberland Row, York (where the chimneys are also separated by the stairs).

The front passage was usually still rather narrow, with a partition of panelling separating it from the front room, and an arch or spanning entablature level with the back of this room (supporting the transverse wall). In some towns the door sometimes opened directly from the street into the front room.

Detached Houses

Free-standing houses for substantial farmers, parsons and professional people were similar in design whether in town or country. Double-fronted and therefore broad in proportions, their centre bay is often fractionally broken forward, and sometimes crowned with a pediment. Inside, the staircase is likely to be more spacious than in the towns; a Dorset house shows one with a type of balustrading that had a vogue in the middle of the century, inspired by Far Eastern work and publicised for furniture by Chippendale, hence termed 'Chinese Chippendale'. Panelling tended to be confined to rather superior houses, unlike in the towns.

88–9 The Circus, Bath (1754), by John Wood I; S Lodge, Dorchester (c.1760)

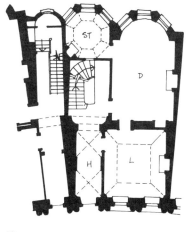

Doorcases

For detached houses even more than terraced ones, the main decorative feature was the doorway. For these, perhaps the most definite change was a general one: they tended to get smaller. There were also changes in types, though many overlaps too.

The classic Palladian arrangement was one which had been relatively rare in the previous phase: a triangular pediment on half-columns. Slightly less grand was a shallower version with pilasters rather than half-columns. Alternatively, the pediment could be supported on consoles. Simpler still was a slight pediment placed over an architrave, often with a pulvinated frieze between.

A cornice, heavy or light in profile, could take the place of the pediment, either over consoles or resting over the architrave.

Venetian windows at The Elms, Broad Street, Bampton, Oxfordshire (c.1750)

Within the various frames there might be an arch, or in rustic doorcases the arch might stand alone (see page 127).

Fanlights, both rectangular and semicircular, became commoner as the very tall doors of the Baroque phase tended to give way to smaller, less vertical doors, which left room for a toplight. It is difficult to date glazing patterns, but they seem to have remained simple before around 1760, with radial wooden spokes in fans (see page 113) and vertical bars or arrangements of diagonals in rectangular toplights. For doors, six panels were now a normal complement.

Windows
Centrepieces that were elaborate or that formed a strong vertical feature with the doorcase were rejected, but the central first-floor window as a more or less isolated element was often given special treatment on more substantial houses, sometimes with a section of balustrading below it or with curves joining it to the band beneath.

A motif favoured towards the end of this phase, especially around 1750, and persisting beyond it, was the Venetian window, which consisted of three lights, the central one arched and the side ones usually narrower. This feature of the grandest architecture reached down the social scale as far as farmhouses; in the north it blended with the tradition of the stepped window, the central light often not being arched, merely taller than the side ones. From c.1730 mullions and framing in the north were normally flush and square-section.

Panelling and Plasterwork
Bolection moulding was becoming obsolete by 1730, even in remote Whitehaven on the Cumbrian coast, though in York c.1745 seems to be the last case. Henceforth plain, fielded panelling was standard for principal rooms. Coving to the cornice had also faded out. Instead, ovolo and ogee mouldings underlay the corona almost uniformly: in London up to around 1750, elsewhere for

longer. A dentil band was now often added to the cornice. There was a general move to 'correctness' in this as in other matters of the Classical idiom. In Beverley, for instance, this has been noted as occurring from around 1730. In hallways the cornices of panelling were supposed to be sternly Doric; in the reception rooms they were supposed to be either Ionic, with dentils or simple modillions, or alternatively Corinthian, with more elaborate modillions. Modillions were used only in grander houses, but quite humble homes could have dentils.

The framework of stiles and rails got broader around 1735 and the panels within this got broader too, though often alternating narrow and broad. The chair rail at the top of the dado prevented furniture rubbing against the panelling, but also notionally marked the base of the invisible order around the interior of the house, and as such was termed a surbase. This had mouldings of different kinds around the torus forming its apex; on stairs, it often matched the handrail running level with it. The standard moulding for the skirting board of fielded panelling was a bold ogee topped by a convex one, but many varieties coexisted and sometimes there was a mere bead.

Alongside fielded panelling, there were simpler types. Flat panels might be bordered by an ovolo moulding or several mouldings. There was also flat panelling without mouldings, usually accompanied, at least in secondary rooms, by a cornice reduced to a cyma recta over a smaller ogee, a surbase much as for fielded panelling and by an unmoulded skirting board.

In London and most other parts of the country only rather grand houses now had plasterwork, but Bath was one place where the larger terraced house still often had main rooms with a Palladian treatment of scrolling foliage broken in a mild Rococo caprice, within a geometric frame, as on the mantelpiece on page 126.

Staircases
There were no great changes in staircase design. Probably the nearest to such a change was the shift from square to columnar newels. Through the Palladian period there was also a growing tendency for the rail to curve into a coil at the foot of the staircase, sometimes over balusters, not a newel.

The tendency for balusters to get slimmer continued and spiral balusters gradually got rarer, but an extraordinary variety reigned

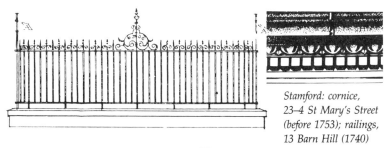

Stamford: cornice, 23–4 St Mary's Street (before 1753); railings, 13 Barn Hill (1740)

and it is impossible to chart a more than local chronological sequence. An open string, with three balusters per tread, was standard, but two balusters per tread remained an alternative (right through the period in York, for instance) and garret and basement flights continued regularly to have the more old-fashioned closed string. Chinese balustrades were introduced in London by 1753 and continued sporadically all over the country into the 1760s and beyond (see page 123). They were used occasionally in Bath, for the sake of cheapness for the top, garret flights and also for internal window guards on staircases.

In London only the grandest houses had stone staircases, but in Bath, from around 1750 and the building of the Circus, they were common in all but the most modest houses. Stone stairs nearly always implied metal balustrades, most designs for which in this period were variations on an S-curve.

Mantelpieces

A shelf integrated with the fireplace surround was now standard. The classic columnar pedimented doorcase arrangement, in miniature and with different proportions, was often adopted for the fireplaces of dignified rooms, with half-columns and an entablature framing the opening and the cornice of the latter forming the shelf. Further elements in this sort of scheme were a central panel in the frieze, a pulvinated frieze and a lugging of the architrave. Dentils and egg-and-dart were favoured for mouldings.

Overmantels continued to be used for the best rooms of more substantial houses, often with flanking scrolls, which could sometimes support the mantelpiece too. Simple marble or stone surrounds, carved with fielded panels and enriched key-block, remained common in less pretentious rooms and houses.

Pattern book mantelpiece with lugged architrave and pulvinated frieze
(B. Langley, 1745)
Wrought-iron stair balustrading, of c.1750 (V & A Museum) and c.1766 (Brock Street, Bath, already with Adam flavour)

Cross-window, quoined, central-entry house: Edgend House, Nelson, Lancashire (c.1753)

Northern Rural Houses

In the brick-built areas of the south there were few significant changes between the first and second thirds of the century. In the north, however, rural houses were in a stage of active evolution.

Even for substantial farmhouses and minor professional-level houses, sash windows had still not been introduced in the northern countryside at the middle of the century, though in other respects houses there were not very different from these further south.

North Scansby Farm, near Halifax, of 1740, serves as an example. It has widely spaced brackets to the eaves, quoins and a band between the storeys, which is ramped up to the central flowery inscription of date and owner's initials. There are flat surrounds to the door and the windows, which are four-light except for the two-light window over the door. Inside, this house has a splendid Classical niche in stone with a gadrooned sill, corresponding to cupboards of wood widespread elsewhere.

In Lancashire, houses were similar. A typical slightly superior small house in Edgend, Nelson, of 1753, is typical, with cross-windows on the first floor and three-light windows below and a keyed-arch doorway. Within, the plan was probably always symmetrical, with a narrow central passage running through from the front door to the dogleg stair.

In the Lake District the somewhat better houses also now came to have vertical windows, as ceilings rose, but it was only towards the end of the century that double-hung sashes were introduced and mullions finally disappeared. The bolection-mould door surround came in briefly as late as the mid-eighteenth century, and the more Palladian architrave and pediment in the latter part of the century, when the square-cut or slightly chamfered doorway were common alternatives.

Scotland

Chessel's Court, 240 Canongate, Edinburgh, of *c.*1748 (restored 1964), is representative of a good quality land of the Palladian period, comprising 'mansion' (or superior) flats. The exterior is of harled rubble with flat window surrounds. The round arch of the quoined doorway is echoed by the windows above it, which have keystones and impost blocks. The top window is in the standard wallhead chimney feature, flanked by narrower windows, creating a kind of dispersed Venetian window. Inside by the entrance is a newel stair. The panelling consists of a low dado surmounted by rails and stiles of pine enclosing plaster panels. (Panelling often consisted of plaster frames towards the middle of the century.) Fireplaces here usually consist of marble slips and pulvinated frieze, with a painting or stucco relief in a frame that was generally lugged and heavily enriched.

Shaped gables were outmoded by the mid-century, but house fronts in country towns often resembled Chessel's Court in having a central wallhead chimney gable, sometimes pedimented, especially in west-central Scotland, for instance on weavers' terraces in Paisley (now lost) and High Street, Kirkintilloch (still surviving). Even when there was no wallhead chimney quite often there was a central gable. An instance is Broughton House, High Street, Kirkcudbright, of a little after 1750.

Houses in country towns and the better manses of the country, as well as the houses of the smaller lairds, also often resembled Chessel's Court in their doorways. Such is 16 Canongate, Jedburgh, of 1729, or a house of 1760 with quoined margins in Front Street, Inveraray, or the Manse, Pelmont, Stirlingshire, of 1735 – and, as late as c.1770, 61 High Street, Huntly. The Manse, Pelmont, is worth noting for its stone staircase with iron balustrade and mahogany handrail. Such houses were now generally double-depth, though sometimes extra space was gained by a rear wing to form a T-plan.

Lesser houses were still often entered at first-floor level by a forestair. A house of 1749 in Cross Wynd, Falkland stands for many others that have survived. It follows the now general pattern in presenting a straight eaves lengthwise to the street. Montrose was probably exceptional by 1760 when it was criticised for its houses being 'in that bad style of building with gable ends to the street': gables were now obsolete. Equally, Dunfermline was unusual in still having partly timber-framed houses with 'furze' roofs in the eighteenth century.

Humbler country houses were still single-storey, but the better ones were now constructed with lime mortar though still limited to 'but' or kitchen and 'ben' or inner room. An example is the Burns Cottage, Alloway, built personally by the poet's farming father in 1756-7. The byre is alongside. Construction here was of clay, still widely used to build houses, sometimes erected wet in shuttering. For instance, all but the very best houses in Erroll in the eighteenth century were built by this method. Clay houses were common in Kincardine, Ayrshire, and in Berwickshire too, and continued into the nineteenth century. Clay could also be combined with wattle in what were termed creel houses or basket houses, one variety having inner walls of wattle and stakes cased in turf, to which divots were pinned like slates. There was even a

Orkney Croft, with probably 18th-century box-bed (c.1905; Orkney Library)

Great House at Kirkpatrick, Dunbartonshire, constructed of wattles.

The less good houses were of cruck construction, usually, it seems, now scarfed rather than of single timbers as in the previous century – if Stirlingshire is representative. The walls of such houses were sometimes of turf, with stone buttresses or posts to support the crucks, if Findlater, writing about Peebleshire fifty years before he published his *General View* in 1802 is a guide to general practice. More normally, the walls were of dry-stone masonry or of rubble lain in clay mortar, as in parts of England.

An idea of the interiors of but and ben houses is given by a mid-eighteenth century description of Deanburnhaugh, Roxburghshire:

'The walls were 5 or 5½ feet high with two windows, one with twelve the other with four panes; then a window in the back wall. The floors were clay with two or three flagstones laid round in front of the grate . . . two box beds were placed so as to leave a passage of three feet to the 'ben end', which also mostly contained another bed and, if they had a cow, the milk press . . . Three feet from the bottom of the chimney there was placed what was called the crook-tree, made sometimes of iron but more mostly of wood.'

[From this a chain hung with adjustable termination for cooking.]

ADAM, THE INDUSTRIAL REVOLUTION AND THE PROGRESS OF THE UNIFIED TERRACE

Around 1760, house design in Britain underwent the most abrupt changes so far, at least in the now greatly expanding towns. Panelling virtually ceased, there were radically new types of front doorway and staircase balustrading, and balconettes and bow windows were introduced. More generally, there was a transformation to a new decorative vocabulary of a wiry lightness, based in part on the inspiration of ancient Greece.

Many people were involved in this revolution of taste, but above all the Scotsman, Robert Adam, who had more impact on the appearance of the ordinary house in Britain than any other single individual before or since. His success and the change of fashion he spearheaded only came about, however, because they were in step with the burgeoning Industrial Revolution, which meant a substantial step forward in the mechanisation of the building trades. Taste and economics combined to produce simpler and slighter, more fine-drawn, forms. Houses became more elegant, but also lost something of enlivening craftsmanship.

Alongside what may be termed the Adam revolution was another important strand of development. Much more of an evolution out of the previous Palladian phase, this was focused on Bath, where John Wood the Younger carried on the work of his pioneering father. He was at the forefront of a great blossoming of the unified terrace in which Adam (and his brother James) also played a part. In particular, he invented the crescent, which was quickly imitated all over the country.

The End of Panelling; the Stick Baluster

It was indoors that the greatest change of all occurred with the disappearance of panelling from walls. In London it had gone by the middle of 1760s. Only the dado, and subsequently only the dado rail, was left, except in humbler houses, which often retained panelled partitions in the front passage. Wallpaper, taxed from 1712 but never quite ousted, took the place of panelling, and by the end of the century was to be found in quite modest homes.

On staircases, almost as striking as the disappearance of panelling was the change from turned balusters to simple square ones. This change however, was not so universal.

Doorways

Two new doorcase types dominated the period. The first, which became a standard type for medium-sized town houses all over Britain until around 1830, was introduced around 1750, somewhat ahead of the other innovations discussed. It was a condensed version of the long-established type of doorcase that consisted of an archway framed by half-columns and topped by a pediment. The head of the archway was now introduced into the open base

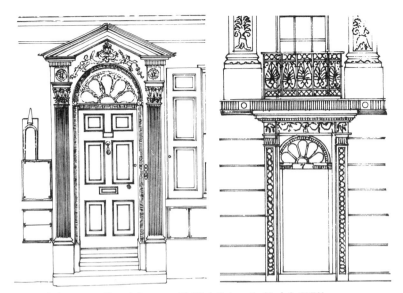

(a) Arch-in-open-pediment doorway: 23 High Petergate, York (c.1779)
(b) 7 Adam St, Adelphi scheme, London (1768, by R. and J. Adam); with balconette

of the pediment. Who invented this type of doorcase is unclear. It may have been Robert Taylor. The first dated example seems to be 43 Parliament Street, Westminster, of 1753, which is ascribed to him. It has a depressed arch.

The other doorcase innovation was more radical. It was to turn the whole arrangement of archway and doorcase inside out, with the doorcase set within the arch and under the fanlight. Taylor crops up in this connection too. He designed a precursor of this type for a big house in Lincoln's Inn Fields in 1754. It was the Adam brothers, however, who popularised it when they applied it to their larger terrace houses in and around Portland Place (see page 132). Under a greatly enlarged fanlight they put sidelights each side of attenuated columns. In later, less grand, versions the sidelights were omitted or the colonettes became mere pilaster strips. A variant form popular in provincial towns for smaller houses without sidelights had quarter-columns against the sides of the arch.

Balconies

A new wish to break down the barriers between the insides of houses and the surrounding parkland led to the main rooms of country houses being transferred from the first floor down to the ground and their windowsills being lowered towards ground level. In terraced town houses this innovation had its counterpart in first-floor windows extending down to the floor. These were protected by a window guard, set only a few inches from the window, or by a balcony, also of iron, which projected only a little further and was hardly wider than the window – hence the term balconette. The Adam brothers employed balconettes on the Adelphi scheme of 1768 (see figure, previous page) and in their subsequent London housing. They soon spread to Bath and elsewhere.

Both balconettes and broader balconies became highly popular in the succeeding Regency period, when, to conform with current taste, they were frequently added to existing houses, and windows were frequently cut down. In consequence, it is difficult to be sure when such features are original.

Façade Design

To some extent it is true to say that the Jonesian temple front scheme came to its fullest realisation only when the Palladians, who modelled themselves on Jones, were being swept aside by Adam and other exponents of post-Palladian taste. For now, more than ever, house fronts really did read as divided into base, order and attic.

In the first place, the sills of the first-floor windows were regularly linked in a band that read as the top of the pedestal from which the implied order rose. This had been done by John Wood in Queen Square as early as 1728, but without any wide following. Often this sill band was duplicated by another just below it, as at Mansfield Street.

Further to reinforce the notion of the podium, the ground floor now regularly began to be given round-headed windows, often uniform with the doorway arch to increase the overall regularity. (Queen's Square was again a precedent.) Albion Place, London, of 1772-c.90, by Mylne, is an early example. Windows on one or more

7 Mansfield Street, London; early 1770s, by Robert Adam (Peter Wyld)

upper storeys also sometimes came to be arched, as at Finsbury Square, London, of 1789-90, by George Dance the younger, which had rectangular windows within the arches (demolished).

Brick Houses

Externally, perhaps the most important change in brick-built houses was the character of the brickwork, a change very much dictated by a combination of taste and technical advance. The red, uneven brickwork that had given warmth and texture to early Georgian houses had already started giving way to smoother, more regular facing bricks of yellow-brown in the more up-to-date London housing in the middle of the century; this change was more or less accomplished by 1760. A minority of houses were taken one step further, by being built of white bricks (actually grey). These had first appeared in the early part of the century in Hertford, but their vogue only gathered pace at the end of the century.

The same cool taste for fine lines led from around 1760 to around 1820 to the practice of 'tucking', whereby putty was used to give the illusion of ultra-fine mortar joints. Yet another, more aesthetically neutral factor for change in brickwork was the 1784 Brick Tax, levied per unit, which led to an increase in the thickness of bricks to 3 or even 3¼ inches; they only shrank again when the tax was doubled on large bricks in 1803.

The 1774 Building Act

The tendency towards simplicity was confirmed by the 1774 London Building Act – unsurprisingly, as it was drafted by the architects Taylor and Dance, themselves exponents of the new refinement. To give further protection against fire, windows not only had to be set back, but the frames now had to be recessed (or 'rebated') into the surrounding brickwork. Apart from doorcases, external woodwork was banned.

The Act repealed its predecessor of 1667, but it continued the four categories of house instituted by that Act, now termed 'rates' and numerically reversed, so that the first-rate house was the largest and a fourth-rate one the smallest. By its requirements for each rate, the Act gave further impetus to standardisation.

Away from London, stone lintels and key-blocks remained widespread, and even gained new territory. For instance, in Farnham, lintels, usually painted, came to be adopted in the aftermath of the 1774 Act. In York, the new sill-band co-existed with the old band between first and second storeys.

Stone Houses

The new taste for smoothness affected stone as well as brick frontages. In Bath, still the place where the finest and most innovative domestic architecture was to be found, windows and doors were often cut flush into the stonework to minimise projections. Architraves tended to vanish, while sills were smoothed into a continuous band. Doorways were sometimes also clean-cut rectangles and sometimes simple arches no wider than the door, though it has to be added that Bath also clung to Palladian types of half-column door.

Interest was given to the façade in new ways. Occasionally tablets or cameos were carved in the stonework, as in Marlborough and Northumberland Buildings of probably before 1790 and 1778 respectively. Both of these terraces also have some of the first-floor windows within incised arches. Ground floors were often rusticated, frequently with arched openings, some of the windows being arched too and some rectangular. An overall cornice with smallish, close-set modillions was standard. Above would be a low parapet or balustrade. To accommodate the steep slopes of Bath, the cornice and plat bands were often ramped from one house to the next. Alternatively, they were discontinuous.

The Venetian window was popular for first floors or otherwise standard houses. This could have the interesting corollary of tripartite windows on the third, top floor without an arch to the middle light as this would collide with the overall cornice. There are examples in Brock Street (1764-70) which also has Venetian windows on lower floors with middle lights which are taller than the side lights but also flat-headed.

In nearby Bristol, house design was similar if more modest - indeed Thomas Paty, who with his son William was responsible for many Bristol streets of the 1780s, had long worked as a mason in Bath. Among differences were a greater liking for the arched open-pediment doorway and the use of pilaster strips to mitigate the discontinuity of cornices and bands on a slope.

At the other end of the limestone belt, Stamford's houses also evolved to a new smoothness. From around 1760 only plat bands or sill bands were proud of the surface.

Crescents and Palace Fronts
Perhaps partly to make up for the general plainness of the standard house front, rows of houses were now increasingly unified, either by the palace front formula of emphasised centrepieces and terminal sections or by the novel layout of the crescent. After the isolated examples of the palace front in the Palladian period, it was John Wood the younger in Bath and, once again, the Adam brothers who provided the impetus.

Wood bent the unified terrace into a moon-like curve in his Royal Crescent of 1767-75. He invented this layout on a very bold scale in the wake of his father's Circus, conceivably prompted by the Rococo collarbone motif (used in Bath plasterwork) or perhaps merely pragmatically following the contour to keep to the level in a sloping area. The invention was a success, and was quickly followed by other crescents, including one in London by Dance, in his small-scale Minories scheme, of 1767-8, one in the estate village of Lowther, by Adam, of 1768-71, and the Crescent, Buxton,

Derbyshire, by John Carr, of 1779-84. Twenty were laid out between 1788 and 1800, half of them in Bath and Bristol.

In terms of palace front elevation treatment, Royal Crescent, with its giant order, no pediment and virtually no other stress at the middle or ends, was not so spectacularly influential. The Adam brothers were more significant in this respect. Their Adelphi Terrace of 1768-72 had decorated pilasters at the middle and ends and pilaster strips over these in an attic storey, but dispensed with pediments as Wood had, though the main terrace was framed by the pedimented return fronts of the two streets at right angles (one of which survives the barbarous demolition of 1936). Portland Place (1776, by Robert and James Adam) was closer to the convention set by Queen Square, with temple fronts at centre and ends, the former pedimented.

In the same year, London at last caught up with Bath in achieving a palace-front square, with Bedford Square, the general design for which was by Thomas Leverton. It, too, echoed Queen Square in having central pedimented temple fronts, but the doorways with their radial Coade stone blocks (see pages 137-9) contribute almost as much to the visual impact.

Back in Bath, Camden Crescent of 1788, by John Eveleigh, had both a continuous giant order and central pediment, but Lansdown Crescent of 1789-93, by John Palmer, had only the slightest central pedimented temple front and was generally so suavely smooth that the arched lamp standards register as its chief articulation. Its terminations were punctuated by shallow bows, a muted variation on the bold convex feature, or large bow, on the centre of another Bath terrace, Somersetshire Building of 1782 by

Lansdown Crescent, Bath (1789–93, by John Palmer)

Thomas Baldwin. Adam likewise incorporated bows in his proposals for Bath, but the idea was not widely followed.

In his last years, Adam set a new pattern of palace front terrace, combining the idea of the temple front with that of the triumphal arch, by inscribing segmental and round heads and thermal motifs within the order. This had already been done in a mild way in Portland Place. It was more strongly effected in 1790 at Fitzroy Square (stone-faced, remarkably for London) and in 1791 at Charlotte Square in Edinburgh, a main feature of the New Town.

Detached Houses

Sometimes, perhaps especially in Wales, even rows of plain sash windows were acceptable, but there was a tendency in this phase to play a number of characteristic variations on plain fronts for detached or double-fronted houses in town or country. The simplest one for three-bay fronts was to make the side windows tripartite. Another tactic was to make the central upper window round-headed. In tune with the prevailing simplicity, there was seldom any surrounding enrichment to this window, except maybe by impost and key-blocks, as at 90 West Street, Farnham. Bay windows were also spreading. From being hidden on the rear, as at Queen Square, Bath, with the windows well separated on each cheek of the bay, these were now placed on visible fronts, and the windows closely joined. Country examples begin around 1750. A little later they occurred in towns, where space permitted.

Bow windows were being applied to house fronts in the southeast from around 1760, before Bath.

The Venetian window, already favoured by the Palladians, and the thermal window, espoused by Adam, were included on detached or double-fronted houses of the 1760s and later. Representative is a house in Grantham where the columned porch is flanked by Venetian windows, the first floor has five conventional windows and the top floor has a thermal window each side. Substantial farmhouses all over the country had similar designs.

Materials and Construction

Welsh slates – yet another element of slenderness and mechanical finish – began to be used in London on a large scale from about 1760, and subsequently all over the country. They could be cut to very thin and precise rectangles, had been used in nearby Chester since the fourteenth century and in Shropshire in the fifteenth century, and – a little inexplicably – in Beverley by the 1740s, but only became widespread after 1760. Slate-hanging was adopted in the late eighteenth century, as weatherproofing, mainly in Devon and Cornwall, but also sometimes in the Lake District.

Mathematical tiles, looking like bricks, but actually interlocking tiles, were widely used in the south-east to disguise unfashionable timber-framed houses. The earliest known are of 1724, but they mostly date from the fifty years after 1760, especially after the 1784

Brick Tax. Weatherboarding was also boosted by the tax. It was popular in East Anglia as well as the south-east.

The introduction of chimney pots was one component in the sweeping changes around 1760. Downpipes received a further boost from an Act of Parliament of 1763. An inverted bell shape for rainwater heads was adopted from the middle of the century. Window glazing bars became even slighter.

The new Decorative Vocabulary

Alongside the more mechanical finish of façades in the last third of the century, and their tendency to unrelieved surface, new types of enrichment developed in compensation. This was not a little assisted by new techniques of multiple production. Others, such as 'Athenian' Stuart, were pioneers of the new vocabulary, but the Adam brothers played the principal role, partly through commercial involvement.

The anthemion was the commonest motif in the new vocabulary, ubiquitously applied both to ironwork and in plasterwork or carving. Also characteristic was wider and shallower dentillation of cornices. Fluted bands took the place of more conventional cornices to mark the top of the invisible order over the first and second floors on grander houses, as on Lansdown Crescent. Plat bands were also often fluted or given a Vitruvian scroll or other ornament. Consoles became elongated.

The use of stucco meant a big change to brick houses, contributing in turn to other changes. Various patent renders had been used in a very limited way during the mid-eighteenth century; but large-scale production only began in 1765 with David Wark's invention of patent render in 1765 and Liardet's in 1773, the patents for both of which were acquired by the Adam brothers. Stucco was originated as a substitute for expensive stone, which was more esteemed than brick but too expensive to use away from the areas where it could be quarried. To imitate stone, stucco was scored in imitation of ashlar joints and painted stone-colour.

Stucco was initially used for decorative elements of the design and, quite often, to face the whole of the ground floor. Thus used, it gave more reality to the notion of the ground floor being the podium to the Classical temple front. It was laid on plain or as flat rustication, the latter being traditional in stone. The Adam brothers applied stucco to the ground storey of Portland Place and adjacent streets from the early 1770s onwards, possibly influenced by the now fashionable Bath, where John Wood's Queen Square had already had a rusticated ground floor in 1729. Stucco on the ground floor became standard treatment for all but the most modest brick houses until the mid-nineteenth century.

A natural extension to imitation ashlar was the imitation of carved ornament in multiple castings of patent compositions, of which much the most important was that of Mrs Eleanor Coade, who took over a moribund firm in 1769, or just before, and produced a vast quantity of mouldings, especially keystone head-reliefs, but also rusticated voussoirs and moulded imposts.

Doorcases

There were a number of significant variations on the two main types that had revolutionised doorcase design. The Adam brothers themselves adapted a little-used Palladian type – an arch enclosed by pilasters and entablature – but transformed it with their free handling of its elements and their characteristic embellishments. One version can be seen on a surviving part of the Adelphi scheme (see page 131). Similar doorways with a square opening and often Ionic fluted pilasters are also to be found. Alternatively, the entablature could be supported on consoles.

Making use of Coade stone, was a type of doorway developed from the Gibbs surround. It consisted of an arch punctuated by rusticated blocks in Coade stone. On a grand scale, such doorcases are an important element in the design of Bedford Square; on a more modest scale at 27 New Road, Whitechapel, also in London, they are equally effective.

All these doorcases could be decorated with applied composition enrichments.

Fanlights and Other Decoration

Fanlights were now usually of metal. It was Adam who pioneered its use, which facilitated his favourite Grecian type of ornament, especially the anthemion motif. This was a point of importance, as fans were now often a key decorative feature of a house. They were soon available in cast iron, which made for large-scale production. The Adam brothers used radial patterns, with arrow spokes and semicircle terminations, a type that became highly popular. The same pattern in simple but elegant form was the cobweb, sometimes echoed identically in the glazing bars of round-headed windows. Patterns based on intersecting circles were also typical (for example, in Colebrook Row, London, of 1768). Joseph Bottomley published a pattern book of metal fans in 1794.

Wooden fans also persisted. In particular, patterns of short loops were common in various parts of the country, especially East Anglia, and were disseminated by John Crunden's *Convenient and Ornamental Architecture* of 1770. This type is associated with the pre-Adam arch-in-open-pediment doorway (see figure, page 121). Crunden also showed Gothic patterns of intersecting glazing bars, such as also featured in round-headed windows.

Plasterwork

With the disappearance of panelling, plaster cornices of slighter profile took their place. Sometimes there were diminutive modillions but more common was an oblique band of leaves or similar motifs. In better rooms a decorative band bordering the ceiling was now usually introduced, and sometimes a frieze at the top of the

Coade Stone embellishment, 27 New Road, Whitechapel, London (1800–10)

wall. Fluting, palmette and anthemion motifs became standard under the influence of the Adam brothers. They also led the way in making up their designs from ready-cast pieces, which were then stuck on. One firm that supplied such products was Wolstenholme of York, which sold composition urns for 8 shillings to 9 shillings a dozen, and swags (or drops) for 6d. or 3d. each.

Sometimes the walls retained a shadow of panelling in the form of planted frames, as well as the surviving dado rail.

For more lavish rooms, ox skulls, vases, lyres and other more sculptural forms were used. For these, decoration might be extended across the ceiling. Here again the depth of relief would be much less than previously. Likely components were a central rose; a larger circular or polygonal central panel; delicate concentric husk bands, or similar, in convex loops, swags or intersecting arcs; and, in outer areas, quadrant and detached panels, filled with rinceaux, urns and the like and maybe interspersed with roundels.

Wallpaper was also increasingly used as panelling retreated. Even in a provincial town like Beverley, walls were papered rather than panelled by around 1765, though chimney breasts still had wood or plaster panels through the 1760s.

Mantelpieces

Applied and composition ornament were also much used on painted wooden mantelpieces, employing many of the same motifs, especially garlands across the frieze. At the sides would be colonettes, commonly Ionic and fluted, or panels. The mid-panel of earlier mantelpieces was now often a figurative relief. Paterae or cameos at the corners were also common. Where there were colonettes, the shelf was often broken forward over them in segmental curves.

Marble mantelpieces were now to be found not just in mansions, but in superior terraced houses. They sometimes had inlaid decoration (Greek fret, for instance). The designs for them were generally similar to the wooden mantelpieces, but in independent-minded Bath elongated consoles sometimes served in place of columns (for example, in the library of 1 Royal Crescent).

Grates underwent a considerable change. Industrialisation had two effects. On the one hand, coal was now the main fuel, at least in the towns, and a smaller grate higher above the hearth was called for. On the other hand, cast-iron parts could now be mass-produced for use all over the country, especially by the Dale company of Coalbrookdale and Carron of Falkirk. The latter, founded in 1759, had the Adam brothers as directors and John Adam as a designer. Two characteristic grates were developed, both flanked by shelves (or hobs), which took up the now surplus space and provided a surface on which kettles or pans could be kept hot: the hourglass (figure, page 139) and the double ogee.

Internal Woodwork and Staircases

By 1770 it was typical to add a second bead to architraves, next to the large ogee moulding. Soon a quirk (linear incision) was also added to the large ogee by the Adam brothers and up-to-date designers. A compressed and quirked ovolo was also fashionable from around 1770. Window reveals were splayed, at first slightly, then more sharply in the Regency period.

Complementing the plain verticals of stick balusters went sweeping curves of handrails and – quite often – of curving walls too. Stairs were sometimes sited mid-house and toplit. Handrails approximated to a cylindrical shape and newels also tended to have a simple profile.

Over much of the country, however, turned balusters continued. In York, for instance, instead of a change to stick balusters there was a standardisation around 1760 to two types with slender columns above the knop, one with a bulb below it, the other with an urn. In Bath, a lightly moulded type was prevalent in the 1770s. Everywhere the carved tread end died away. Instead, various simple linear ornament was applied, frequently a double curve or a simple version of the Vitruvian scroll.

Water Closets

For the first time water closets ceased to be a rare luxury and spread to many middling homes, thanks to technological advance. The S-bend water trap, patented by Alexander Cumming in 1775, was one key element to the practicality of the device; the handle-operated flap or valve, patented shortly afterwards by Bramah, was the other.

Industrial Housing in the North

Most domestic architecture in the thirty-five years or so under consideration does not call for separate discussion. On the one hand the new taste found similar expression in the north to that elsewhere, mainly in better houses and in the towns, though even cottages could boast simple versions of the double-ogee type of fireplace, for instance. On the other hand, most modest rural housing was little affected. The Industrial Revolution did, however, create a new category of workers' housing in the north. An early instance was in North Street, Cromford, Derbyshire, where in 1771 Arkright erected some houses with bipartite sash windows separated by flat mullions, and some with casements.

Developments in textile workers' housing may be followed in some detail in West Yorkshire, where it has been closely studied. Here, as on the Lancashire side of the Pennines as well as in Derbyshire, early industrialisation created characteristic so-called 'weavers' housing, both in the form of cottages and of larger ranges. Such housing was used by other textile workers as well as weavers. Representative of weavers' cottage design is 32 and 33 Oldfield, Honley, a semi-detached pair of the mid-eighteenth century. The upper windows are twice the width of the lower ones to light the home looms or other apparatus. Downstairs each cottage had a living room and a scullery. Sometimes, it seems, there was a shared workroom extending over several cottages.

Among larger ranges of textile workers' dwellings was a type that was to have a large progeny: the back to back (whereby rows of dwellings were butted together back to back, with windows of each set looking only one way). An early example is on Huddersfield Road, Thongsbridge, dated 1790 in an elegant inscription – the only ornamental feature of the exterior.

An alternative economy dwelling was the back-to-earth, built into a steep bank, which allowed ground-level access to the workroom or upper dwelling from the high level at the back, through 'taking-in doors'. An example is at West Laithe, Hepton-stall, which has single-storey vaulted under-dwellings and two-storeyed upper ones. The homes in such ranges could be as small as the Honley cottages or be larger by a whole extra storey. The front of this one is slightly enlivened by minimalist versions of the straight-headed Venetian window so widespread in the north, the central light being only fractionally taller than the sidelights.

The window surrounds and mullions here and in the other housing under discussion are uniform square slabs, set flush with the wall. They would originally have appeared less severe than they do now because they would have had small panes. By the end of the century, cottages were being fitted with sashes, though held open by wedges, not hung. The middle light of the rectangular Venetian window was suited to these.

The use of water power meant that textile workers came to be employed in mills, rather than working at home. Partly because many mills had to be away from existing settlements (to obtain a good water flow), owners often erected rows of cottages, which were usually two-storeyed with no back door and a single room on each floor; they differed from the weavers' cottages in not having large upper windows. There was such a row at the first mill in West Yorkshire, at Addingham, erected shortly after 1787.

Scotland

Workers' housing was also being systematically erected here in the later eighteenth century. Windows were vertical sashes, by contrast with the North of England, and the stairs were usually in a circular projection at the rear. Examples may be viewed at the Livingstone Centre, Blantyre, and at Robert Owen's model New Lanark. Urban tenements were fairly similar, only much taller. A Glasgow example (below) is representative in its plan. The front often continued to bear a central gabled wallhead chimney. Below this there might be a round-headed window on the first floor and below that an arched pend (vehicular through-passage).

In Edinburgh, a great leap forward was taken with the laying out of the New Town in a regular grid of Classical streets from 1767. At first the houses followed simple Palladian designs and were not entirely uniform, though controlled in dimensions. However, standards of finish were rising, with rubble and dressings giving way to droved (horizontally tooled) ashlar. And after Adam's Charlotte Square, begun in 1791, the unified terrace became usual. Bowed features came in at the same time, as at 39-43 North Castle Street, of 1790-93, where they flank a central pediment. Some ranges were pilastered, some had columned porches, many were plain.

Venetian windows were to be found, if somewhat less widely than in England, both in the towns and the country. Carlyle's birthplace in Ecclefechan is a good example, built by 1791, with a central pend for symmetrical effect. The kitchen within shows a typical country fireplace with plain corbeled lintel similar to those in stone-built areas of England and Wales (for instance at North Street, Cromford). All over Scotland a great 'improvement', as it was termed, took place, with the better types of house rapidly taking the place of inferior ones.

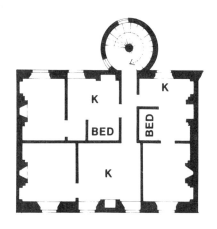

394 Gallowgate, Glasgow (1771); upper floor plan of three-storey tenement, typical till c.1850, when stairs became non-projecting and dogleg (after F. Worsdall; K = kitchen)

THE REGENCY PHASE, *c.*1795-*c.*1835

The Regency strictly lasted only from 1811 to 1820, while the Prince of Wales was Regent because of the lunacy of his father. As a stylistic term, however, it is generally extended backwards at least to 1800, and forwards through the Prince Regent's own reign as George IV (1820-30) and beyond. Evolving in the wake of Robert Adam's death in 1792 and initially influenced by the taste for starkness in other arts in around 1792, it was an intermediate stage between the fine-drawn elegance of the Adam period and the rotund richness of Victorian taste. Verandas, continuous balconies and enlarged windows were characteristic features from around 1795. Giant order terraces, all-over stucco and the Greek Revival came to the fore after 1800; proportions tended to get broader and decoration, in England, distinctly lusher.

The Terrace in Scotland

In architecture, Scotland was not just the equal of England in the Regency period but at the forefront of European achievement – as it had already become in philosophy, economics and literature.

Edinburgh was now taking over from Bath as the prime centre of the ashlar-faced terrace, with a galaxy of architects from 1802 onwards designing a huge area of airy, sober, impressive terraces in and around the New Town. The main difference was a more hard-edged unity and, as time went on, a stronger Greek flavour. At first the pattern set by Adam was closely followed, if without some of his more individual touches. Ground floors were rusticated, and partly or wholly round-arched – often with the windows recessed, reinforcing the solidity of the implied temple base. Above this, a giant order was applied to centre and end sections of the grander terraces, often with an attic storey added to these for emphasis, and sometimes a central pediment. Balustrading and window cornices or pedimented surrounds were other elements applied to different stretches of the terrace to balance the composition. Thermal windows were often incorporated in the wallhead chimneys of end sections or return fronts (which were often divided into tenements).

Royal Terrace, Edinburgh
(1819, by Playfair;
plan overleaf)

*Carlton Street, Edinburgh
(1824, by James Milne)*

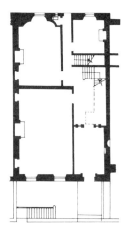

12 *Royal Terrace, with toplit mid stair typical of Scotland (after RCAHMS)*

Playfair was one of the leaders among the architects of the New Town. His Royal Terrace of 1819 is one of the most impressive terraces, with very much the rhythm of Charlotte Square, but simpler and perhaps stronger. Such palace front terraces were interspersed with lower ranges, which conformed to the same pattern, but without an order and generally without emphasised sections. They were often graced by continuous or discontinuous first-floor balconies. Carlton Street is a good example of the way in which the lucid, geometric forms of balcony fronts, railings and toplights added up to an elegant unity. Typical is the way in which the doorway exactly matches the windows openings, though the type of doorcase which is set within an archway under a more lacy fanlight is also common.

On the basic theme of the linear terrace the Edinburgh architects played imaginative variations. There were squares, crescents, circuses and angled layouts. The grandest of the last type is Moray Place, of 1822, by another key architect, James Gillespie Graham.

Edinburgh is where Scottish urbanism supremely flourished in the first quarter of the century, but by the early 1820s good terraces were beginning to be found in all the larger Scottish towns.

Nash

In England the key architectural figure, backed by the Regent himself, was John Nash, who was especially important both for terrace design and as the arch exponent of stucco, invariably applied all over on his terrace fronts. Though his work was less fine-drawn than that of the Scots, in the years 1812-27 around Regent's Park in London Nash took the unified terrace to its apogee, characterised by showy central and terminal sections and a plentiful use of giant columns. Much like the Scots, he emphasised the end sections by breaking them forward or upwards, sometimes pedimenting them, as in Hanover Terrace of 1822-3. He usually applied pilaster strips to the attics. His most adventurous terrace, Sussex Place, he crowned with domes; he also angled forward the end sections, like Moray Place of the same year. He often applied giant columns to centre and ends but sometimes to the stretches between instead; he frequently set them well forward of the wall surface, aligned with the front edge of the balconies.

All Nash's big terraces had balconies on the first floor. In Park Crescent of 1812-22 the balconies were supported by a continuous colonnade of coupled columns aligned with the area railings; other terraces had colonnades or arcades beneath the balconies. The majority of his balconies were fronted with balusters, rather than railings; he also often set balustrades above his top cornice. This made for a heavier look, as did his window architraves, elaborate cornices and the like, but he used a wide Classical vocabulary in sparing combinations, to produce pleasing variety and contrast.

Brighton saw the greatest amount of wholly stuccoed terracing outside London, with rather lax designs featuring groups of giant columns and bow windows; Brunswick Terrace, 1830 by C.A. Busby, has a giant order extending end to end. The layout tended to laxity too, a local speciality being a bottle-shaped square, open to the sea at the bottom, the sides of a wider outer rectangular section sloping inwards to a narrower inner one.

Elsewhere, the palace front terrace probably had its most notable exposition in Newcastle, especially at Leazes Park by T. Oliver, of 1829-30, which is crisply severe in a Scottish spirit, though with detailing all of its own. It dispenses with any order at all on one front, relying on forward and upward breaks in its massing. It is important for its plan, which is a square turned inside out.

Window Innovations
Most terrace housing, even outside the stone-built areas, remained unstuccoed and was not given unifying treatment, but continued

Hanover Terrace, London (1822–3, by John Nash): a palace-front terrace

more in the patterns set by the late eighteenth century. There was, however, one crucial change eschewed in all the unified-terrace designs so far considered, which retained strict symmetry in the arrangement of window and door openings. In 1795 George Dance designed a row of houses in Chiswell Street, London, in which the two ground-floor windows were offset in order to accommodate the front door. Earlier, there might have been three windows above the three ground-floor openings; the Window Tax may have reduced the number.

By around 1810, non-alignment between ground floor and the windows above was common in London, especially in the case of a single ground-floor window, which could not otherwise easily be central to the front room. Non-alignment was often made less obvious by continuous balconies, as well as by the stuccoing which marked off the ground floor from the upper storeys.

Window Tax probably had its biggest effect between 1798, when its scope was widened to include houses with only six windows, and 1825, when it was reduced. It should be borne in mind in relation to a number of Regency window arrangements.

The tripartite window continued to gain ground, especially as a means of enlarging a single ground floor window; the type was previously restricted to the corners of terraces, as in Bath, or to the wider end-bays of unified compositions. One divided by colonettes was popular in Birmingham in the last years of the eighteenth century. In Bath, in a notable step towards the Victorian Italianate style, Thomas Baldwin used tripartite windows on all three storeys of Bathwick Street of 1790 and pedimented those on the first floor.

Another means of enlarging windows and thus making a single-window frontage more acceptable also met the Regency taste for broader proportions. This was the use of sixteen-pane sash windows in place of the twelve-pane windows of the eighteenth century. They could be adopted for the ground floor alone or all the way up. There are examples as early as the 1780s and 1790s in Manchester (St James's Square) and of around 1800 in Hull (in courtyard housing). External shutters occur in the latter case, a vogue that extended from before 1800 to c.1830. Wider windows were now often given segmental heads.

Bay windows became much commoner, especially in southern seaside towns, both in canted form and bowed. Bow windows were to be found on brick and stucco-fronted houses nearly everywhere. Such was the strength and pervasiveness of national fashions now that they spread to such remote areas as the North Yorkshire moors as early as c.1800 on gentry houses, and little later on others.

Round-headed windows lit staircases, even in York, where they were otherwise rare. These were sometimes greatly elongated, to light several landings, which produced a striking effect and again saved money on Window Tax.

The pattern of glazing bars was also changing. The conventional oblong pane was beginning to be found boring. By around 1820 many windows, though retaining the twelve-pane pattern, had wider proportions and almost square panes. More drastic was the introduction of 'margin glazing'. It featured in Doyle and Underwood's 1810 catalogue, in metal French windows, and was soon popular for other non-sash varieties. It had become sufficiently

Brunswick Square, Brighton (1825, by C A Busby): the whole front bowed; Greek revival detail

standard by 1825 to be included in Elsam's *Practical Builder* of that year. It was used in the oblong fanlights that were being reintroduced at about the same time. Often coloured glass was fitted in the margin panes. Margin glazing was probably most prevalent as late as the 1840s, by then used widely on ordinary sash windows, and only died away after the middle of the century.

Non-sash windows were often cast iron by the end of the eighteenth century, especially for cottage housing, which tended to have small windows of sixteen panes, with the central four opening (figure, page 82). More picturesque, and more often surviving, are iron casements with Gothic interlace or margin-glazing.

The Semi-Detached and its Kin

Contrary to what is often stated, urban pairs of houses had been built right back to the seventeenth century, but they had been sporadic and single. As early as 1724 pairs of estate cottages were put up in rows at New Houghton, Norfolk. Others followed. Rows of semis in the town seem only to have started at the same time as other variations on the standard terrace, towards 1800.

An important innovation of as early as around *c.*1790 was that of the quasi-semi-detached row, pioneered by William Paty (and probably his son Thomas) in Bristol and by Michael Searles in Gloucester Circus, Greenwich. In this arrangement a terrace is given the appearance of a series of semi-detached houses by lowering and setting back the contiguous side bays of adjoining houses (in which the front doors are usually set). A characteristic example at Wharton Street, London, of *c.*1840 incidentally shows how the Regency style overlapped with the onset of Victorian taste. These houses also have crowning pediments stressing the unity of the pair, a feature possibly also originated by Searles. They were often applied to genuine semi-detached houses.

A related Regency innovation, favoured perhaps more in Bristol than elsewhere, was the row of four houses treated as a unified composition, with centre or ends broken forward, often with a

Quasi-semi-detached terrace:
Wharton Street, London (c.1840)

balcony (maybe on pillars) across the middle. Full-length three-light first-floor windows and giant orders of shallow pilasters applied across the front were characteristic of pairs as well as foursomes in Bristol, where stone remained in fashion.

Searles was applying the lowered, set-back side bays of the quasi-semi to semis themselves as early as 1792. Such treatment was widespread by the 1820s for standard brick houses and even more so for the carefully varied, stuccoed developments of suburbs from the 1830s onwards. As at Wharton Street, doorways in this sort of house were now frequently recessed behind piers and entablature. It was in such suburbs that modulations evolved from the unified terrace were beginning to merge with a tradition derived from the rural cottage and villa.

From Cottage Orné to Suburban Semi

What was to be a long line of descent began with the whimsical design of estate cottages, not for the sake of the occupants but to enhance the surroundings of the landlord's great house. Hence the term cottage orné. The word 'cottage' first occurred in print in 1765, in America. Whimsy was imparted by stylistic features of the past, especially Gothic, and exaggerated borrowings from traditional rural cottages, especially very steep gables. Many designs for such cottages were published in around 1800, notably Plaw's and Laing's. A sprinkling of cottages ornés were erected at Sidmouth in around c.1805 and Nash created a hamlet of them at Blaise, near Bristol, at the same time; but the turning point came when Nash brought them to town with Park Village East and West, begun in 1824, on the fringe of his Regent's Park scheme.

Along with the Gothic houses that anticipated Victorian taste, Nash included Classical houses in this picturesque allsorts, which he took from another tributary to the great suburban stream. This was the villa tradition originating in substantial piles like Chiswick House in the early eighteenth century, which had evolved into the wealthy man's villa on the outskirts of the city and was now being reduced into being the only home, or the principal one, of professional people, as improved roads and coach services and then the railways made it feasible to live further from work. Such a point seems to have been reached in about 1790 around Liverpool or in Clapham, to the southwest of London. Whether detached or semi-detached, these 'villas' were generally Classical in design, stuccoed and with a deep eaves, with slender, often paired, brackets or none, and tended to have a wide-spaced order of pilasters, perhaps limited to a framing pair, sometimes with incised decoration. On the façades large shallow arches, both round-headed and segmental, were often cut, on the ground floor, as at Keats House, Hampstead, of the 1820s, and sometimes through both storeys. Double-fronted rectories and the like in the country were similar.

Typical semi-detached pair in 'villa' taste of c.1825

Provincial Towns

In most areas, towns were abreast of standard developments, even though there was a persistence of such regional flavours as the shaped stone or stucco window lintels of the Midlands and the north, often with decorated keystones.

In northern towns, brick terraces similar to those in other parts of the country were beginning to appear, but there was still much housing in coursed rubble with flat window surrounds and simple cornice-headed or arched doorways.

Fanlights and Doorcases

The Regency produced a new style of fanlight, characterised by concentric bands and loops. Especially typical were teardrop and batswing patterns, but also different from the radial delicacy of the previous phase (still widespread) were the plain vertical bars with semicircular heads and bases, and tangential or intersecting circles (all these types featured in Underwood and Doyle's catalogue of 1813). Simpler circle patterns were common in Scotland (see figure, page 144). Diagonal bars were common in oblong fanlights, becoming a standard form in the decade 1830-40.

The most modest houses had plain arched doorways, with perhaps a decorative frieze below the fan. Very slightly more elaborate was a continuous cove within the arch. Much commoner were quarter-columns inset each side of the arch, usually with narrow grooving and shallow capitals of the Doric order. Grander

Surrey Square, London; Regency doorway and curvilinear fan

Standard Regency finials

150

versions, found in Liverpool, for instance, had half-columns. Inset colonettes were also common, especially in the north, generally under segmental arches. Also in the north the more traditional entablature and half-columns persisted widely, usually enclosing an arched opening. A different approach was the recessed door combined with pilasters under a flat head, with an oblong toplight and often with panelled reveals. This suited houses where the ground-floor windows were flat-headed.

Six-panel doors remained the norm, but many had flush panels with reeded surrounds (early examples are 41-2 Kensington Square, London, 1804-5). Two innovations – often combined – were doors of two vertical panels and doors with circular, oval or (most commonly) round-headed panels. A vertical moulding down the centre was sometimes adopted to simulate double doors.

The Greek Revival

Originating in the personal work of leading architects in around 1800, this 'strong' Regency style appeared in ordinary domestic architecture in the second decade of the nineteenth century. Adam had introduced Greek motifs, but from around 1802 a taste developed for a more thoroughgoing adoption of Greek features, especially of the Doric order, to produce a heavy and austere manner that was a long way from Adam delicacy.

The revival was manifested chiefly in large and expensive buildings such as Hamilton's High School in Edinburgh. Its effect on ordinary houses was less obvious. Greek Doric, it is true, was widely used for doorcases and porches, following the example of Nash, as it continued to be in the subsequent period on what were otherwise Italianate houses. Sometimes on the detached residences of rich professional families and the like the revival took more definite form, especially in Scotland. There, heavy Doric-columned porches were also common on terraced housing. They were not allowed to break up the regularity of the terrace, however, being recessed halfway into the hallway. Occasionally a fuller display of a Doric order was made. St Bernard's Crescent, Edinburgh, is perhaps the most splendid example.

In England, the Greek Revival was mainly manifested in the use of incised linear motifs (shown on page 150) and in block-like mouldings such as terrace centrepieces on which names were inscribed, as well as in acroteria on pediments and, most commonly, in the studding of doors and on railings and iron balusters.

Railings and Ironwork

The most characteristic Regency railings had Greek-inspired spear finials of various types, sometimes combined with plant heads on the stanchions, though the plain tapered square finial and urn-topped stanchions persisted to the end of the period. Also still widespread was latticework, often with arrow heads and tails added in lead.

These and a rich variety of other patterns were notably to be found in Cheltenham, fashionable and expanding in the Regency period. Among these other patterns were palmettes, intersecting ovals and circles and Gothic arches, frets of different designs, and, after around 1820, elongated scrolls and heart-and-honeysuckle (see figure, page 146). The last, introduced by Adam back in 1768, was markedly popular wherever balconies were used. It was not withdrawn until after 1868, though it was last used on a Cheltenham terrace in 1840-44. Many of the patterns of the previous twenty years were illustrated in *The Smith and Founder's Director* of 1824, by L. N. Cottingham; a large proportion were made by Carron, if Kent is typical.

The veranda was highly characteristic of the Regency. It seems to have been introduced in around 1795, as an elaboration of the continuous balcony. (One was added to the Adelphi by 1795-6, when Malton drew it.) Roofed in copper or zinc, it became a typical feature of resorts like Brighton (where its popularity persisted longer than elsewhere) and Cheltenham (where, surprisingly, the earliest known example, at Berkeley Place, London Road, was no earlier than shortly before 1820). Related to the veranda was the ironwork porch with tent-like hood, also very characteristic of Cheltenham, where it was introduced, it seems, by 1816-17.

Among minor features, bell-pulls were introduced at this date. Boot-scrapers also seem to have become a standard feature during the Regency. Cast-iron gutters were a more important innovation. In areas of the north such as York an eaves cornice consisting of an ornate gutter supported on paired shaped brackets was popular and characteristic (for example, 136-44 The Mount, 1824); this popularity continued until the middle of the century.

Interiors

Plans remained much the same, but stairs were even more likely than in the Adam period to rise in an elegant spiral sweep when space permitted, often producing a bow on the exterior. This treatment was especially favoured in Scotland. An innovation that swept the country was the opening of front and rear reception rooms into one another by means of broad archways with folding doors.

Decorative mouldings at the edges of the ceiling, rather than the top of the wall, were pioneered in around 1795 by Henry Holland and his cousin Richard. Holland also used pea beading (like rows of peas), characteristic of the Regency period. Ceiling roses became general in principal rooms of ordinary houses, not just in grand houses. This was especially the case when pendant gas lights were introduced (for example, in 1824 in York, where roses were often made of cast iron, oddly enough).

There was little change to ordinary wooden staircases, now highly standardised. Thus the designs in Nicholson's *New Practical Builder* of 1825 differ little from those of *c*.1770 and continued to be

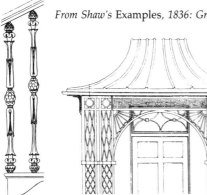

From Shaw's Examples, *1836: Greek Revival stair balustrading*

Tent porch: The Limes, Kingston-on-Thames (c.1825) with Greek key and lattice panels

followed down to 1840 and beyond. In some parts of England, turned balusters were still popular.

Cast-iron balusters were now sometimes introduced in houses of no special size or splendour. In Brighton a Greek key pattern was in use by around 1800 and in York there was a notable blossoming, including lattice panels, scroll-and-palmette (*c.*1834) and crossed arrows, and serpent and palmette patterns. Henry Shaw in his *Examples of Ornamental Metal Work* of 1836 shows a range representative of the end of the period.

The standard Regency mantelpiece had small roundels of concentric circles at the angles and horizontal and vertical mouldings to the lintel and side panels respectively, a pattern already established in 1795 in London. Cast-iron technology enabled the hob-grates within them to be more elaborate; typical are the reeded decoration and slightly more lavish lion's heads at Cadogan Street, London, of around 1825. Roundels or paterae were also applied to doorways in some more substantial houses (especially in Scotland). In principal rooms, mantelpieces of plain marble slips and the simplest pilaster treatment were standard; slightly more lavish examples have scrolled brackets.

Water closets now became normal beyond the homes of the affluent; the developer Cubitt installed them in all his houses from about 1824 (though he did not cater for the poorer classes).

The Rural North, Scotland and Wales

In farmhouses in the north, corbels were beginning to disappear from fireplaces, leaving flat surrounds with simple mouldings. Four-panel or plain battened doors were the norm.

Modest houses in Scotland were plainer than in England, being generally of harled masonry, with decoration confined to the doorcase, flat window surrounds and carved skewputs. One-storey houses remained much more common than south of the border, even sometimes for manses. In parts of Wales too, especially on Anglesey, single-storey houses were the rural norm. At St Fagans may be seen a cottage, which is essentially single-room, but is sub-divided by two cupboard beds at one end, on top of which boards form a loft (*croglofft*) reached by a ladder.

5 THE VICTORIAN HOUSE

The Victorian period, in the design of houses as in other kinds of architecture, saw an unprecedented multiplicity of style and feature, with borrowings from many different lands and eras. It also witnessed a new stylistic divergence between the housing of the poor, which in its simplicity evolved only slowly away from Georgian norms, and the more elaborate houses of the middle and upper classes. Nevertheless a pattern can be discerned in all this variety, and chronology is the best basis for charting it: deviations, subdivisions and regional specialities being noted as we go along. Whatever variety of features was to be found during any given phase, running through it was a common taste of the time, sometimes strongly, sometimes weakly, but nearly always discernible by one characteristic or another.

Three main phases can be made out in the welter of variety: Italianate, High Victorian and Redbrick. The starting-point of each is relatively definite, but it is important to note that each partly overlapped with its successor and, especially in the case of more modest housing, partly merged into it.

There are a few key features which run right through the Victorian period. Omnipresent was the S-profile panel mould (already in use in the late 1820s) — round door panels, on architraves and on skirting boards. Equally characteristic were the horns introduced on the upper leaves of sash windows, which came in as glazing bars went out (making up for the loss of stiffening). These also had an S-profile. In Scotland, the bay dormer was an additional leitmotif (see figure, page 170). Its introduction is difficult to date, as it was often added to existing houses, but was probably in the 1820s. (It had reached a house in Hope Street, Lanark by 1833.)

Strong Italianate: Lypiatt Terrace, Cheltenham (c.1845, probably by R W Jearrad)

THE ITALIANATE PHASE, c.1830 ONWARDS

Italianate is a term used to indicate inspiration from those aspects of the architecture of the Italian Renaissance that answered the taste of the early Victorians for enrichment of the façade, round-arch windows and an asymmetrical silhouette – in fact whatever was less purely Classical. Inspiration was particularly drawn from the informal villas of the countryside and the more highly embellished buildings divergent from the spacious simplicity of the Renaissance mainstream.

At its strongest, the Italianate was especially characterised by three features. The first was that of little square towers reminiscent of Italian rural villas. These were often found on larger, detached suburban houses and had figured in books of designs from c.1800 onwards, an impetus being given by J. C. Loudon's *Encyclopaedia of Cottage, Farm and Villa Architecture* of 1833. They also sometimes featured as terminal features on terraces or crowning the side bays of semi-detached pairs. The two other prime features were round-arched windows and strongly projecting, often richly bracketed eaves and cornices. Groupings of window openings either with narrow openings flanking the main opening or in paired openings, round-arched or not, were also characteristic. (The tripartite Venetian window of Georgian tradition, however, was rare.) Nash's Park Village East already had grouped round-arched windows and other Italianate features in c.1824.

Quoins were also favoured, as in Lyppiatt Terrace, Cheltenham, of around 1845, which has towers at each end and projecting gable roofs to the four intermediate pavilions, as well as round-headed windows throughout, some coupled or tripled. Such window forms were widely applied to many terraces and semi-detached houses in the Clifton area of nearby Bristol by 1855, where individual houses were sometimes given towers. Coupled and tripled round-headed windows were also found, for instance, on Blenheim Terrace, Bradford, by S. Jackson, of 1865, also stone-fronted.

In a weaker form, the term Italianate is applied to a wide range of work, only vaguely Italian in derivation, but part of the same movement of taste. In this wider sense the style had two aspects. First, there were characteristics already found in some Regency architecture, but now taken a degree further: heavier, more enriched detail, wider proportions and a liking for a rounding of angles. Second, accented individual features began to break up the plain regularity of the Classical terrace and the unified compositions of the Nash tradition.

The Line grows Thick

Wider proportions were accentuated by large windowpanes. These were made possible by the falling price of plate glass, especially with the removal of duty in 1845. (Between 1844 and 1849 plate glass fell in price by three-quarters.) There were now usually only four panes, two to each sash, and in wealthier houses, especially, there might be only one pane to each sash. Sashes also began to give way to large-pane casements, and first-floor balconies continued to have French windows. Conservatories now often graced the hinder parts of superior houses.

Lusher decoration meant that eaves cornices became more elaborate, and for larger houses were often crowned with balustrading (for instance, on the east side of Onslow Square London, of 1846.) Balustrading was likewise used for balcony fronts, along with other weighty stuccoed or stone designs. Quoins and vermiculated rustication lent richness of texture.

The most universal form of enrichment, applied to all but the humblest houses, was the stucco surround, with or without bracketed cornices, applied to at least the main windows.

Rounding applied on the largest and smallest scales. The S-curve moulding was standard, especially on door panels and architraves; corners of cupboards and of rooms were rounded (for instance towards the ground-floor passage); the corners of houses were also sometimes rounded (Wapping Pier, London, as early as 1811).

De-Unifying the Terrace

The Italianate in its weak sense meant that accented individual features began to break up the plain regularity of the classical terrace and the unified compositions of the Nash tradition. The two particular features that had this latter effect were big columned porches (as in Belgrave Square, London, 1827) and bay windows, which spread slowly after the early instance of Royal Crescent, Brighton, of 1799, becoming standard in seaside towns by the 1840s and very common in the more expensive, stucco-fronted terraces going up elsewhere in the 1840s and 1850s alongside the less affluent brick terraces that continued the Georgian flat front. South Kensington abounds in the type. An example from its final decade is Stafford Terrace, a little to the north, which displays Italianate proportions at their broadest and window panes at their largest. The bay window spread to suburban houses in London by the 1860s.

In the same spirit, houses were now regularly built with rear extensions. These had often been added to existing houses from the eighteenth century onwards, but by about 1850 larger houses in London were being built with rear extensions and they were quickly spreading elsewhere. Lancaster Terrace of 1857 was an early example: the extensions of neighbouring houses were coupled under a single roof, as was to be the usual pattern. In the provinces the roof was usually lean-to, in London more often gabled. In the former type the outer room was lower. By around 1860 there were already two-part extensions and extensions on both sides of the rear. In both cases the rear of the house was put into still deeper shadow. In larger London houses the rooms in the extensions were two-thirds the height of the main storeys and were reached from the half-landings.

The tight, varied forms of square and crescent tended to give way to plain grids of streets or squares split by roads or otherwise loosely arranged — following Eaton Square, London, of 1827.

Middling Houses

As ever, smaller, less grand houses tended to be not only simpler but more old-fashioned. Stucco was usually limited to the surrounds of openings. Front doors were often recessed, which may be regarded as an economical equivalent of the columned porch. Away from London, in houses of little pretension, windows were often framed by mouldings not so very different from the keyed lintels of the eighteenth century.

In northern England brick continued to advance at the expense of stone, but otherwise early Victorian housing was often marked by no more than the popularity of bay windows and rear extensions and by a change of proportions and detail from previous work.

Italianate Detail

Decorated fanlights virtually disappeared with the onset of the Italianate, being replaced by plain rectangular overlights. There were, for instance, no fanlights in the big houses designed by Basevi in Thurloe Square (1840) or Egerton Crescent (1843), both in South Kensington. Humbler homes followed suit.

Railings lost the crispness of the Regency by employing lusher forms and enriching existing patterns, so that, for instance, an encrusted version of the anthemion appeared in Cheltenham by

Linley Sambourne House, 18 Stafford Terrace, Kensington, London (c.1870); bay windows, wide proportions and eaves balustrading typical of mild Italianate

Lorn Road, London (1841): the Gothic alternative. Median Rd, London (1866): fleur-de-lys finial, typical c.1830-85; anthemion panel

1834 (Pittville Lawn). Responding to Victorian liking for the curvacious rather than the geometric, an S-curve was widely given to balcony fronts.

The main influence on fireplaces was the Rococo. In the principal rooms of larger houses they were often outward-swelling (bombé) or at least boasted lushly naturalistic floral brackets. A round-arched opening was standard in the 1850s and 1860s.

The Neo-Gothic Sidestream

Against the background of its more serious application to churches after 1815, Gothic came to be an occasional style for ordinary houses. At this stage it was nearly always neo-Tudor in kind, which allowed window heads to be flat rather than pointed, and the differences from Classical counterparts were in general only superficial. Groups of such houses were composed in Lonsdale Square, London (1838), and Brook Street, Stoke-on-Trent (1837). The latter is quasi-semi-detached, with transmullioned windows and paired doors under Tudor arches in the recessed sections. More widespread were individual houses, or more often semi-detached pairs, dressed in Gothic to lend variety to what might internally be identical to the interior of their Classical neighbour – a development of the Regency villa that led onwards to twentieth-century suburban variegation.

The Scottish Classical Afterburn

In Scotland a taut, disciplined, imaginative Neo-Classical tradition swept on, regardless of the relaxed, profuse Victorianism dominant in England. In rapidly growing Glasgow, as previously in Edinburgh, the convenience of porches was not allowed to break up the unity of the terrace: they were partially or wholly recessed. By the 1870s bay windows were being admitted, but they were shallow or rectangular and sometimes merged into adjacent elements of the frontage; in any event, they were firmly subordinated to the overall design. Detail remained fine-cut, respectful of formal geometry, the Ionic and Doric orders were favoured, motifs tended to be Grecian and when they were eclectic leant to the Egyptian that had been a variation for the Neo-Classicists of around 1805.

Many terraces were given unified compositions, still using many of the permutations pioneered by Nash and Playfair, but in a somewhat more hard-edged manner and with a more functional consideration of the amenity of the interiors, which Nash notoriously sacrificed to the outward show. Partly for this reason there were far fewer giant columns. Imaginative layout continued. Grosvenor Terrace of 1855, for instance, was a re-interpretation of John Wood's application of the Colosseum in his Circus. Crown Circus, by James Thomson, of 1858, was a convex variation on the crescent, with a colonnade set against the ground floor.

The greatest architect active in Glasgow, and arguably the greatest of all Victorian architects, Alexander (Greek) Thomson, went way beyond British precedent. In particular, he took up Schinkel's idea of windows as openings between a row of piers, the glazing extending as nearly as possible the whole distance from one pier to the next (see figure, page 169).

Great Western Terrace, Glasgow, by Thomson (1869): an example of the Scottish Classical afterburn by its greatest exponent

HIGH VICTORIAN, c.1855 ONWARDS

High Victorian was almost the opposite of Scottish Classicism. It was the climax of Victorianism, in enrichment, in harshness of anti-classical proportion and asymmetry and in craggy individualism between buildings and within them. In these characteristics it accentuated existing tendencies; but it also tended to jettison features of the previous phase that were at odds with its taste. After the Italianate phase, when Classical proportions and compositional principles were set aside, now the Classical architectural vocabulary itself was on the retreat, replaced by motifs drawn from every past style and none.

Fractured Forms

Faceted, asymmetrical forms were favoured for both the overall shape of houses and for the smaller parts of them. Whereas the Classical designer had tried to impose symmetry on the elevation, High Victorians deliberately sought asymmetry. What was desired is suggested by E. L. Blackburne, writing about the model houses featured in his *Suburban and Rural Architecture* of 1869: 'the object of the designer has been to obtain as much picturesqueness of outline and play of light and shade as is possible in houses of so small a class'. Bay windows became even more popular, reaching the level of so-called 'By-law housing', around 1870.

Asymmetry and the fractured effect were easiest in the more expensive detached or semi-detached houses, where the bay-

60 Banbury Rd, North Oxford (1869) by William Wilkinson: steep-pitched, gabled Gothic, with stilted heads to ground-floor windows

*Charlotte Street, Bristol (c.1870);
strong Italianate terrace blending
into chamfered High Victorian*

windowed section could be crowned with a gable and the side
section with front door could be set back, while subsidiary
features, often slanting or gabled again, could further break up the
overall shape.

Gables produced a sought-after broken roofline and went with
a steep pitch. Whereas under the Classical impulse, with its restful
horizontals, the trend running from the Middle Ages to the early
nineteenth century had been for the roof pitches of ordinary
domestic architecture to become ever lower, down to the 30° pitch
that was standard between c.1820 and c.1850, this new trend went
into reverse, following the lead set many decades before by the
cottage orné and the Gothic sidestream. By around 1875 a pitch of
up to 60° became normal for more prosperous houses. (Economy
forbade this in the case of cheaper houses).

Polychromy
In a parallel shift, colours and materials were chosen for variety
and contrast, strength of colour and texture. Tiles were reintroduced in place of slates when the extra cost could be afforded. By the
1870s, all-over stucco was going out even for the London
conservative; instead the hard texture of crimson and grey pressed
brick was in, as were horizontal banding in single or double
courses (for example, Rosebury Road, Exeter, as late as 1896-8) and
moulded decoration on bricks, used from the 1840s onwards.

The Stilted Head and Chamfer

The most widespread manifestation of High Victorianism was the stilted window head, a raising of the lintel on short extensions of the jamb above the capitals (see figure, page 160). In modest housing this was frequently the only manifestation, but it persisted strongly, however, as styles at the humbler level have done so often, at least into the 1880s and 1890s, when smarter architecture had moved on.

An even simpler method of achieving a similar effect was to give the lintel a chamfer – an embellishment that was almost as much a defining characteristic of High Victorianism as the stilted head.

Gothic and Spiky Detail

Gothic, and the opportunities it gave for angularity and polychromy, suited the High Victorian, but was used selectively and reinterpreted freely, partly for practical reasons. Porches were frequently adorned with colonettes of Gothic derivation. The mass-produced pre-cast capitals on these, as on the bay windows, were commonly Early English stiff-leaf in form, which eventually merged into the floral decoration of the succeeding Redbrick style. Cost and convenience inhibited a more widespread use of pointed arches, but occasionally porches and windows had Gothic heads, especially on larger houses, for instance in north Oxford.

In northern England the tradition of stone architecture encouraged the revival of mullions, often, however, with large, sash-fitted lights. A good example is Hunter Street, Carnforth, of around c.1860, where the door lintels are also characteristically peaked, the first floor has a sill band and the end houses have an extra, gable-fronted storey, a common feature of the period. In this case a small mid-point gable is to be found too.

Gothic or not, roofs were commonly given tile or cast-iron cresting and finials. The whole house was also often gable-fronted in a way rare since the seventeenth century. Gables tended to be given bargeboards of crushing aspect.

Craggy Features and Period Costume

In larger houses of more or less loosely Classical design, cragginess was imparted by heavily stucco-framed dormers flush with the balustrade, combined occasionally with what the Scots would term wallhead chimney stacks. Such dormers are found as early as c.1840 in Holland Park, London. In smaller houses top-floor windows sometimes cut through the cornice to form semi-dormers (for example, Wharncliffe Street, Sunderland, c.1850s, and in Lancaster as late as 1888). Even in Scotland, assertive dormers modified the bay-windowed, Italianate Belgrave Crescent, Edinburgh, of 1874 by John Chesser.

Detail was often of great richness as well as very mixed derivation or invention.

In the north, a prevalent feature was the guttering that doubled

Spring Back, Hull (c.1870)

as cornice, supported on small, square, wide-spaced corbels (in Lancaster, for example, ranging from pre-1864 to 1888).

Among the styles now being drawn upon for the first time, the most notable was that of mansard-roof French Classicism, following a revival in France itself, where it has come to be named Second Empire after Napoleon III (1848-70). French detail was used to embellish the otherwise standard Italianate Lancaster Gate, London, of 1857. Twin terraces on Clapham Common North Side, London, were given full-blown French roofs in 1860, by Knowles.

Interiors

Plasterwork mirrored the character of external detail; spikiness was characteristic, as in the ceiling at New Walk, Hull (1876), which also has Rococo inspiration in its double band with corner scrolling. Staircase balustrades tended to grotesque extremes of bulbous newels. The main influence on fireplaces continued to be the Rococo, but Gothic was now prevalent too.

Linley Sambourne House, Stafford Terrace, London (c.1870)

Ceiling rose, Grazebrook Rd, London, late 1860s

163

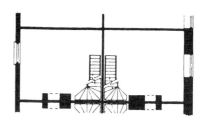

Back-to-back, Victoria
Avenue, Llanidloes, Powys;
1832/40; first-floor
(J. Lowe)

Victorian Workers' Houses

These remained so plain that the successive phases of Victorian taste left little mark, especially in the north, where stone was predominant right through the century. As late as 1875 elevations could essentially follow the Georgian pattern, except that they were built of machine-made brick, had large-pane sashes and were devoid of even the smallest touch of decoration. For the smallest houses, casement windows were the rule. Slates continued to be used except where local tiles were cheap.

In Scotland and the north-east especially, single-storey cottages remained common for the humblest homes into the twentieth century, and the single-room-deep plan was as widespread as the double depth (in north Wales often being double-fronted). In many areas the front door opened straight into the front room and the stairs were either between front and back rooms or open to the back room. Rear extensions were rare right through the century.

One plan that became very common in the industrial towns of the north and Midlands was the back-to-back, beginning in the late eighteenth century, particularly in Manchester and Nottingham (over half the houses in the latter being of this type by around 1840). Normally the front door led into the only room on the ground floor. The stairs were in the dark at the back. Back-to-backs were sometimes three storeys high and sometimes built for middle-class occupation. In Liverpool they had basements forming separate, unhealthy dwellings. Back-to-backs, like other northern workers' terraces, were often arranged in rows at right-angles to the street, with 'courts' or alleys between – in Hull as late as 1926.

By-laws were beginnng to set standards for workers' housing by the mid-nineteenth century – hence the term 'By-law housing': the lowest category, for which local regulations tended increasingly to determine the pattern. Such by-laws progressively outlawed back-to-backs from the 1840s onwards (for example, in Nottingham in 1846, in Birmingham in 1864); they remained dominant in North-west Yorkshire, however, till the late nineteenth century and were still being built in Leeds into the 1930s.

The toilets for back-to-backs were in separate blocks, either in one part of the terrace or, more often, in detached clusters. This separate provision was common to other types of northern terrace, as was the absence of rear gardens. Normally the toilet, together with the coal shed and often the wash-house too, was in a back yard, either lean-to against the house or detached. Access for delivery of coal and removal of sewage was by arched passages between the houses or from back alleys.

THE RED BRICK PHASE, *c*.1875 ONWARDS

The dominant strand in late nineteenth-century domestic architecture was rather misleadingly given the label Queen Anne Revival at the time of its birth and has never quite shaken it off. The historical inspiration was in fact twofold: the Classical brick houses of the seventeenth- and early eighteenth-century Low Countries as well as their equivalent in Britain (likewise dating from both sides of 1700, not just the reign of Queen Anne of 1702-14). In its strong form, the style should perhaps be termed Neo-1700.

The new taste represented a reaction against High Victorianism but also a continuation of many of its features. It represented a rejection of the harshness of High Victorianism in favour of the warmer and gentler character of Classical domestic architecture, but in choosing within the Classical tradition to revive the verticality, panelwork and contrasts of purple and red brick of Queen Anne and the narrow gable fronts and floral decoration of the Low Countries the new fashion remained true to Victorian taste.

The most important key to the shifts of the period was the widespread liking for house fronts of red, in reaction against stucco, stock brick and High Victorian polychromy alike. This red-shift extended beyond Neo-1700. It largely applied to its rural counterpart, known as the Old English style, otherwise characterised by mock-timbered and tile-hung upper storeys (if tending more to the salmon pink in that case). It even applied to some extent in the stone-built areas of Britain. There is a good case, therefore, for terming the movement of taste at its broadest the Redbrick style.

Neo-1700

A turning point to the new fashion in its most definite, Neo-1700, form has been identified in the appropriately named Red House, Bayswater Road, London, of 1871, by J. J. Stevenson, who was to be one of the fashion's principal exponents along with the more brilliant and protean Norman Shaw. It took this definite form in the homes of the better-off, who could afford its components: a crowning shaped gable; bay windows, often on shaped stone brackets or as bellied oriels; balconies, also on shaped brackets, with railings or balustrades; recessed or projecting porches with shaped entries (not columns), and often additional openings in the sides or over the arch; vertical ribbing or shafts, particularly to end-of-terrace chimney stacks; and many trimmings in the way of little scrolly pediments, floral panels, window aprons, gable-head pargeting and the like – in stone, cut brick, terracotta and plaster. French windows gave onto the balconies. Other windows were sometimes of 'Flemish' form, sometimes mullioned. For the rest, large-paned sash windows remained the norm, but the glazing bars of the upper half were often arranged in patterns, or in small panes, as was the case when casements took their place.

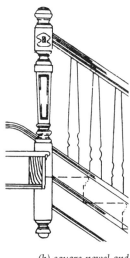

Neo-1700: (a) 5-7
Cadogan Gardens,
London (1892,
by F. Knight),

(b) square newel and
splat balusters
(G. Middleton, Modern Buildings, 1906-10)

These lush frontages, usually varied from one house to the next, went up in the late 1870s, and the 1880s and 1890s, over the richer areas of west London and Hampstead and to a lesser extent in other towns of brick-built England.

It is noteworthy that the backs of these houses were frequently far plainer and not readily distinguishable from those of the High Victorian phase, though if anything they were even more heavily girt with rear extensions. While the fronts were faced in red brick of rich and varied hues, the backs were of stock brick drabness.

Bathrooms were still not included in some of the most opulent terraces around 1880, but by 1900 they were a regular feature even of small houses.

After 1900, large houses became smoother and blander, modulating towards Neo-Georgian, with shallow bow windows, rounded gables and strongly horizontal stone cornices and bands of egg-and-dart.

At the more modest level of speculative housing, at which the style burgeoned on a massive scale from around 1880, Neo-1700 naturally took simpler Redbrick forms, and indeed there was often an imperceptible merging from High Victorian to the new style. The outline and internal plan of the terrace house remained the same, with a one or two-storeyed bay window and a rear extension at the back of the passage. Sometimes the change amounted to

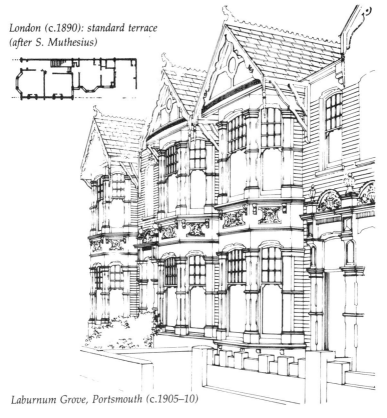

London (c.1890): standard terrace (after S. Muthesius)

Laburnum Grove, Portsmouth (c.1905–10)

little more than a liking for warm red brick, together with simplified forms of the embellishment seen on the bigger Neo-1700 houses, especially sunflower and similar smiling motifs, small panes in the upper sashes of windows, and shallow scalloping of the window heads (in the manner of early eighteenth-century houses).

Laburnum Grove in Portsmouth, of c.1905, a particularly lush example, looks back to the chamfers of High Victorianism but also forward to the rising Suburban style in its mock timber gables overshadowing the bay windows.

Decorative features such as lintels were now often set flush with the wall surface and there was a taste for incised decoration of a stencil type on these dressings. Even on small houses bay windows were quite often square, rather than canted. Where there was no bay window, openings were more likely to be aligned one above another in eighteenth-century fashion. By the 1890s, decorated tilework was a widespread embellishment to the side walls of recessed porches.

Porches on middling houses were, however, now more often projecting rather than recessed, often being constructed of timber openwork, incorporating rows of balusters like early seventeenth-century porches (only more attenuated; see figure, page 73). They often also projected on smaller houses, by virtue of being

Dallas Road, Lancaster
(1900)

integrated with the adjacent bay windows under a common roof, as in houses of 1895 in Lancaster. Another solution was the use of moulded asymmetrical struts. A simple example dates from around 1893, in Birmingham, on early council-built workers' housing without bay windows. Between the two is the strutted porch unconnected with the adjacent bay, as at Dallas Road, Lancaster, probably of *c.*1900. The curve is characteristic. So is the stained glass panel, though its position is unusual.

The Old English Style

As far back as 1850, precursors of the rural counterpart of Neo-1700 by Devey had been built at Penshurst, and already by around 1867 the recipe for what was to be termed the Old English style had been developed. An indication that it was a counterpart of Neo-1700 is that its principal progenitor was Norman Shaw, the man in the forefront of the urban style. The ingredients were mock-timbering to the upper storey (which was jettied), tile-hung gables, tall chimneys and mullioned windows, often with leaded lights.

Mock timbering also found its way into towns, most notably in Chester, where rich timber frontages erected in the Rows from around 1860 onwards blended convincingly with their genuine seventeenth-century neighbours. In suburbs and small towns Old English and Neo-1700 merged together. Influential early examples were at Bedford Park on the western fringes of London, a carefully planned development begun in 1875. Here the forms were simpler, with fewer gables and bays and more tile-hanging and white-painted woodwork. The houses were detached or semi-detached.

Three characteristics were pointers to the future of suburban housing. There were no basements. The entrance halls were spacious in proportion to the other rooms. And there were relatively ample front gardens, bounded by brick piers and wooden paling, rather than railings.

The Redbrick style, because it was one of brick, tile and mock timbering, and drew on predominantly southern traditions, naturally had a muted effect on the stone-building areas of Britain. In Keswick, for instance, there is an area of terraces dating from the 1890s with chamfered window heads, gables of several varieties, slate roofs, tile cresting and bay windows in moderation. The combination of colours from the different materials employed is bold but benign: sawn slate rubble facing, the red of sandstone dressings and the blue of a brick eaves band. The result contrasts with High Victorian polychromy (though never handicapped by industrial grime), but has little specific in common with Redbrick taste.

Scotland

The type of house in the Redbrick taste that spread practically everywhere was that of the bay-window terrace. There are plenty of examples in stone-built Aberdeen, for instance. Something of the flavour of Redbrick was imparted to other housing not only by more use of red and pink stone but also by a restrained introduction of the curvilinear and a trace of Baroque swagger.

On tenements, bay windows, previously rare, were standard by the 1880s. They were often given bellied soffits (already in 1858 in Kent Road, Glasgow) or peaked roofs (as in the Marchmont area of Edinburgh). Bow windows were also favoured (for instance in splendid reiteration along Greenock's Sandringham Terrace of 1900-1901 and its continuations). Slightly more ornate were high-pitched roofs and detail of French derivation. More in the hard-edged Classical tradition were the geometric three-quarter circles some tenements had on their corners (for example, Saltoun Street, Glasgow). All these variations made for the greater window area favoured at the end of the nineteenth century.

Saltoun Street, Glasgow
(1897, by Adam & Short),
with pier-to-pier
glazing

Candiehead, Stirlingshire (probably c.1895): Redbrick features in rural Scotland

In the 1890s, as in the recessed porches of English and Welsh houses, tiled dados were introduced into tenement closes (common passages leading to the stairs). Internal arrangements improved, but plans did not much alter. Water closets were increasingly installed from the 1870s, either on the half-landings, for communal use and forming a narrow projection, often of cast iron or brick, or within the houses (a Scottish term for flats), but lit from the staircase.

Interiors

Bolection mouldings were used round fireplaces of middling size to some extent, and mantelshelves of early eighteenth-century type, but otherwise not much was drawn either from the reign of Queen Anne or from the Netherlands. The typical feature of the Redbrick interior was a rather elaborate type of fireplace. This was likely to have a moulded iron hood, tiles on the slanting sides with floral, or curvilinear decoration, and, most characteristically, an overmantel of multiple shelving supported by shaped brackets.

Grates within the fireplace changed in around 1870, with the supersession of the arched opening by a smaller rectangular opening surrounded or flanked by tiles. This change was associated with lower grates, set closer to the floor, either with a solid hearth-brick base, removing the air supply from below altogether, and dependent on high-grade coal, or an ash-pan with adjustable air vent (introduced a little later). Around 1880 canopies, either flat or bellied, were introduced, in conjunction with projecting grates.

A characteristic feature of the stronger versions of Redbrick was the introduction of a picture rail at a level that left space for a broad frieze above it. (Previously pictures had been suspended from the very top of the wall or – in the middle of the century – from metal rails fixed in front of the wall.) An innovation of the same date by no means limited to Neo-1700 houses was that of embossed wallpaper made of tough patent materials, used in all types of houses except the humblest, originally in imitation of leather wallcoverings: Lincrusta of 1877, used below the dado rail of passageways and staircases, and Anaglypta of a decade later, mostly used on ceilings. Slightly more ornate interiors often had ceiling ribwork of late sixteenth- or early seventeenth-century type.

Stained Glass

A characteristic feature of the broader Redbrick taste was the use of stained glass. This was to be found especially in the upper panels of front doors, in the toplights and sidelights around them and on staircase windows giving onto the narrow gaps between semi-detached pairs. The pale tints and sometimes langorous treatment of the favoured bird and foliage subject matter were part of what was lampooned as greenery-yallery. Like the associated furnishing, it was influenced by later Pre-Raphaelitism, particularly by Morris, himself a major designer of wallpaper, textiles and furniture. The stained glass on the Lancaster house (page 168) is of simpler character and later date.

Neo-Adam

This was a style, limited as yet to interior decoration, that ran more or less in tandem with Neo-1700 from around 1875 (being found, for instance, in South Kensington by 1877). Cast-iron mantelpieces (first manufactured in around 1850) were available in this style.

Doorways

The upper parts of front doors were often divided by a pattern of glazing bars like the upper parts of windows. At the bottom a single horizontal panel was common, sometimes peaked as well as fielded and surrounded by raised mouldings of complex profile (see figure, page 168).

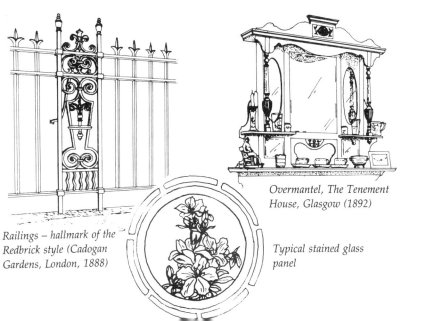

Railings – hallmark of the Redbrick style (Cadogan Gardens, London, 1888)

Overmantel, The Tenement House, Glasgow (1892)

Typical stained glass panel

6 THE TWENTIETH-CENTURY HOUSE

The huge majority of ordinary twentieth-century houses have been designed in what can only be described as the Suburban style. This evolved out of the Arts and Crafts movement in the first years of the century and had still only partially developed into something substantially different as the century was drawing to a close. Its prodigious success is masked by the low critical esteem it has enjoyed and the fact that noted architects have almost always worked in some other idiom.

By comparison, Functionalism (otherwise termed the Modern Movement) has been far less successful. Though dominant for flats and offices in the third quarter of the century, it has contributed only a tiny minority of ordinary houses, except in the New Towns of the 1950s and 1960s, and in a marginal role on urban council estates; since 1970 it has been on the retreat in the face of the stylistic revival whose various tendencies are gathered under the Post-Modern label.

The other main alternative to the Suburban, almost throughout the century, has been Neo-Georgian. Considerably more successful than Functionalism in the design of houses, it has been the commonest style for terraced housing in the inner city; elsewhere it has been either the chief alternative to the Suburban or – especially for the better-off – an ingredient in the Suburban style itself.

A typical Voysey house: Tilehurst, Bushey Grange Road, Bushey, Herts (1903) with tiled roof, roughcast walls and leaded iron casements

THE ARTS AND CRAFTS STYLE
AND ITS SUBURBAN PROGENY

The Arts and Crafts style emerged almost imperceptibly out of Old English and Neo-1700 – a smoother, quieter, less russet offspring of the two. Eschewing the busy deployment of period motifs practised by the Victorians in favour of a new feeling for overall form, the style took its main inspiration from simple traditional rural architecture, especially of the seventeenth century (about which books were beginning to appear in the first years of the twentieth century). There was a fundamental shift from the verticality characteristic of Redbrick to a taste for the horizontal and the ground-hugging that went hand in hand with a preference for the rural over the urban.

In terms of materials, the change meant that red brick gave way to pebbledash, and sash windows to casements. Eventually the yearning for rusticity also meant that fake timbering, though usually scorned by the proponents of the Arts and Crafts movement proper, became the hallmark of the mass of less discriminating housing. In terms of housing types there was a shift from terraced housing, which became a rarity, to the suburban non-basement semi-detached, which became the norm.

Three stages may be delineated in the progress of the new style. First came an early strong form, largely embodied in a smallish number of rural houses designed by architects for individual clients. Next, a plainer, more economical version burgeoned with the 'garden city' movement, from 1902 till the outbreak of the First World War in 1914. Finally, the style was applied in popularised form in a huge suburban sprawl all over Britain from 1918.

Early Arts and Crafts

The strong version of Arts and Crafts began as early as 1885, pre-eminently in the work of Voysey. Many of its features were to be endlessly repeated in the Suburban stage: catslide roofs (originated by 1890), often sweeping over the porch; gables overhanging polygonal bay windows; doorways recessed behind wide arches on low jambs; iron stays strutting upwards to the eaves or downwards to support slab door hoods; strap hinges and motifs such as lozenges in gable heads and hearts on fittings.

The narrow passage and dogleg staircase standard since the seventeenth century were discarded in favour of a square hallway with its own window, with the stairs usually rising steeply round two sides or even in a single flight, in either case starting immediately inside the door, with winders there and at the angle with the second flight, if there was one. Stained woodwork was widespread for stairs and elsewhere. Even more standard were square balusters and newel posts. The posts might taper somewhat and even more probably would be crowned with flat caps. Both these were Voysey features, as were broad, flat balusters.

Stair-type for the new century, at Bournville, Birmingham, proto-Garden City (c.1900, by W. A. Harvey)

The sitting-room fireplace often had a horizontal version of the wooden Redbrick fireplace, with shelving (or cupboards) at each side rather than above, and with tapered rather than curvilinear parts. Sometimes there would be an inglenook, maybe with its own miniature window, and with settle or windowseat, all inspired by seventeenth-century equivalents. The floor was often of hardwood parquet.

The Garden City Phase

Nearly all the work by the first Arts and Crafts architects was for detached houses for well-to-do families, but Voysey himself played a part in the second stage of the style, when it was applied to multiple housing for those of middling or modest wealth. In 1904 he designed a double range of houses for miners at Whitworth, West Yorkshire, which helped set the pattern for low-cost housing with its rendered fronts and façade gables interspersed with dormers, a crisp version of traditional Cotswold cottages.

The second stage had already been launched, however, in the series of garden cities projects from 1901 onwards, which were largely the progeny of the partners and brothers-in-law Barry Parker and Raymond Unwin. They too designed cottages normally with both front and rear flat and with façade gables rather than bay windows. At New Earswick, in 1902, characteristic internal features included living rooms extending from front to back, which became a feature not so much of small houses as of middling ones. The adoption of the through room was an alternative to the folding doors of Victorian houses. At Letchworth, from 1903, and at Hampstead Garden Suburb, from 1905, these rooms included huge bressumers spanning the fireplaces.

Garden cities and municipal estates of similar character were built in many different parts of the country. In London a notable example was the Totterdown Fields Estate, Tooting, of 1903-11.

It is striking that here and at other London County Council estates the windows were predominantly sash, continuing the Neo-1700 usage, rather than following the Arts and Crafts preference for casements. Horizontality was often imparted, however, by grouping the sashes in pairs or threes.

Typical Arts and Crafts cottages of the second, pre-1914 stage had a combined kitchen and sitting room, together with a separate scullery, small compartments for larder and coal and an external earth or water closet. Alternatively they might have a living room and separate kitchen. Slightly larger cottages also had a parlour, only used on special occasions. Upstairs, three small bedrooms were common.

Art Nouveau
By around 1890 Art Nouveau was adding a somewhat extraneous ingredient to the widening Arts and Crafts range, in matters of detail and interior design. The tendril or molten lines of this occasionally sickly style were to be found in stained glass panels

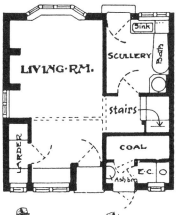

Garden City planning at New Earswick, York: houses of 1902 by Parker and Unwin – no rear extension; through livingroom; a bath, but still only an earth closet (E.C.)

and on the metalwork of fireplace hoods, door and window ironmongery and light fittings. They were also to be found on tilework, especially on the walls of recessed porches and around fireplaces. [Although among serious artists the Art Nouveau had fizzled out by 1914, its impact on the ordinary home actually widened in the following decades.]

The Suburban Explosion
In 1918 there began the third stages of the Arts and Crafts style, that of its mass popularisation. The garden city formula, hitherto applied in carefully planned enclaves, and often complete with communal buildings such as churches, was translated into the sprawl of dormitory suburbs, either in shaplessly non-geometric streets without focus or simply unrolled along the roads radiating from towns in 'ribbon development'.

Common to most suburban houses built between the First and Second World Wars was the spreading hipped roof that sat on them. This was usually tiled, but sometimes slated; pantiles were an occasional variant, especially in the 1930s. Below the roof nearly all houses had flat rears, but council houses were more likely to have flat fronts too, whereas speculative houses almost always had bay windows.

The internal layout of the two types was also very similar, following closely the pattern set by the garden city estates. The living room now usually had French windows to the garden. The kitchen tended to be a tiny room opening from the hall, with back door and larder on one side and one corner taken up by the coke boiler (see plan, page 181).

1920s Council Housing
Under the Housing Act of 1919, local authorities were required, not merely empowered, to provide housing. The Tudor Walters Report of 1918, drafted by Unwin, set the scene through its recommended standards. For example, 70 feet (21 metres) was laid down as the minimum distance across streets from the fronts of houses on one side to those on the other, which guaranteed a surburban diffuseness to the vast majority of both council and private housing for the next half-century.

The Report recommended that every house should contain a living room, parlour and scullery and at least three bedrooms; a bathroom and larder were both regarded as essential.

The monotony of a grid of long terraces with rear access from back alleys was to be avoided; instead culs-de-sac were suggested and through-passages for ranges of more than two houses. Sample façade designs, of garden city character, were widely followed.

1920s Speculative Housing
The main difference from council housing was not in size but in a greater continuity with the pre-war Redbrick, Old English and Art Nouveau. The Redbrick terrace pattern of bay window with porch

Coquet Terrace, Newcastle; c.1905, but doors and much else typical into the 1920s

alongside continued to be standard. It was constructed, however, in cheaper, less solid fashion. Gone were the moulded capitals set in solid brickwork. In their place was fake timbering, in the gable, if not more extensively, and weatherboarding (usually with the lower edges unsawn) or tile-hanging under the bay windows and possibly in the gable. The rest of the front was usually pebble-dashed or rendered, which concealed the use of cheap pink brick, though often there was a brick edging to the porch arch.

The windows were always casement, never sash; sometimes of wood, but often of metal, which had been introduced in Arts and Crafts houses before 1914 in imitation of seventeenth-century windows and from 1918 were mass-produced. Panes were usually small and sometimes leaded. A shallow curve was often given to the inner edge of the top of the frame. The Redbrick arrangement of large panes below small panes was often followed, with the latter in flaps above the casements.

A key shift in methods of construction was the spread in the use of cavity walls, which Voysey and others had eschewed. The leading speculative builders Costains had adopted them by 1924.

Larger houses were more spacious and sprawling. L-shaped sitting rooms were sometimes favoured, following the lead of the garden city layouts of Parker and Unwin. Hatches between kitchen and dining room were common.

Stained Glass

Art Nouveau, though short-lived as a fashion in high art, had a long afterlife in the detail of modest homes, especially in the leaded glazing of front doors. In a different vein, popular motifs for stained glass in the period between the First and Second World Wars were a galleon with billowed sail, children in Dutch costume, windmills, flowers and generalised heraldry. In the 1920s and 1930s, especially in the north of England, stick-on leaded glazing

177

was applied to the upper parts of windows and elsewhere, of elongated Art Nouveau patterns, rather than pictorial matter.

Paving and Fencing
Around suburban houses there was very often crazy paving (the earliest use of the term found by the *Oxford English Dictionary* was of 1923). Rather than railings there were often low walls of composition stone, sometimes pink or some other pastel shade, or chain hanging from short posts.

Neo-Georgian
This alternative to Arts and Crafts emerged from Queen Anne around 1900, with paler brickwork and daintier, drier detail, and was much less three-dimensional and more horizontal.

The key feature for nearly all Neo-Georgian houses was the doorcase, usually underscaled by eighteenth-century standards. Simple flat hoods on shaped brackets were standard and often found on otherwise non-Classical cottages of the Parker and Unwin type. For middle-class housing, decorative fans were reintroduced, often of metal or stick-on leading. Period authenticity was not attempted, features of different dates being selected as convenient and especially as fitted modest budgets. There was some partiality for Adam motifs, however, such as the scalloped lunette above windows. Occasionally margin glazing was revived.

Internally, Adam-style mantelpieces continued to be favoured by many well-to-do people of middlebrow tastes, as they had been since the 1870s. Glazed corner cupboards were also characteristic. At a less expensive level, the coved cornice was very widespread.

Neo-Georgian, like so many other styles, blended into others. It would be impossible to describe them all; moreover, many of the varieties defy succinct labels. One that evoked the Mediterranean often had pantiled roofs, sometimes with coloured glazes, such as bright green, and Spanish-style ironwork (for instance in round-arched openings to garden walls). Neo-Tudor developed out of Old English without the softening effect of the Arts and Crafts movement and was adapted to pale red brick and composition stone mullions. Its key internal feature, the Tudor-arch fireplace, again usually in some composition material, had a much wider currency than the sub-style as a whole (see figure, page 181).

Neo-Georgian at Coombe Park, Kingston-on-Thames (c.1935, by G. J. M. Viner)

Bungalows

After 1918, bungalows, first introduced under that name in 1869, were adopted as ordinary homes by many people, not just for holiday use. Their design followed other suburban housing.

Scotland

Domestic architecture in Scotland strongly converged with English practice after 1918. The building of tenement housing diminished to a small trickle and cottages became the staple, as in England. Unwin himself had worked in Scotland before and during the First World War. Differences from England included less fake-timbering and more all-over render, the latter true to the tradition of harling, but without the all-important colour-wash.

THE 1930s

Modern for the Minority

Complete absence of ornament or stylistic feature first occurred in domestic architecture on the Continent in around 1910. It was based on the idea of truth to the nature of materials, design in terms of pure form and the idea that beauty arises from fitness for function: hence the label Functionalism. It was largely motivated by dissatisfaction with the period styles that made such a confused jumble of later nineteenth-century urban development.

In Britain, there were a few forerunners of Functionalism at the beginning of the 1920s that related to certain transitional designs of a geometric kind between Art Nouveau and the Functional – several erected by the Crittall metal window company. However, the earliest houses of wholly Functionalist character date from around 1930. They remained a tiny number till the Second World War put a virtual stop to all house building. Most of them were heavily influenced by Le Corbusier, the Swiss architect who practised in Paris.

Now thought of as constructed of concrete, they were in fact mostly rendered and white-painted, which gave them a concrete look. A few were built in brick; there was also occasional use of timber boarding. The roofs were nearly always flat. Windows were usually metal. Panes were large and usually arranged in horizontal bands, unbroken by the mullions of Arts and Crafts windows, and recalling the radical horizontal glazing of around 1600 (see page 75). Often there would also be a conspicuous vertical window. Sometimes, if functionally desirable, a window turned round a corner, since modern construction needed no longer to be load-bearing at the corners.

One of the best examples, free of the awkwardness and derivative character of most of the others, is Sun House, Frognal, Hampstead, of 1936, by Maxwell Fry. This is quite a large house. Indeed, nearly all Functionalist houses before the Second World

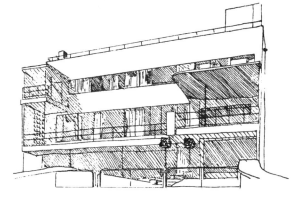

Sun House, Frognal,
London (1936,
by Maxwell Fry)

War were for private clients of a certain wealth. Building societies were even more hostile than planning authorities.

Internally, the Functionalist house tended to be yet starker in effect than externally. Open-planning was favoured, or at least a sitting room of maximum size. The fireplace was largely de-throned, the up-to-date electric fire taking the place of an open hearth. Stairs were often open-tread and rose within the living room; in larger houses they were sometimes spiral.

Modernistic

This disparaging term was given at the time to design that aped the characteristics of Functionalism without acceptance of its ideas – that in fact stood its ideas on their head since it used 'modern' features as stylistic elements. (The term Art Deco was introduced in the 1960s to give the style a more acceptable image, but it is taken from the historically distinct 1925 Exposition des Arts Decoratifs in Paris. It is sometimes confusingly used to embrace both Modern and Modernistic.)

The basic layout of the Suburban house was retained, including, as often as not, the pitched roof, but this was clothed in clichés taken from Functionalist work in place of fake timbering and the like. Thus windows were wrapped around corners or were stepped up geometrically, as they are in an example in Cullomp-ton, Devon. Metal windows divided into horizontal panes were characteristic, in contrast to the large, undivided panes of Func-tionalism. Streamlined effects were much prized. So was the sunburst motif, to be found in the bars of glazed front doors, as well as on wooden and metalwork garden gates, and even in stained-glass design.

Internally, stepwork and curved corners were also popular - indeed more widely than in Modernistic exteriors – especially for the tilework of fireplaces or bathrooms, frequently asymmetrically. Flush doors were favoured, as they were by the Functionalists; so were solid panels below the banister rails. Both these features were often applied to older houses, to give them an up-to-date look.

Modernistic houses were much more numerous than Functional-ist houses in the 1930s, but, unlike Functionalism, the fashion did not survive the war.

Greenwich Road, Cardiff (1924),
typical of both 1920s and 1930s

Modernistic: Willand
Road, Cullompton, Devon
(1936)

The more Traditional Suburban House

Very little stylistic change took place between the 1920s and 1930s, but improvements in the standard of living had some effect. The exterior was now frequently widened to include an integral garage, generally with an additional bedroom over it.

By 1934, the New Ideal Homesteads house-building company was offering gas and electric power points at the fireplaces, tiled surrounds and a back-boiler to the dining-room fireplace to supply hot water, a kitchen tiled to dado height, tiled fireplaces in the two main bedrooms and a heated linen cupboard. The tiled fireplaces were often of mottled brown, with rounded corners to the standard stepped outline. By 1939 some 75 per cent of houses were wired for electricity, compared with 2 per cent in 1910.

Built-in furniture became more widespread, especially wardrobes and kitchen storage units. Narrow bands of coloured trim were often applied to these and similar edging was found in bathroom tiling.

Oakwood: house type built by Costains (1928)
Tudor-arch fireplace with stepped tilework (1930s)

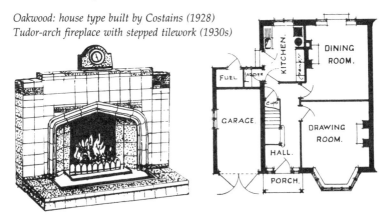

POSTWAR: 1945-1970

The Arts and Crafts permeation has virtually continued to the present day as the predominant style of housing. Both the internal planning and the external layout of the great mass of suburban housing differed little after the Second World War from before. Partly under the influence of Functionalism, there was a tendency to plainness, and small panes gave way to whole-casement panes and to picture windows; brick was preferred to render.

1940s' and 1950s' Utility

To a certain degree Functionalism came to predominance in the first decade after the War when only council housing was permitted, but most of what was built should be termed utilitarian rather than Functionalist, as it was bereft of adornment out of economy rather than principle and tended to lack the positive design of abstract shape that was the essence of the Functionalist idea.

For a while, in the late 1940s and the 1950s, front gables became rare and smaller houses became little more than brick boxes, still generally, however, very much in the garden city mould. The New Towns designed to take the surplus populations of the conurbations, long regarded as overcrowded, were naturally particularly close to the model, the cottage form still being transplanted to an urban context. Characteristic of the 1950s were plain slab door hoods, often extended across the neighbouring window and down to the ground on both sides to form a kind of picture frame.

What did differ, was the layout of inner-city council estates. In

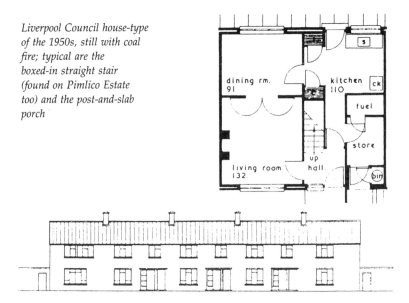

Liverpool Council house-type of the 1950s, still with coal fire; typical are the boxed-in straight stair (found on Pimlico Estate too) and the post-and-slab porch

these, following the doctrine of Corbusier and others, housing was no longer aligned with streets but disposed on open ground, the various blocks, whether of flats or houses, turned inwards to relate to one another. Unlike suburban council housing, they were often of a very positive design, with flat roofs and panelled exteriors or exteriors made up of prefabricated elements.

1955-1970: Variety Resumes

When private housing began to be built again in the early 1950s, Functionalists produced houses for individual clients more three-dimensional and lively than early postwar work and more varied in materials and form than pre-war. The influence of Mies van der Rohe and the sleekness of glazed geometry, exemplified in Dowson's Long Wall (overleaf), was foremost among many strands.

In multiple housing too, Functionalists also began to enliven the flatness of postwar utility, especially by the use of panelwork above and below windows (of tiles, weatherboarding or corrugated plastic). Eric Lyons pioneered work in this more friendly vein for the Span developers, which influenced public housing and, fleetingly, the mass of developers' suburban.

At first suburban housing tended to be rather muted, without the pre-war bay window, but the 'traditional' inclination revived, and a fairly continuous spectrum was soon established all the way from utilitarian to speculators' Tudor and Neo-Georgian.

*Pimlico Estate, Westminster (1945-55,
by Powell and Moya)*

Long Wall, Long Melford, Suffolk, with timber windows and roof (1963, by Philip Dowson)

More than ever after 1945, Neo-Georgian carried a genteel flavour; as Functionalism became the norm for council housing in the 1940s, so Neo-Georgian became especially associated with the private-sector houses of the better off. Perhaps in consequence, its widest application of all was to come in a single, easily installed feature. This was the front door with a fanlight cut into its head, instead of being set in the arch above the door. Although contrary to all Classical logic and precedent, this had the advantage of fitting the standard square-headed opening of post-1914 houses. From *c.*1970, it became increasingly popular, inserted as a touch of elegance in many non-Classical homes, including Functionalist council flats and houses.

NEO-VERNACULAR, POST-MODERN AND TOYTOWN

Around 1970, the Modernists' command of the high ground of British architecture was fairly abruptly broken. Henceforth it was not just the speculative developers of suburban housing who were free to ignore the tenets of Functionalism, or the tiny number of maverick architects who had persisted with Classical designs. All architects now felt unconstrained. They tended to move in their new freedom in three directions, sometimes gathered under the single label of Post-Modern, at least in their more developed form, but it is worth distinguishing them, as follows: Neo-Vernacular, what may be termed Period Echoes, and Post-Modernism in a strong sense.

Neo-Vernacular

This was the earliest tendency of the three and can be regarded as much as an evolution of Functionalism as a rejection of it. It developed during the 1970s, partly under the influence of the growing conservation movement, and especially the enthusiasm for the humbler kind of old buildings of the countryside, which were coming to be termed vernacular, but also as part of the reaction to the grimness and aridity of post-1945 building.

Pitched roofs, often with projecting eaves, were favoured; so too were the traditional textured surfaces of brick and wood, the latter nearly always stained rather than painted. The window frames,

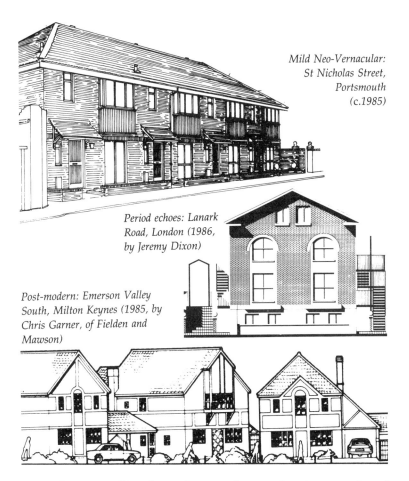

Mild Neo-Vernacular:
St Nicholas Street,
Portsmouth
(c.1985)

Period echoes: Lanark
Road, London (1986,
by Jeremy Dixon)

Post-modern: Emerson Valley
South, Milton Keynes (1985, by
Chris Garner, of Fielden and
Mawson)

now also generally of wood, were frequently given cambered heads, a feature that became very widespread in the following decades in housing that belonged to all tendencies and none. After the flatness of the 1940s and 1950s and the more stark tendency towards the heavily gridlike of the 1960s, there was a reversion to projecting features: porches on strutted supports, windows bayed out or cantilevered out from the walls. A typical example is St Nicholas Street, Portsmouth. In a parallel shift, increased use of cross wings, façade gablets and roofs uniting porch and garage lent a more villagy touch to the broader mass of developers' housing.

Period Echoes

It became increasingly common to give buildings elements reminiscent of past periods of architecture. There was no question of adopting a past style wholeheartedly, in the manner of the Gothic Revivalists, nor of dressing buildings in elaborate period costume in the way that flourished down to 1914 and beyond; it was more a matter of incorporating small touches based on historic styles – echoes, in fact. The earliest such reminiscence was of Neo-

Victorian, mainly characterised by bands of coloured brickwork and gabled dormers. An even less complete imitation was Neo-Redbrick, featuring salmon pink and shaped gables. More individualistically, but influentially, Jeremy Dixon echoed the stepped gables of Dutch tradition in London at St Marks Road (1976-9) and also at Compass Point, Isle of Dogs (1988) – as well as early nineteenth-century Neo-Classicism in his Lanark Road flats.

Post Modern

In its narrower sense, Post-Modernism had a large Neo-Classical component, but as part of a geometric-flavoured vocabulary, rather than any period evocation. It started in the United States of America and its spread to Britain was a manifestation of a general increase in Americal cultural influence. Its proponents repudiated the abstinence from stylistic feature of Functionalism, indeed upheld a freedom from all aesthetic tenets. As with the Neo-Vernacularists, pitched roofs were reinstated.

In marked contrast with their Neo-Georgian predecessors, the Post-Modernists married their Classicism to modern technology and modern finishes, often strongly coloured. In harmony with economic necessity, their Classical features were a matter of geometry rather than of decorative detail. The linear suggestion of a pediment, often in split form, was pervasive. Round-arched and other semicircular features were also favoured, particularly for glazed toplighting – reminiscent more of the Crystal Palace than the eighteenth century. Openings stepped outwards towards the top; circular windows and tall, protruding V-shaped windows were other recurring features. Many of these motifs had an early display in a strong form at Thematic House, in West London, of 1979-85, designed by two leading Post-Modernists, Charles Jencks and Terry Farrell. In trying to reintroduce stylistic force, the Post-Modernists were in danger of producing a vocabulary of clichés.

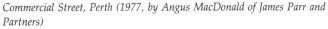

Commercial Street, Perth (1977, by Angus MacDonald of James Parr and Partners)

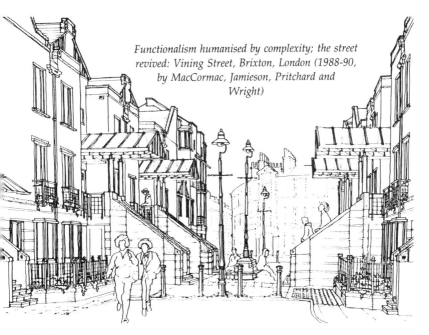

Functionalism humanised by complexity; the street revived: Vining Street, Brixton, London (1988-90, by MacCormac, Jamieson, Pritchard and Wright)

Toytown

By far the greatest number of houses being put up in the early 1990s continued to be styled in a slightly modified utilitarian manner, and flavoured, especially if slightly more expensive, with features of Neo-Vernacular, Post-Modern, mock-timber or Neo-Georgian, all of which might be included in a single development. Significantly, the semi-detached house was no longer so preponderant, comprising only twenty per cent of new houses. Forty per cent were detached. At their plainest, such houses could be aptly described as Toytown, and varied hardly at all between town and country. The standardisation of domestic architecture that had been advancing ever since 1700 was now almost complete. Often, houses in the new developments were butted against one another in staggered or cross-built versions of the village row.

Standing far above the general run of such housing, but providing an early model for others, was a group in Perth. It ranges from small five-storey blocks of flats to single-storey cottages of traditional Scottish form. It is built in sand-blasted pinky-beige concrete blocks, with lead-covered dormers, stained wood windows and slate roofs. Facing away from the river, onto the road, are the rounded projections of stair turrets – another Scots touch. Those schemes that have followed down the same road have seldom succeeded in being so organically embedded in the landscape or so carefully designed to be native to the locality.

Internally, there was an upturn in period detail, usually loosely Georgian, in the 1980s. Reflecting greater wealth were bathrooms ensuite with bedrooms and utility rooms ensuite with kitchens. Arched openings between reception rooms were favoured.

187

BIBLIOGRAPHY

GENERAL

Ayres, James, *The Shell Book of the Home in Britain: decoration, design and construction of vernacular interiors, 1500–1850*, 1981

Barley, Maurice, *The English Farmhouse and Cottage*, 1961

Barley, Maurice, *Houses and History*, 1986

Brunskill, R. W., *Illustrated Handbook of Vernacular Architecture*, (1970) 1978

Calloway, Stephen (ed.), *The Elements of Style: an encyclopedia of domestic architectural details*, 1991

Chapman, S. D. (ed.), *The History of Working-class Housing*, 1971

Cook, Olive, and Smith, Edwin, *The English House through Seven Centuries*, (1968) 1984

Girouard, Mark, *The English Town*, 1990

Iredale, David, and J. Barrett, *Discovering Your Old House*, (1968) 1991

Lloyd, Nathaniel, *A History of the English House*, (1931), 1985

Mercer, Eric, *Vernacular Architecture* (Royal Commission on Historical Monuments), 1975

Powell, Christopher, *Discovering Cottage Architecture*, 1984

Quiney, Anthony, *Period Houses*, 1989

Quiney, Anthony, *The Traditional Buildings of England*, 1990

CONSTRUCTION AND MATERIALS

Alcock, N. W. (ed.) *Cruck Construction: an introduction and a catalogue* (CBA Research Report 42), 1981

Bankart, George, *The Art of the Plasterer*, 1914

Brunskill, R., and P. Crawley, *Timber Building in Britain*, 1985

Clifton-Taylor, Alec, *The Pattern of English Building*, (1962) 1987

Clifton-Taylor, Alec, and R. Brunskill, *English Brickwork*, 1977

Gardner, J. S., *English Ironwork of the 17th and 18th Centuries*, 1911

Harris, Richard, *Discovering Timber Frame Houses*, 1978

Hewett, Cecil A., *English Historic Carpentry*, 1980

Lloyd, Nathaniel, *A History of English Brickwork*, 1925

Kelly, Alison, *Mrs Coade's Stone*, 1990

McCann, John, *Cob and Clay Buildings*, 1983

Sambrook, John, *Fanlights*, 1989

BY PERIOD
Prehistoric and Medieval

Beresford, Maurice, and J. G. Hurst, *Deserted Medieval Villages*, 1971

Dyer, C. 'English peasant buildings in the later Middle Ages' *Medieval Archaeology*, 1986, pp. 19-45

Longworth, Ian and J. Cherry (eds), *Archaeology in Britain since 1945*, 1986

Platt, Colin, *Medieval English Towns*, 1976

Rahtz, P. A., 'Buildings and rural settlement', in Wilson, D. M. (ed.) *The Archaeology of Anglo-Saxon England*, 1976

Smith, John T., P. Faulkner and Anthony Emery, *Studies in Medieval Domestic Architecture*, 1975

Wood, Margaret, *The Mediaeval House*, (1965) 1983

Classical

Cruickshank, D. and N. Burton, *Life in the Georgian City*, 1990

Louw, H., 'The Origin of the Sash Window', *Architectural History*, 1983, pp. 49–72

Reid, Richard, *The Georgian House and its Details*, 1989

Reiff, Daniel, *Small Georgian Houses in England and Virginia*, 1986

Summerson, J., *Architecture in Britain, 1530–1830*, (1953) 1984

Victorian and Twentieth century

Barrett, Helena, and Phillips, John, *Suburban Style: the British home, 1840–1960*, 1987

Burnett, J., *A Social History of Housing 1815–1970*, (1978) 1980

Gould, Jeremy, *The Modern House in Britain, 1914–39*, 1977

Muthesius, Stefan, *The English Terraced House*, 1982

Service, Alastair, *Edwardian Interiors*, 1985

GEOGRAPHICAL

Scotland

Dunbar, John, *The Architecture of Scotland*, London (1966) 1978

Fenton, A., and B. Walker, *The Rural Architecture of Scotland*, 1981

Gifford, J., *Edinburgh* (Buildings of Scotland series), 1984

Gifford, J., *Fife* (Buildings of Scotland series), 1988

Gomme, Andor, and David Walker, *Architecture of Glasgow*, (1968) 1987

MacGibbon, D. and T. Ross, *The Castellated and Domestic Architecture of Scotland*, 5 vols, 1887–92

McKean, Charles, (ed.), RIAS Architectural Guides to Scotland (series), 13 vols, 1982-92

McKean, Charles, *The Scottish 1930s*, 1988

McWilliam, Colin, *Lothian* (Buildings of Scotland series), 1978

McWilliam, Colin, *Scottish Townscape*, 1975

Royal Commission on Ancient and Historical Monuments in Scotland (RCAHMS), *Argyll*, 5 vols., 1971–84

RCAHMS, *Edinburgh*, 1951

RCAHMS, *Stirlingshire*, 1963

Williamson, Elizabeth, A. Riches and M. Higgs, *Glasgow*, (Buildings of Scotland series), 1990
Worsdall, Frank, *The Glasgow Tenement*, (1979) 1991

Wales

Fox, Cyril, and Lord Raglan, *Monmouthshire Houses*, National Museum of Wales, 1951–4
Haslam, Richard, *Powys*, 1979
Hilling, John B., *Cardiff and the Valleys: architecture and townscape*, 1973
Hilling, John B., *The Historic Architecture of Wales*, 1976
Hubbard, Edward, *Clwyd*, 1986
Lowe, J. B., *Welsh Industrial Workers' Housing, 1775–1875*, 1977
Royal Commission on Ancient and Historical Monuments in Wales, *Glamorgan*, vols IIIii (1982) and IVii (1988)
Smith, Peter, *Houses in the Welsh Countryside*, (1975) 1988

The North of England

Brunskill, R. W., *Vernacular Architecture of the Lake District*, 1974
Caffyn, L., *Workers' Housing in West Yorkshire, 1750–1920*, 1986
Denyer, Susan, *Traditional Buildings and Life in The Lake District*, 1991
Giles, C., *Rural Houses of West Yorkshire, 1400–1830*, 1986
Hall, I. and E., *A New Picture of Georgian Hull*, 1973
Hall, I. and E., *Historic Beverley*, (1971), 1981
Harrison, B., and Hutton, Barbara, *Vernacular Houses in North Yorkshire and Cleveland*, 1984
Pearson, Sarah, *Rural Houses of the Lancashire Pennines*, 1985
Pevsner, N. et al, *Northumberland*, (1957) 1992
RCHM, *Houses of the North Yorkshire Moors*, 1987
RCHM, *City of York*, vols. III, IV and V, 1972, 1975 and 1981
Wrathmell, Stuart, *Wharram*, 1989

The Midlands

Pevsner, N., *Leicestershire and Rutland*, (1960) 1984
Pevsner, N., and J. Harris, *Lincolnshire*, (1964) 1989
RCHM, *Northamptonshire*, vol. 6 (North) 1984
RCHM, *The Town of Stamford*, 1977

East Anglia

Parker, V., *The Making of King's Lynn*, 1971
Smith, J. T. *English Houses, 1200–1800: the Hertfordshire evidence*, 1992

London

Beattie, Susan, *A Revolution in London Housing*, 1980
Byrne, Andrew, *London's Georgian Houses*, 1987
Cherry, Bridget, and N. Pevsner, *London 2: South*, 1983

Cherry, Bridget, and N. Pevsner, *London 3: North West*, 1991

Cruickshank, Dan, and Wyld, Peter, *London: the art of Georgian building*, 1975

Kelsall, A. F. 'The London house plan in the later 17th century', *Post-Medieval Archaeology*, 1974, pp. 80–91

Schofield, John, *The Building of London from the Conquest to the Great Fire*, 1984

Summerson, John, *Georgian London*, (1945), 1988

Summerson, John, 'The London suburban villa', in *The Unromantic Castle and other Essays*, 1990

The Survey of London, 42 vols., 1900–1986

The South and South-east of England

Lewis, Elizabeth, and Roberts, K., *Medieval Hall Houses in the Winchester Area*, 1988

Martin, D., and Martin, B., *Historical Buildings in Eastern Sussex*, Rape of Hastings Architectural Survey, vols 1–6, 1980–91

Mason, R. T., *Framed houses of the Weald*, (1964) 1969

RCHM, *Salisbury*, vol. I, 1981

The South-west and the Limestone Belt

Beacham, Peter (ed.), *Devon Building*, 1990

Chatwin, Amina, *Cheltenham Ornamental Ironwork*, 1975

Chesher, V. M., and F. J., *The Cornishman's House*, 1968

Gomme, Andor, M. Jenner and B. Little, *Bristol: an architectural history*, 1979

Hall, L. J., *The Rural Houses of North Avon and South Gloucestershire, 1400–1700*, 1983

Ison, Walter, *The Georgian Buildings of Bath, 1700–1830*, (1948) 1980

Laithwaite, Michael, 'The buildings of Burford', in A. M. Everitt (ed.), *Perspectives in Urban History*, 1973

Leach, R., *Early Industrial Housing: the Trinity area of Frome*, RCHM 1981

Portman, Derek, *Exeter Houses 1400–1600*, 1966

Taylor, R., 'Town houses in Taunton, 1500–1700', *Post Medieval Archaeology*, 1974, pp.63–79.

Wood-Jones, Raymond, *Traditional Domestic Architecture of the Banbury Region*, 1963

Open-air Museums and Smaller Houses Open to the Public

A few houses somewhat larger than those discussed in the text are included for the relevant light they shed.

For opening seasons, times and charges, the appropriate annual handbooks should be consulted. Entries in these may be listed either under the name of the house or under the locality. Here, houses are listed by locality, except for open-air museums, which are listed by name. Houses managed by the National Trust (NT) and National Trust for Scotland (NTS) are indicated.

OPEN-AIR MUSEUMS

Anglo-Saxon Village, West Stow, Suffolk, reconstruction of excavated settlement of *c.* 420–650 including four houses (0284 728718)

Auchindrain, Old Highland Township, Inveraray, Argyll, Highlands, simple houses from the eighteenth century onwards, including several longhouses

Avoncroft Museum of Buildings, Stoke Heath, Bromsgrove, Hereford and Worcester, including fifteenth-century town house, frame of Welsh aisled hall, 1946 prefab, etc. (0527 31886)

Beamish: North of England Open Air Museum, near Chester-le-Street, Co. Durham, including nineteenth-century town houses and pit cottages, and eighteenth-century farmhouse (0207 231811)

Butser Archaeological Farm, Bascomb Copse, Chalton, Portsmouth, reconstructed Iron Age house (0705 598838)

Chiltern Open Air Museum, Newland Park, Gorelands Lane, Chalfont St Giles, Buckinghamshire, (including reconstructed Iron Age House, farm buildings) (02407 71117)

Church Farm Museum, Skegness, Lincolnshire, (including farmhouse of *c.*1760 and mud-and-stud cottage of *c.*1790 (0754 66658)

Chysauster Ancient Village Gulval, Cornwall, excavated Neolithic stone houses (0736 61889)

Cregneash Village Folk Museum, Port St Mary, Isle of Man, including nineteenth-century crofter-fisherman's house and farmhouse (0624 75522)

David Livingstone Centre, Station Road, Strathclyde, tenement block and cottage row of 1785 (0698 823140)

Highland Folk Museum, Kingussie, Highland eighteenth-century factor's house, nineteenth-century farmhouse and reconstructed Black House (0540 661307)

Museum of East Anglian Life, Stowmarket, Suffolk, includes restored fourteenth-century Edgar's Farmhouse, among reconstructed farm and industrial buildings and displays (0449 612229)

New Lanark Conservation Village, Lanark, Strathclyde, model industrial village, started 1785, continued by Robert Owen from 1800; includes exteriors of four ranges of workers' housing and two detached houses (0555 61345)

Ryedale Folk Museum, Hutton-le-Hole, North Yorkshire, includes re-erected late sixteenth-century open-hall manor house, seventeenth-century longhouse, recreated pre-seventeenth-century longhouse and cruck cottage furnished as in nineteenth century (07515 367)

Weald and Downland Open Air Museum, Singleton, Chichester, West Sussex, includes seven complete houses, from thirteenth to seventeenth century, and fifteenth-century detached kitchen, among over thirty re-erected buildings (024 363 348)

Welsh Folk Museum, St Fagans, near Cardiff, includes six re-erected houses, from c.1470 to 1762, also Elizabethan mansion and late nineteenth-century farmhouse in situ (0222 569441)

York Castle Museum, Eye of York, includes two recreated streets, using original shopfronts and furnishing, and five period rooms (0904 653611).

HOUSES IN ENGLAND

Avon

Bath: *Royal Crescent*, 1767–74, two floors restored and furnished (0225 428126)

Bristol: *Georgian House*, 7 Great George Street, a sugar merchant's house of 1789–91, probably by William Paty

Cambridgeshire

Wisbech: *Peckover House*, a large furnished detached town house of c.1722 (NT; 0945 583463)

Cheshire

Chester: *Grosvenor Museum*, Grosvenor Street, Chester, at rear of which is a Georgian house of c.1680 (0244 321616)

Nantwich: *Church's Mansion*, 1577, restaurant

Cornwall

Launceston: *Lawrence House*, 9 Castle Street, 1653, with Mayor's Parlour (NT; 0566 773277/773047)

Tintagel: *Old Post Office*, a small manor house, probably early fifteenth century (NT; 0840 770024)

Cumbria

Ambleside: *Hill Top*, Sawrey, a seventeenth-century farmhouse, home of Beatrix Potter (NT 09666 269)

Carlisle: *Old Tullie House*, Castle Street, 1689 with Victorian extensions (0228 34781)

Cockermouth: *Wordsworth House*, 1745, birthplace of Wordsworth with seven rooms of eighteenth-century furnishing (NT; 053 94 32628)

Troutbeck: *Townend*, a seventeenth-century farmhouse, with added woodwork of the late nineteenth century (NT; 05394 32628)

Derbyshire

Bakewell: *Old House Museum*, Cunningham Place, 1534–35, enlarged before 1594 with an extension of *c.*1620, the home of Richard Arkwright (0629 813647)

Chesterfield: *Peacock Heritage Centre*, Low Pavement, sixteenth century, timber-framed (0246 207777)

Derby: *Pickford's House Museum*, 41 Friargate, 1769–70, furnished (0332 255363)

Devon

Dartmouth: *Town Museum*, The Butterwalk, house of 1640 with original panelling and ceilings

Exeter: *Rougemont House Museum of Costume and Lace*, Castle Street, period room settings in a Georgian house

Marlborough: *Yarde, Kingsbridge*, a farmhouse of *c.*1700

Plymouth: *Elizabethan House*, 32 New Street, a sixteenth-century house with contemporary furniture (0752 264878)

Plymouth: *Merchant's House*, 33 St Andrew's Street, sixteenth or early seventeenth-century, social history museum (0752 264878)

Totnes: *(Elizabethan) Museum*, 70 Fore Street, late sixteenth- or early seventeenth-century house with furniture and mixed exhibits (0803 863821)

Dorset

Dorchester: *Dawnay House*, Puddletown, 1725 (0305 269741)

Higher Bockhampton: *Hardy's Cottage*, 1800 with addition of 1840 (NT; 0305 262366)

Poole: *Scaplen's Court*, High Street, exhibits of everyday life in fifteenth-century merchant's house (0202 675151)

Wimborne Minster: *Priest's House Museum*, 23 High Street, partly Tudor (0202 882533)

Essex

Coggeshall: *Paycock's*, a lavish merchant's house of *c.*1500 (NT; 0376 561305)

Colchester: *Hollytrees Museum*, 1718, with exhibits of later social history (0206 712493)

Harlow: *Harlow Museum*, Passmores House, Third Avenue, a Tudor and Georgian farmhouse (0279 446422)

Gloucestershire

Cheltenham: *Gustav Holst Birthplace Museum*, an early nineteenth-century two-storey stuccoed house with period furnishings (0242 524846)

Sturminster Newton: *Fiddleford Manor (or Mill)*, fourteenth-century hall and solar with elaborate cusped roofs; sixteenth-century alterations (0258 72597)

Gloucester: *Folk Museum*, 99–103 Westgate Street, partly furnished group of fifteenth- and sixteenth-century houses (0452 26467)

Newent: *The Shambles Museum*, 20 Church Street, early eighteenth-century, furnished as late Victorian tradesman's house with reconstruction of Victorian shops at the rear

Tewkesbury: *The Little Museum*, Church Street, an early sixteenth-century merchant's cottage, annexe to John Moore Countryside Museum, in the same restored range

Greater Manchester

Rochdale Museum: *Sparrow Hill*, interiors and varied collections in eighteenth-century vicarage (0706 47474)

Hampshire

Alton: *Jane Austen's House*, Chawton, mainly later eighteenth-century (0420 83262)

Portsmouth: *Dickens Museum*, 393 Commercial Road, 1805, the birthplace of Dickens, showing furnishing of the time (0705 827261)

Southampton: *Medieval Merchant's House*, 58 French Street, restored house of c1290, with furniture reconstructions

Southampton: *Tudor House Museum*, St Michael's Square, historical exhibits in a sixteenth-century house (0703 24216)

Hereford and Worcester

Bromyard: *Lower Brockhampton*, a small timber-framed manor house of *c*.1400 (NT)

Hereford: *The Old House*, High Town, 1621, furnished (0432 268121)

Whitney-on-Wye: *Cwmmau Farmhouse*, Brilley, early seventeenth-century, timber-framed (NT, limited opening)

Worcester: *Elgar Birthplace*, Crown East Lane, Lower Broadheath, small mid-nineteenth-century house

Worcester: *Tudor House Museum*, Friar Street, a fifteenth-century timber-framed house with furnishing and exhibits of various periods

Humberside

Barton on Humber: *Baysgarth Museum*, Baysgarth Park, Caistor Road, an eighteenth-century town house and cottage (0652 32318)

Epworth: *The Old Rectory*, 1709, the childhood home of John and Charles Wesley (0427 872268)

Hull: *Wilberforce House and Georgian Houses*, 23–5 High Street, the birthplace of William Wilberforce, probably post-1656, with a big staircase of *c*.1760; the adjoining Georgian Houses of the 1750s have furniture and silver collections (0482 22237)

Isle of Man

Ramsey: *Grove Rural Life Museum*, Andreas Road, early Victorian house, with Victorian period rooms

Kent

Margate: *Tudor House and Museum*, King Street, timber-framed house of *c.*1525 with early seventeenth-century interiors (0843 225511 x 2520)
Tenterden: *Smallhythe Place*, sixteenth-century timber-framed house, home of Ellen Terry (NT; 05806 2334)

Lancashire

Lancaster: *Cottage Museum*, 15 Castle Hill, half of a house of 1759, divided *c.*1825–30, furnished as an artisan's cottage of 1825 (0524 64637)

Leicestershire

Donington-le-Heath: *Manor House*, dating from *c.*1280 with sixteenth- and seventeenth-century alterations (0530 31259)
Leicester: *Museum of Costume*, Wygston's House, Applegate, St Nicholas Circle, late sixteenth-century and early nineteenth-century (0533 554100)

Lincolnshire

Colsterworth: *Woolsthorpe Manor*, a large early seventeenth-century farmhouse, birthplace of Isaac Newton (NT; 0476 860338)

London

Brent: *Grange Museum of Community History*, Neasden Lane, NW10, a stable converted to a gothic cottage *c.*1810; displays include a Victorian parlour and 1930s lounge (081 452 8311)
Carshalton: *Little Holland House*, 40 Beeches Avenue, a 1904 house designed for himself by the Arts and Crafts artist Frank Dickinson
Chelsea: *Carlyle's House*, 24 Cheyne Row, a typical terraced house of 1708, with the furnishing of Carlyle's time (1834–81) and relics (071 352 7087)
Chiswick: *Hogarth's House*, Hogarth Lane, Great West Road, W4, a small detached house of 1700, which was Hogarth's country home 1749–74 (081 994 6757)
City of London: *Dr Johnson's House*, 17 Gough Square, EC4, a single-depth house of *c.*1700 in a City court, which was Johnson's home 1749–59 (071 353 3745)
Greenwich: *Fan Museum*, 12 Crooms Hill, SE10, two terraced houses of 1721, carefully restored (081 858 7879)
Hampstead: *Freud Museum*, 20 Maresfield Gardens, NW3, a detached Neo-Georgian house of 1920, which was Freud's resi-

dence 1938 till his death in 1939, containing furniture from Vienna (071 435 2002)

Hampstead: *Hampstead Museum*, Burgh House, New End Square, NW3, a detached house of 1703 (071 431 0144)

Hampstead: *Keats House*, Keats Grove, NW3, a semi-detached pair of 1815–16, one the home of Keats, 1818–20, the other that of his fiancée; the pair were united, and a drawing room and conservatory added, in 1838; the furnishings are of Keats' time

Holborn: *The Dickens House Museum*, 48 Doughty Street, WC1, 1802 terraced house, home of Dickens 1837–9, with furnishing of his time (071 405 2127)

Kensington: *Linley Sambourne House*, 18 Stafford Terrace, built in the 1860s with interior and furnishing designed after 1874

Sutton: *Whitehall*, 1 Malden Road, Cheam, Surrey, a timber-framed house of *c.*1500 (081 643 1236)

Norfolk

Great Yarmouth: *Elizabethan House Museum*, 4 South Quay (0493 855746)

Great Yarmouth: *Old Merchants' House and the Row 111 houses*, South Quay, early seventeenth-century merchants' houses (0493 857900)

Norwich: *Strangers' Hall*, Charing Cross, a hall house of *c.*1540; rooms of *c.*1627, 1659, 1748 and *c.*1840, each with furnishing of the time (0603 667229)

Thetford: *The Ancient House Museum*, White Hart Street, probably built shortly after 1500 (0842 752599)

Nottinghamshire

Eastwood: *D. H. Lawrence's Birthplace Museum*, 8a Victoria Street, a small house of the 1850s with furnishing of *c.*1885, (0773 763312)

Oxfordshire

Witney: *Cogges Manor Farm Museum*, Church Lane, Cogges, including a manor of the thirteenth century and later (0993 772602)

Shropshire

Shrewsbury: *Clive House Museum*, home of Clive of India, built in 1752 around medieval fabric

Telford: *Rosehill House*, part of the Ironbridge Gorge Museum, an early nineteenth-century restored ironmaster's house (095245 3522/2751)

Somerset

Axbridge Museum: King John's Hunting Lodge, an urban range of *c.*1500

Staffordshire

Lichfield: *Donegal House*, Bore Street, a cloth merchant's house of 1730 (0543 252109)
Lichfield: *Dr Johnson's Birthplace*, Breadmarket Street, 1707–8, a house over bookshop that has hardly altered
Shallowford: *Isaac Walton's Cottage*, a probably seventeenth-century timber-framed single-storey cottage with attic
Stafford: *Ancient High House*, a large timber-framed house of 1595

Suffolk

Bury St Edmunds: *Moyse's Hall Museum*, Cornhill, a twelfth-century house, considerably restored
Sudbury: *Gainsborough's House*, Gainsborough Street, the birthplace of the painter, dating from the early eighteenth century, with earlier fabric

Surrey

Guildford House, 155 High Street, *c.*1660. Lavish town house of *c.*1660, restored 1992–3 (0483 444740)

East Sussex

Lewes: *Anne of Cleves House*, Southover High Street, Lewes, an early sixteenth-century timber-framed open-hall house, with transferred Elizabethan staircase and additions of 1599 and later, plus furniture (0273 474379)
Seaford: *Alfriston Clergy House*, Polegate, a Wealden house of *c.*1360 (NT)

West Sussex

Chichester: *Pallant House*, 9 North Pallant, a large furnished town house of 1712–13 (0243 774557)
West Hoathly: *Priest House*, an early fifteenth-century timber-framed open-hall house, with chimney and floor inserted in the later sixteenth century and mainly eighteenth- and nineteenth-century furnishing (0342 810479)

Warwickshire

Stratford-on-Avon: *Shakespeare Birthplace Trust properties –*
Anne Hathaway's Cottage, Shottery, with crucks of 1463; mainly sixteenth- and seventeenth-century
Hall's Croft, Old Town, late sixteenth-century timber-framed doctor's house, with early seventeenth-century addition
Mary Arden's House (Shakespeare Countryside Museum), Wilmcote, an early sixteenth-century timber-framed house
Shakespeare's Birthplace, Healey Street, a restored timber-framed sixteenth-century house (0789 204016)

West Midlands

Yardley: *Blakesley Hall*, Blakesley Road, a large timber-framed yeoman house of *c*.1575, partly furnished, with a display on timber building methods (021 783 2193)

Wiltshire

Salisbury: *Mompesson House*, Cathedral Close, a small mansion of 1700, with a wing of the mid-eighteenth century (NT)
Swindon: *Railway Village Museum*, 34 Faringdon Road, an early 1860s railwayman's house furnished as in 1900 (0793 526161 x 3189)

North Yorkshire

York: *Fairfax House*, Castlegate, a small mansion by John Carr, of *c*.1762 (0904 655543)

South Yorkshire

Sheffield: *Bishop's House*, Meersbrook Park, a Tudor timber-framed house (0742 557701)

West Yorkshire

Cleckheaton: *Red House*, Oxford Road, Gomersal, a Regency house furnished as in the 1830s (0274 872165)
Coxwold: *Shandy Hall*, the home of Sterne from 1760, a timber-framed fifteenth-century open hall, cased in stone in the seventeenth century, altered by Sterne (03476 465)
Haworth Parsonage, 1778 and later, the home of the Brontës (0535 642323)

HOUSES IN WALES

Dyfed

Haverfordwest: *Penrhos Cottage*, Llanycefn, Maenchlochog, a turf cottage, probably of the early nineteenth century that was cased in stone, probably in 1849, with furnishing of *c*.1937–68 (0437 731328)
Tenby: *Merchant's House*, superior late fifteenth-century stone-built house (0834 2279)

Mid Glamorgan

Merthyr Tydfyl: *Joseph Parry's Birthplace*, 4 Chapel Row, George-town, early nineteenth-century house furnished as in Parry's childhood in the 1840s (0685 83704)

Gwynedd

Betws-y-Coed: *Ty Mawr*, Wybrnant, open-hall, stone-walled house of *c*.1545, remodelled as storeyed house, late sixteenth or

early seventeenth century (NT, 069 03 213)
Criccieth: *High Cottage* (The New Lloyd George Museum), Llanystumdwy, early nineteenth-century, furnished as childhood home of Lloyd George in the 1870s

HOUSES IN SCOTLAND

Borders

Jedburgh: *Mary Queen of Scots House*, Queen Street, a sixteenth-century tower house

Dumfries and Galloway

Dumfries: *Burns House*, c.1745; Burns lived there for three years, till his death in 1796 (0387 55297)
Dumfries: *Old Bridge House Museum*, seventeenth-century; six period rooms (0387 56904)
Dumfries: *Sanquhar Museum*, 1735
Ecclefechan: *Arched House*, by 1791; small pair of cottages, linked by arch; childhood home of Carlyle (NTS; 05763 666)
Kirkcudbright: *Broughton House*, High Street, a mid-eighteenth century furnished town house (0557 30437)

Fife

Culross: *The Study*, a 1633 house with panelled, furnished room with painted ceiling (NTS; 0383 880359)
Dunfermline: *Andrew Carnegie Birthplace Museum*, junction of Moodie Street and Priory Lane, an early nineteenth-century weaver's cottage (0383 724302)

Grampian

Aberdeen: *James Dun's House*, 61 Schoolhill, 1769 (0224 646333)
Aberdeen: *Provost Skene's House* Guestrow, off Broad Street, ranges of 1629 and c.1670 (with plasterwork), Georgian panelling, furnished (0224 641086)

Highland

Cromarty: *Hugh Miller's Cottage*, 1711, furnished (NTS; 03817 245)
Culloden: *Old Leanach Cottage*, an early eighteenth-century furnished cruck cottage (NTS; 0463 790607)
Glencoe: *Glencoe and North Lorn Folk Museum*, an eighteenth-century (or later) thatched, restored cruck cottage
Lewis: *The Black House*, Arnol, a primitive stone house of c.1875

Lothian

Edinburgh: *Georgian House*, 7 Charlotte Square, in a square designed by Adam, 1791; the house was built in 1796 (NTS; 031 225 2160)

Edinburgh: *Gladstone's Land*, 483 Lawnmarket, a six-storey apartment house of 1617–20 (NTS; 031 226 5856)
Edinburgh: *John Knox House Museum*, Royal Mile, a house of the early and mid-sixteenth century, with later alterations (031 556 6961)

Orkney

Corrigall: part of Orkney Farm and Folk Museum, a restored eighteenth to nineteenth-century farmstead
Kirkbuster: part of Orkney Farm and Folk Museum, a restored farmstead of 1723
Knap of Howar, excavated Neolithic stone houses
Skara Brae, excavated Neolithic stone houses

Shetland

Dunrossness: *Shetland Croft House Museum*, Voe, a restored croft of *c*.1870s (0595 5057)

Strathclyde

Alloway: *Burns' Cottage*, Burns' birthplace, 1759; built shortly before
Biggar: *Greenhill Covenanter's House*, Burn Braes, a two-storey re-erected farmhouse from the upper Clyde valley, seventeenth century, but much altered.
Glasgow: *Provand's Lordship*, 3 Castle Street, a large house, built 1471 (041 552 8819)
Glasgow: *Tenement House*, 145 Buccleugh Street, Garnethill, a first-floor furnished flat of 1892 (NTS; 041 333 0183)
Helensburgh: *The Hill House*, Upper Colquhoun Street, built in 1902–4, a large house by Mackintosh (NTS; 0436 3900)
Kilbarchan: *Weaver's Cottage*, The Cross, an eighteenth-century craftsman's house (NTS; 050 57 5588)
Kirkoswald: *Souter Johnnie's House*, the thatched home, of *c*.1785, of the souter (cobbler) of Burns's 'Tam o'Shanter' (NTS; 065 56 603)
Tarbolton *Bachelors' Club*, seventeenth-century thatched house (NTS; 0292 541/940)

Tayside

Glamis: *Angus Folk Museum*, a row of restored nineteenth-century cottages (NTS; 030 784 288)

GLOSSARY, SUBJECT INDEX AND
READY-REFERENCE GUIDE TO DATING

Date-spans are for the ordinary run of smaller houses, not mansions or rarities (and often conjectural or subject to regional or other qualification). They generally apply to Scotland (Sc.) only as specified. Definitions are provided if not given in the text. Many features, though defined separately, are grouped under general headings in CAPITALS for date-spans (e.g. ROOF, PLAN, WINDOW). Cross-references are also capitalised. Illustrations (in bold) are only indexed when not signalled in the text. (C = century, fl. = flourished, rev. = revived.)

Acroterion, pl. -ia (Greek; blocks at ends or top of pediment, crowned by statues or mouldings): fl. 1810–1840, **145**, 151

Anaglypta: introd. 1887, 171

Anthemion (Greek; fan pattern, with spokes turning inwards, based on stamens of honeysuckle): from c.1760, **131**, 137, 139, **146**, 152, dwindling from c.1845–1935, 157–8

Apron (a panel below a window): Artisan, mid-17C, 98; c.1695–c.1730, 110, **112**; rev. c.1875–1935, 165

Arcading: 89, 90, 145

Arch – two-centred (simple Gothic one, formed by intersecting compass arcs from two centres) – four-centered (shallow one set out from four centres, two broad arcs being flanked by two tight ones) – ogee (two double curves, peaking at centre) – three-centred (with rounded top; set out in three arcs)

Arch brace: 19, **31**, **37**, **38**, **43**

Architrave (Classical framing used round doors and windows, taken from the lowest of the three main parts of an entablature): tending to vanish from stone façades c.1760, 133; second bead added c.1770, 140; quirk added c.1775, 140; compressed and quirked ones, from c.1770, 140; elaborate window ones of Nash, 145; panel mould applied to, late 1820s–1920s, 154

Arris (corner where two surfaces meet)

Art Nouveau (style based on nature, rather than historical precedent, esp. elongated, sinuous tendrils): c.1890–1940, **168**, 175–6, 176–7

Artisan Classicism: c.1615–1710, 74, 93, 96–7, **96**, 98

Ashlar (stone worked to a smooth face and even joints): 120, 141, 143; pargeted imitation, c.1660–1700, 100; stucco imitation c.1765–1840, 137

Astragal (glazing bar): 89

Attic (in a Classical house, a half-storey above the order or main cornice; also used of GARRET)

Back-to-backs (two rows of houses butted back-to-back, so without rear windows): see LAYOUT

Bacon-smoking chamber: 16C to 18C, 64

BALCONY: roof ones fl. c.1580–1710, 102–3; first-floor balconies, with BALUSTERS, mid-17C, 95, with RAILINGS, c.1620–1700, 101–2, 106; balconettes, c.1768–1845, esp. with anthemion, 131–2, **146–147**, also latticework c.1780–1830, palmettes, intersecting circles and ovals, frets and Gothic arches c.1815–40, 144, 151–2; longer balconies

Crown post: **19**, 36; see ROOF

Crow-stepping (stepped GABLE coping)

Crucks: **19**, 14; see ROOF

Cusping (sharp points between adjoining curves): on barge boards, wind braces, c.1330–, **38**, 43, 44, **44**; on close panelling, c.1580–1680, 73

Cyma recta (double-curve moulding, concave above convex)

Dado (PANELLING on bottom portion of wall)

Dais canopy or beam (COVE or JETTY, or moulded beam, over dais area at top end of hall, raised in grander houses): 17, 50

Daub, see WATTLE

Decorated style: c.1300–, 43, 49, 50

Dendrochronology: 21–2, 30, 31, 34, 36, 40, **46**, 48

Dentillation (band of small toothlike blocks in cornices): increased use, c.1730–60, externally, 119, **125**, internally 125, 126, **139**

Divot (turf roof tile – Sc.) 15, 129

DOOR: – external: with bar-bolt, by 3100/2500 BC, 9; primitive, of wicker, rushes, etc, **13**, 14; ledged or battened (planks and cross boards) norm till rise of panel, c.1600, and thereafter for poor, 153, rev., c.1890–1914, **175**; ten-panel, late 17C to c.1730 (sometimes St Andrew's Cross, **113**, **121**), 106; six-panel, c.1725–1830s, **113**, **119**, 124, **131–2**, **146**; four-panel, occas. flush with reeded margins, or with round panel, or simulated double doors or studded, c.1810–30s, 151; with two arched panels, c.1820–70s, 151; four-panel or battened, for farmhouses c.1800, 153; four-panel with panel-moulds (sometimes Gothic-arched), late 1820s–1890, 158; with stained glass panels, bolection moulding, aprons, peaked bottom panel or small panes in top, c.1875–1914, and later, **168**, 171, **181**; with glazed roundel or moulded vertical panels, c.1910–30, **177**; with slit, stepped or sunburst glazing, 1930s, 180; flush or with large glazed panels, by Functionalists, 1930s–, widespread 1945–70, 180, **182**; with fan in head or vertical barring c.1970–, 184;

– internal: matching small square panelling, 17C, **87**; two-panel (also three-and four-), 17C to earlier 18C, 107

DOORWAY: superior ones round-ARCHed to c.1200, **26–7**; two-centred, c.1175–, fading mid-14C–, **24**, 29, **30**, 49; four-centred, mid 1380s-, fading late 17C, 45, 55, **62**, 63, 85, **78**; ogee-headed, c.1380-late 17C, **43**, 49, **84**; three-centred, late 14C–, typ. of late 15C, **54**, 55; Classically detailed, c.1600–, 69; ornate-headed, c.1590–1710, 84–5, **84**; heavy, round-arch, early 17C, fading 18C, 85; roll moulding typ. in Sc., 17C, 77, 90, also bead, 91; keyed arch, c.1640–1830, 95, 105; broken-pediment, c.1670–1730, 105, in Sc., 117; swan-neck, c.1660–1720, 105, 112–3; pediment hood, 1660–, 105; arched hood, c.1660–1750 and occas. later, **99**, 105, ·**124**; cornice only, c.1660–, 105, 120, 150; plain or bolection surround, c.1640–1730, **92**, 94, 105, 114, 127, 144; fluted pilaster, esp. c.1680–1730, 112–13; bracketed hood/canopy, c.1680–1730 (often with shell, c.1680–1725), **111**, 112; with ramped architrave, c.1680–1730, 112; segmental pediment, fluted pilasters, c.1680, fading from 1725, **113**; architraved, often lugged, c.1690–1750, 120, in Sc. to 1760s, 116; Gibbs surround, (occas. early 17C) by 1722, to c.1765, 113, 138, **121**; in N, recessed, with panelled reveals, pilasters and entablature, c.1745–1850, 119, 149; smaller from *c.*1730, 123; pediment on columns or simpler, esp. *c.*1730–50 (Bath till later), 123, 127, 134, 151; arch in open pediment, *c.*1750–1820s, 130–31, 134; recessed within arch, with sidelights, *c.*1765–1800, **131**, 138; simple arch, *c.*1730–, esp. *c.*1775–1840, **127**, 133–4, **143**, 144, 150; chamfered, in Lakes, late 18C, 127; quarter or half-columns or colonettes in arch (often segmental), *c.*1800–40, 150–51; Doric half-columns in Sc., usually semi-recessed, 151; recessed behind pilasters and entablature on middling houses, *c.*1825–80, 157; with stilted or pointed heads, *c.*1850–1914, **160**, 162; recessed behind wide arches on low jambs or with slab hoods, *c.*1890–1940, 173; Georgian rev., usually under-scaled, often with hood on shaped brackets, *c.*1895–, 178; concrete slab hoods, often on slender post, *c.*1940–60, 182; under strutted pentice hoods, *c.*1970–, 185

Doric order: 1. fluted Roman, fl. 1680–1730, 113, **114**, 125; 2. unfluted Roman, fl. 1730–1880, **112**, **143**, **145**; 3. Greek (with broad flutes, no base and slab capital), fl. 1810–40, in Sc. to 1870s, 151, 159

Dormers (window rising out of roof slope): introd. 16C, 69, 70; in Scotland, by 16C, 67; in two tiers, *c.*1660–1710, 104; eaves-slicing, *c.*1850–1914, 162

Downpipe (drainpipe): 49, 101, 137

Drop (cluster of flowers, etc hanging from point): 139

Dragon tie: 24, 34, **34**

Drip-mould, or hood-mould (pre-Classical horizontal moulding over windows, doors, to throw off water; 'continuous' = across several openings): 78, 85

Drystone (without mortar): 9, 11, 13–15, **13**, 129

Dutch GABLE: 96

Early English (first phase of Gothic, *c.*1175–1315, with two-centred ARCHES)

Earthfast, 10, 23–4, 29

Eaves (overhang of roof slope): cavetto and ogival, in Sc., 91; balustraded, *c.*1640–*c.*1700, 102–3 and again *c.*1815–80, 143, **144**, 145, 156; deep, flat, often with paired slender brackets or none, *c.*1805–45, 149, **150**; strutted with iron stays, *c.*1890–1920s, 173; projecting, *c.*1970–, 184

Egg and dart: from *c.*1600, **69**, esp. 1730–60, **125**, 126; rev. *c.*1875–1940, 166

Egyptian Revival: occas. *c.*1810–30; in Scotland, mid-19C, 159

Electricity: lighting, 1890s–, **174**, 176, 181; fires etc., *c.*1912–, 180, 181

English bond (alternating headers and stretchers in every course of BRICK)

Fanlight (toplight, etc): leaded, often matching top of window, prob. by *c.*1600, to *c.*1700, 95, 105–6; vertical bars, ?*c.*1640–1730, 113, **115**, **119**, 124, and *c.*1820–45, 148; diagonals, *c.*1720–60, 124, and *c.*1820–50, 150; waggon-wheel *c.*1723–60, 113; fretted-radial *c.*1725–50, 113; short wooden loops, *c.*1750–80, **121**, 138; metal-radial, *c.*1765–1810, 131, 138, 144; intersecting or tangential circles, *c.*1765–1830, 138, esp. in Sc., 144, 150; cobweb, *c.*1770–1840, 138; oblong re-introd. (sometimes MARGIN-GLAZED) *c.*1820–40s, 150; teardrop, batswing or concentric band, *c.*1810–30, **146**, 150; rounded-end barring, *c.*1810–40s, 150; single-pane, 1830s–70s, 157; stained glass (or multi-pane), *c.*1875–1914, 171; Neo-Georgian, often in leading or metal separate from glazing, c.1900–, 178; cut in top of door, c.1970–, 184

Finials (upward terminations to gables, railings etc)

FIREPLACE: open-hearth norm till 16C, 17, 32, 34, 52, 80, in Sc., till 18C, 129; in first-floor stone houses, segmental-headed superseded by hooded, c.1190–, 27, 32, **46**; spread in towns, in 14C, 47–8, 49; shouldered jambs, early 15C, 51; four-centred lintels, 14C–17C, 64, 85, **87**; roll-moulded, in Scotland, 16C–17C, 68, 91; flat lintel, plain or chamfered, to c.1700, 77, 85; fluting above, 17C, 83; flanked by columns or pilasters, c.1580 to c.1700, 107; corner, diagonal fireplace early 17C to mid 18C (mid 19C for workers), 114; bolection-moulded, c.1660–1730, 107, 114, in Sc., early 18C, 116 (or moulded corbels); flat-arched, flush stone surrounds, keyed or fielded, c.1680–1760, sometimes with small shelf over (in N. till c.1780), 114, 126, in Sc., 117; circled corner, impost and keystone, in Sc., 18C, 117; raised grate for coal, c.1720–, 140; shelf integrated with surround, often with architrave, pulvinated frieze or central panel, c.1725–65; with Ionic colonettes, Adam motifs or shelf broken forward in curves, c.1765–1800, 139–40; job grate, often hour-glass or double ogee, c.1770–1810, 140; corbels to flat surrounds in rural stone areas, inc. Sc., mid-18C to c.1820, 142;

ribbed jambs and lintels and corner roundels, c.1795–1850, 153; plain marble with flat surround and deep shelf, and very slight mouldings or offsets (scroll brackets for best), c.1805–40, 153; lusher hob grates, with lion heads, etc, c.1810–40, 153; corbels going from rural surrounds, c.1820, 153; metal round arch over grate, and surround often bombé or with floral brackets c.1840–80, 158, 163; lowered grate in rectangular tiled opening, c.1870–, 170, combined with cast-iron canopy over projecting grate, c.1880–, 170; rev. c.1700 shelf and bolection surround, and introd. of multi-shelf overmantel, c.1875–1910, 170; shelving combined horizontally, c.1900–30, 174; Art Nouveau rounded hood, c.1890–1920, 176; Neo-Adam, c.1875–, 171, 178; Neo-Tudor, fl. 1920–50, 178, **181**; flush electric fire supersedes for Funtionalists, c.1930–50, 180; Modernistic: stepped, 1930s, 180

Flemish bond (alternate headers and stretchers in each course of BRICK)

Flemish WINDOW (used in this book for one having arched central light within rectangular whole)

Floating PEDIMENT (one not visually supported by pilasters etc)

Floors: compacted earth, into 17C, 17, 64, 76, into 18C in Sc., 129; tiles, 16C–, 64; stone flags common by 17C, 88; plaster, 16C and 17C, 64, 88; parquet, c.1890–1960, 174

Floorboards: rebated into joists (or beams), 16C, 64; from loose to nailed, 16C–17C, 64, 88; narrowing to 20cm in mid 18C, 122

Fluted bands: on timberwork, esp. overmantels and built-in furniture, c.1580–c.1660, 83; as frieze round rooms and on plat bands etc, c.1760–c.1820, **131**, 137, 139

Forestair (external STAIR to first-floor entrance – Sc.)

Furze (gorse or whin – Sc.)

Gables: – façade gables, fl. c.1580s–1710, 70, 77, 81; rev., c.1890–1930s, 174; gablets, c.1970–, 177; – (crow-)stepped, 17C–18C, 116, occas. rev., 19C–20C, **82**, **166**, 186, in Sc., 16C–18C, 67, 68, 90, 116; – coped, 77; – shaped (inc. Dutch), 96, 98–9, 116, in Sc., c.1668–1755, 117, rev.

1875–1905, 165, **166**; – over Classical fronts, mid-17C to *c.*1720, **97**, 99, **100**, 111; over polygonal window, 75, 77, rev. *c.*1900–1939, **167**, 173

Gadroon (reversed fluting on curve, usually edging)

Galleries: – external, 13C–14C, 33, **46**, in Sc., 16C, or earlier, to late 17C, 67–8, 89–90; – internal, 14C, 39, 46,

Garage: *c.*1910–, 181

Garderobe, see SANITATION

Garland (circular wreath of flowers)

Garret (rooms wholly or partly under roof slope): in London, by 14C, but elsewhere from 16C, 45, 56, 67, 70, 82, 103

Gas: lighting, introd. 1807, 152; fires, fl. 1918–60, 181

Giant order: continuous, *c.*1630–60, 94–5, 97; 1710–30, 111; in Bath, *c.*1730–, 120, 135; elsewhere, *c.*1820–40, 143–5, **147**; at two-bay intervals, *c.*1660–1700, 100; to centre bay *c.*1660–1730, 99, 111; framing front, *c.*1710–30, 111, **112** (slight ones thereafter, 134); for terrace ends and centres, *c.*1765–1840s, 143, 145; on pairs and foursomes, 1812–*c.*1830, 149

GLAZING: mostly absent till late 16C, 17–18, 25, 60; then fast spread, 45, 56, 62, 67, 70, 82, 103; diamond panes, till mid-17C (end of 17C in N.), 70, **97**, **105**, then rectangular, 70, **102**; in Sc., leaded direct till late 17C, then with wooden bars, 89, ground fl. only glazed, early 18C, 116; four and five pane width, *c.*1680–1700, 109; three-pane width, *c.*1700–, 109, **112**; bars narrow from 3cm to 1.5cm, from *c.*1700 to *c.*1775, 109, 137; intersecting bars, *c.*1750–1840, 138, **146**, 148; four-pane width, *c.*1795–, 146–7, **148**, **150**; nearly square pane, *c.*1820–40, 147; margin, sometimes coloured, *c.*1810–60s, **146**, 147–8, rev. *c.*1920–40, 178; fall in price, *c.*1845, 155–6; four and two pane, *c.*1835–1880, 156; extending from pier to pier *c.*1855–80, 159, **169**; small-paned in top of window, *c.*1875–1920s, 165, 167, **170**, 177; leading revived, *c.*1875–1939, 168, 177; camber-headed lights, *c.*1910–40 and 1970–, 177, 184–5; stick-on leading, *c.*1914–40, 177–8; whole-light, Functionalist, *c.*1930–, 179, **180**, general, *c.*1954–, 182, **182–7**; Modernistic horizontal panes, 180; see STAINED GLASS, WINDOWS

Gothic Revival: intersecting glazing, *c.*1750–1840, 138, **146**, 148; cottages ornés, *c.*1775–1850, 149; mainly Neo-Tudor, *c.*1835–60, 158, **158**; and High Victorianism, *c.*1850–80, **160**, 161–2

Great Rebuilding: 57

Greek fret or key (line turned on itself in repeated right angles, forming pattern like ward of key): *c.*1810–40, 139, 153,

Greek Revival: *c.*1810–40 (to *c.*1875 in Sc.), 151, **147**, 159

Grotesques (figures fancifully growing out of ornament): 89

Guilloche (plaited pattern): 63, 89

Gutter: cast-iron, *c.*1810–, 152; forming cornice, in N., *c.*1800–late 19C, 152, 162–3

Hanging lum: Sc., 18C, 16

Harling: Sc., 16C to later 18C in towns, later in country, 91, 116, 153; unpainted, 1920s, 179

Header bond (BRICKS laid with only ends showing)

Heck: in N., 17C-earlier 18C, 79–80, 81, 82–3

Hinge: butterfly or L-shaped, later 17C-early 18C, 107; strap (with long tapering leaf) 17C, into 18C in country, 81; rev. *c.*1890–1920, 173, **175**

Hipped (ends of roof sloped inwards, not gabled)

Hollow; see CAVETTO, MOULDING

Hood mould; see DRIP MOULD

Impost (a horizontal block or band between arch and jamb)

Infill: wattle and daub, to 16C, 20, 45; lath or stone, 14C, 45; brick, from
c.1500, 93

Inglenook (area within large fireplace, often with seat), 174

Ionic (Classical order of usually fluted columns and flat capitals with
scrolls at corners, and dentilled cornice)

Jamb (side of opening)

Jetty: by 1246, 35, **38**, 39–40, 55, **56**; fading later 16C, early 17C, 62, 73–
4; internal, early 14C to 15C, 39, **51**; continuous, 61; to gables, c.1590
into 18C, 74, 75; rev. c.1875–1900 (gables to 1939), 168, **175**

Joints: 21, 24, 34

Joists (lesser timbers supporting floorboards): squarish in section till
c.1600, 64; occas. counterchanged, in 16C, 64; slighter and laid on
edge, from c.1600, 88; plastered, late 16C to mid-17C, 87

Key block/stone (enlarged or emphasised central stone of arch or flat
head of opening): over windows fl. c.1640–1725, **95**, 103, 111–12, **112**,
persisting in provinces to mid 19C, 119, 133, 150

King mullion (central, border one): 60, 71, **81**

Kitchen: often detached till 16C, 23, 29, 45, 47; next hall, 34, **34**, 55, 59,
77; on first floor in London, 14C–15C, 48, 55; in rear wing, 17C, 72,
81; outer room of but and ben, 17C–18C, 91; on ground floor, as
basement ceases, c.1875–, 175, 176, 177, **181**, **182**, 187; with ensuite
utility room, c.1990.

Kneeler: 77, **78**, **81**, 85; in Sc. (as skewputt) 90, 91, 116, 153; persisting
in N. to c.1770, 122, **127**

Knop (knoblike moulding on slender baluster): **114**

Land (large house built on set of flats – Sc.): to mid-18C, 89, 117; see
TENEMENT

Lap joint (one made by a cut halfway into both members to be joined):
to c.1300, 21, 24, 31, 34

Larder: 47, 55; common in small houses by 1920s, 175, 176, **191**

LAYOUT: urban tenement row, by 13C, 48–9; Sc. land, to mid-18C, 89,
117; uniform terrace, c.1640–, 94–5, 118–9; square, c.1630–, **92**, 94–5,
103, 108, 110–12; palace-front, c.1725–1840, 120, 125, 134–6, 143–5;
circus, 1754–c.1840, **123**, 134, 144, 159; crescent, 1767–c.1840, 134–5,
144, 159; rows of semi-det., rural, 1724–, urban, c.1790–, 148–9, 155,
158, 168, 173, 187; quasi-semi, c.1790–1880s, 148–9, 158; back-to-back,
14C case, 48; widespread c.1780–, fading mid 19C to 1930s, 141, 164;
square, inverted, bisected etc, c.1825–90s, 145, 157; unified three-four
houses, c.1820–50, 149; workers' rows in courts, c.1840–70s, 164; 70ft
street width, c.1918–1970, 176; uniform terrace fades, 1875–, 166, esp
1918–, 173, set inside Council estates, c.1945–80, 182–3; shift from
grid of streets to culs-de-sac and curves, c.1905–, 176; cross-butting
etc, street (and court) rev., 1970s–, 187

Lighting: see ELECTRICITY, GAS

Lime mortar: in rural Sc. introd. by 1625, in better tenant houses by
late 17C, 91, in humble houses by mid-18c, 128

Lincrusta: 1877–c.1914, 171

Linenfold (carved representation of loosely pleated piece of cloth):

59–60, 77, 81; three-cell, 61, 77, 80–81; in Sc. towns, corner turret stairs and forestairs, enclosed or open galleries and two rooms per storey (often as tenements), by mid-16C, to c.1700, 66–7, 89–91; with outshuts, from early 17C, 76, 82–3, in N to c.1820, 115–6; in urban Sc., galleries outlawed 1674, 89–90, in country, linear two and three unit houses, with end chimneys and rarely upper storeys, early 17C to later 18C, 91, 128; heck-entry, early 17C to mid-18C, 80, 81, 82–3; urban with chimney and stair between front and back room, from c.1560, waning from c.1680, **72**, 97, 108, 122; tiny yard by mid stair, c.1640–85, 95, 97, 108; closet wing, c.1680–1750, 114, 122; double-depth, central-entry, urban by mid-17C, 108, rural by c.1650 in Yorks, from late 17C elsewhere, 108, **112**, 115–16, with central passage to dogleg stair, c.1685–, 127; party-wall chimneys and stair at rear of passage, c.1680–1914, 114, **123**; in rural Scotland, single-depth, central-entry from c.1700, usually single-storey, 116; in urban Sc., mid-stair tenements with gable and wallhead chimneys and flats of up to seven rooms, late 17C to mid-18C, 117; forestairs in Sc. to mid-18C, 128; double-depth in country, in Sc. two-room flats in tenement terraces with stairs in rear turnpike, later 18C, 142, **142**; many Sc. houses single-storey to 20C, 116, 128–9, 153, **179**;

broader hallway and mid, toplit stair typical in towns, esp Sc., late 18C-late 19C, **144**; folding doors between front and rear room, early 19C to c.1900, 152, 174; rear extensions: fl. c.1850–1914, 156–7, 166, **167** (rare for workers, 164); direct entry and stairs in back room or middle for workers till late 19C, 141, 164; stair to side of door or round hall, c.1895–1940, 173, **174**, **181**; through-living room or L-plan, c.1900–, 174, 177; Functionalists: open plan, c.1930–, 180; boxed-in stair, galley kitchen, 1945–70, **182**; larger kitchen, ensuite utility room, bedrooms with ensuite bathrooms, c.1990, 187

PLASTERWORK: ribbed or flat bandwork and vine trail, birds, etc, c.1580–1690, 86–7; plainer small-rib, sometimes with central oval and stuck-on foliage, c.1660–1760, 107, but occas. Rococo in mid-18C, 125; Sc. similar, 128; finer relief, Adam motifs, c.1750–90s, 138–9; band at edge of ceiling, c.1795–, 152; ceiling roses spread to middling houses, esp. from c.1820, 152, **163**; pea beading, c.1800–30, 152; spiky, Neo-Rococo, c.1850–1900, 163; Neo-1700 ribwork, c.1875–1910, 171; see CORNICE

Plat band: 85, 103, 118, 120, 121, 127, 132, 133, 137

Plinth (in timber framing, continuous base in brick, stone)

Polychromy (multi-coloured): c.1850, fading from 1880s, **160**, 161, rev., 1980–, 186

PORCH: on black houses, 13; on first floor hall, late 12C, 27; in 13C London, 33; widespread in country, often storeyed, c.1610–1700, 70, 72, **74**, 75, 76, 77, 81; columned, occas. c.1660–, 142, more widely on urban terraces c.1810–, esp. 1835–75, 156; tent-roofed, c.1820–30, 152; recessed, for modest hos., c.1820–80, 151, 157, and c.1900–50 (often for paired doors), 173; in Sc., semi-recessed with Doric half-columns c.1825–80, 151, 158–9; with stilted or pointed heads, colonettes, or loosely Classical arches, c.1850–1914, 162, **163**; for the rich, non-columnar porches with shaped openings, c.1875–1900, 165; for others, timber, with Neo-17C posts or balusters in side, often strutted or linked to bay window, c.1895–1925, 167–8; concrete slab on slender post(s), *c.*1940–60, 182, **182**; strutted or sharing roof-slope with garage, *c.*1970–, 185, **185**

Post and panel, see PLANK

Pulvinated (convex frieze): esp. *c.*1730–60, over doorcase or fireplace, **107**, 116, 126, 128 (Sc.)

Purlin (longitudinal ROOF timber)

Quatrefoil (four-pointed shape, cloverlike): 73

Queen posts (pair of vertical posts in a roof truss): 62

Quirk (a sharp lengthwise cut beside a raised moulding) 68, 140

Quoins (French for corner; slightly projecting or specially worked stones at side edges of façade): 104, **127**, 128, 155, 156

Rafter (sloping timber directly supporting roofing): 24

Rail (a horizontal in joinery)

RAILINGS etc: wood palings common till *c.*1700, **92**, 95; alternate twisted and straight uprights, spike finials and simple scrolled dec., *c.*1620–1700, **102**, 106; square, tapering finials and urns to stanchions, *c.*1680, fading only 1820s, 113, **135**; dec. with curves broken in right angles, scrolls and foliage, *c.*1695–1760, 113, **125**; Adamesque, *c.*1770–1810, **135**, 137; with arched lamp standards, *c.*1760–1815, 135; spear and javelin finials typical *c.*1820–40, latter fading only *c.*1860, 151; encrusted anthemion etc, *c.*1835–70, 157–8; fleur-de-lys finials, *c.*1830–85, **158**; more geometric in Sc., *c.*1840–80, 159; Neo-1700, with wavy uprights in panels, *c.*1875–1910, **171**; palings rev., in suburbs *c.*1875–, 168; low composition walls, *c.*1910–40, 178; post and chain, *c.*1925–50, 178; Spanish-style gates etc, *c.*1920–40, 178; sunburst motif (gates, toprails), 1930s, 180

Rainwater head (enlarged open top of drain-pipe): inverted bell succeeds box, *c.*1750–1800, 137

Ramp (sharp upward curve, of architrave, plat band, handrail etc): fl. *c.*1680–1840, 113, **113**, **123**, 134

Rates (sizes, under 1774 Act): 133

Reeding (parallel ridges, reedlike, forming low-relief or flush moulding): *c.*1800–1830, 151

Render (external surfacing with sand and lime or cement): 174, 177, 179; see HARLING

Reserved, or sunk, CHAMFER (inset SPLAY)

Reveal (the inside face of an opening)

Rinceau (French; scrolling foliage pattern): 139

Rococo (playful style of dec., of short curves, etc., asym. in detail): *c.*1750–70, 125, 134; rev., *c.*1840–80, 158, 163

Roll MOULDING (tubelike – half round, or more)

ROOF: tentlike, 9, 10–11; raised cruck 12–14, 52, 53; jointed cruck, 12, 50–51; passing-brace, by late 11C/early 12C, slowly fading from *c.*1275, **23**, 24, 29, 34, 35, 36, 37; cruck (full or non-specific), before 1200, 14–16, 18–20, 25, 31, **36**, **44**, 51, less for gentry, more in Wales and N, from mid-15C, 53, 54, 62, 76, 80, 83, 91; side-purlin, introd late 13C, standard from 16C, fading from *c.*1700, **19**, 35–6, 37, **38**, 44, 62, **62**; crown-post, later 13C to mid-16C, **19**, 36–7, 40, 53, 62; king post, by *c.*1325, 37, mainly northern from *c.*1400 (fading 1600), 52, 53, 62; raised aisle, early 14C–, 41; hammer beam, *c.*1300 into 15C (in Wales to *c.*1600), 41–2; base-cruck, from *c.*1300, fading mid-15C, 42–3; queen-post, esp. mid-16C, 62, 122; A-trusses take place of crucks in Sc., 17C, 91; metal straps for joints, by 1730s; strutted king and queen post typical, in two spans, through 18C, 122; scarfed succeed full crucks in 18C Sc., 129; 35° of 18C slated roofs down to 30° c.1820–50, rising to 60° for cottages ornés, c.1800–30, and on Gothic semis, 1830–60, and terraces, c.1860–80s, 122, 158, 161; finials, cresting, heavy barge-boards, c.1850–90, **160**, 162; catslide (roof slope extended to low level over porch etc.), c.1890–1940, 173, **181**; hipped the norm, 1918–40, 176, **177**, **181**; Functionalist usually flat, c.1930–70, 179, **180**, 183, **184**; pitched frequent for Modernistic, 1930–40, **181**, the norm, c.1970–, 184, 186;

Roofing: stone flags, 50, 52, 84; see SLATES, TILES, THATCH

Rose (ceiling): 139, 152, **163**

Rustication (stonework with rough, raised surface or sunk joints, 'banded' if horizontal only): pargeted, 100; in 17C, 104; to ground floors c.1730–c.1850, 120, **132**, 134, 137, 143, **143–7**

Sanitation: garderobe, for rich by 13C, others, in towns, by 14C, 32, 40, 45, 49, 55; w.c. rare till c.1775 (introd. of S-bend and valve), 140, for all but poor by c.1825, 153; for workers, earth closets till c.1900, 164, 175; in Sc. tenements, w.c. entered or lit from landing, by late 19C, 170

Samson post: 28, 33

Scale and platt (dogleg STAIR – Sc.)

Scalloping (like fluting or edge of shell): in brick window-heads, c.1680–1730, 110, rev., c.1875, 167

Segmental (a curve of less than half a circle)

Scissor braces: 24, 36

Scribing (slight linear MOULDING, incised close to edge): 88

Scroll (tubular MOULDING with longitudinal step, like roll of paper) often paired with hollow moulding: 64

Scullery (room to wash dishes): 141, 175, 176

Second Empire: c.1860–80s, 163

Settle (bench with arm(s) at end and tall back): 80, 174

Shillet: 11, 76

Shingles (wood tiles): at least till later 13C, 28

Shippon; see BYRE

Shutters: internal, open-hall, to 16C, 18, 25; in lower half of window, in Sc., 16–17C, 89; external, ground-floor, occas. through 18C, **131**, widespread (louvred) c.1795–c.1830, 147, then fading

Shuttering (planking holding cob etc as it dries): 128

Side purlin (longitudinal ROOF timber, linking RAFTERS at mid-height)

Sill band: esp. c.1770–1800, 118, 132, 133–4, 162

Skewputt (KNEELER – Sc.)

Skirting board: 125, 154

Slates – roofing: along S. coast, by 12C, 28, in Chester etc from 14C, 136; in Sc. for rich in 17C, 91; spreading, early 18C, 122, usual in London by 1760, 136; less from mid-19C, 161; artificial, c.1945–, **182**; – as cladding: in SW by 17C, in Cumbria etc from late 18C, 136

Smoke bay: late 15C through 16C, 52, 56; in London up to c.1600

Smoke-hood: by mid-15C, fading late 17C, 52, **52**, 59, 65, 79–80, **79**, 83

Solar: 18, 25, 34, 44, 47, 48

Spandrel (triangle between curve of arch and horizontal above)

Spere: 42–3

Spice cupboard: fl. 17C to early 18C, 84

Splay (surface angled out from adjacent one at more than right-angle, e.g. WINDOW reveal, plain slant of MULLION)

Sorts of house: under 1667 Act, 100–101, 103; see RATES

Stained glass: plain in margin panes, c.1810–70, 148; in top lights, door panels, sidelights and stair windows, leaded, patterned or pictorial, c.1870–1940, 168, 171, 177–8; Art Nouveau, c.1890–1930, **168**, 175 (as stick-on to upper window-lights, c.1900–45, 177–8); sunburst, 1930–40, 180

STAIRS: external in most 12C first-floor houses, 25, 27; from door at lower end in better halls, 29; winding, usual in stone houses as soon as ladders superseded, late 12C till the 18th century, 27, 32, 44–5, 49; ladders, 45–6, 67; semi-turret early 17C to c.1720, 51, 77, 80, 83, 88; forestairs, in Sc., by mid-16C, fading mid-18C, 54, 68, 89, 90, 91, 128; in towns, dog-leg (straight flights adjacent to one another joined by landings), c.1640–, 83, 88, 95, 97, 108, 173, in country, **115**, 127; balustrading starts with bobbin and splat, c.1600–1700, **84**, 88, 108, 116;

Classical balusters, introd c.1640 (still on closed string), waisted till c.1660, 95–6, bulbous or spiral c.1650–, 108, slowly waning from c.1700, 114; slender balusters on open string from c.1700, 114, 125–6; newel changing from square to round and rail tending to coil, from early 18C, 125; Chinese Chippendale, c.1750–65, 123, 126; stone steps and curvilinear metal banisters, c.1750–, 126 (Adamesque c.1760–1800), in Sc., 128; stick baluster and rounder handrail, c.1760–1840, 130, 140, 152–3; curved flights, c.1780–c.1830, 140, 152; turned balusters persist in places, slenderer, to c.1830, 140, 153; newel (turnpike) in Sc., to late 18C, 128, 142, **142**, rev. c.1980, 187;

cast-iron balusters, and Greek motifs, spread c.1800–40, 153; bulbous wooden newels, ornate metal balustrades, c.1850–1900, 163; square newels and splat balusters rev., c.1875–1910, **166**; flat or square balusters, c.1895–1940, 173, **174**; flush-panel balustrade, 1930s, 180; Functionalist often open tread or spiral, c.1930–, 180; boxed-in straight flights, 1945–, **182**

Stanchions (in railings, the more substantial uprights)

Stiff-leaf (12C–13C stylised sculptured foliage): mass-produced, c.1870–1900, 162

Stile (vertical timber in joinery)

Stilted (raising of arch or lintel on short extensions of JAMBS above capitals): **160**, 162

Stop chamfers: 63, 85

Strapwork: 86, **98**

String, stair (closed: unbroken slope on which balusters sit, **95**; open: steps open at side, with balusters rising from each, **114**)

Stucco (fine-grained render, to take moulding and paint): on ground floor and for dec. c.1765–c.1860, **131–2**, 137, 146; all over, esp. terraces, c.1810–75, 144–5, 149, 156, 161; for surrounds, esp. bracketed cornice hoods, c.1830–80, 150, 156–7

Superimposed orders (one order above another): fl. 1660–1700, 98, 99–100; framing ones, c.1700–30, 111

Swag (cloth, fruit, etc, hanging in curve): 139

Temple-front: 94, 103, 118, 132, 137, 143

Tenement: 48, 55–6, 67, 89–90, 117; mid-18C–, 127–8, 142, 144, 169–70,

179; see LAND

Terra cotta (fine-grained, hard form of brick, usually for moulded dec., sometimes glazed): occas. *c.*1520–40, fl. 1860–1910, 165

Thatch: general till 16C, 17, 33, 50; in Sc. towns into 17C, 67, 90, through 18C in country, 116, 128; in Lakes, waning *c.*1700, 84

Thermal window or motif (semi-circular window, with two mullions): *c.*1770–1800, 136, 143

Tile: – hanging, by early 18C, 115; on upper storeys, *c.*1875–1918, 165, 168; in recessed porches, often Art Nouveau, *c.*1890–1920, 167, 176; in gable-heads, etc., esp. 1918–39, 177, **181**; in panels, *c.*1955–, 183; – internal: in fireplaces, esp *c.*1870–1914, 170, 176; in Scotland, 170; for mantelpieces, *c.*1925–55, 180, 181; for bathrooms and kitchens, late 19C–, 180, 181; – roofing: by 12C, 28; required, London, 1191+ , 1212, 33; common, London (and Kent) by 14C, 50; reintrod., for better-off, *c.*1850, 161, 164, spreading in 20C, 176; cresting, *c.*1850– 1920s, **167**, 164, 169; see PANTILES

Timber framing: earthfast till *c.*1200, 9–11, 23–4, then footing, 29, 32; box-frame or cruck, 18–20; nearly square timbers till *c.*1300, then fading, 24, 31, 34; mixed box and cruck, in Wales, *c.*1400, 53, box only widespread *c.*1500, 62; persists, in N, in 16C, 65, in Sc., in 16C, 67, in 17C, 89, 104, for Classical houses, later 17C, 100, 104, 105, and beyond, 115; mock, introd. by *c.*1860, 168; see ROOF, WALLFRAMING

Torus (semi-circular moulding): 125

Tower house: 15C–17C, **52**, 54, 56, 67, 89, **90**; see PELE

Transmullioned (with transoms and mullions): 16C to early 18C, 60, 76

Transom (horizontal member dividing WINDOW): 60, 89

Trefoiled (three-pointed shape, cloverlike): 47

Triglyph (unit of three verticals, in DORIC frieze): often on lintel to front doorway or passage *c.*1700–1730, **112–114**

Triumphal arch motif (an arch flanked by smaller ones, within the framework of an order): 136

Truss (timbers framed to form triangular support in ROOF)

Turf walling: 15, 129: see COB

Undercroft (medieval BASEMENT or semi-basement): 33, 34, 46, 48

Urn (ornament based on small pot with lid): on railings, 113; Adamesque, 139

Veranda (balcony with pitched roof on light supports, or similar on ground level) *c.*1795–1840: 152

Vermiculated (rustication pitted with short wormlike curves): 156

Villa (small superior secondary residence near town; imitations thereof): 149, 158

Vitruvian scroll (band of repeat wave pattern): 137, 140

Wainscotting (early term for oak PANELLING, hence applied to 'small square' type): *c.*1550–*c.*1660, 50, 87–8

WALL-FRAMING: large-panel, by late 13C, 30, 34, 43, 53, fading *c.*1450–, 53, 62; St Andrew's Cross, by *c.*1330, through 15C, 44, 53; straight angle braces, till early 14C, 30, 34, 44, curved from *c.*1300, 43–4, 53, straight again, late 17C–, 74; herring bone (parallel) bracing, by end of 14C, fading mid-17C, 53, 73; close-studding, from *c.*1340, **46**, 53–4, **61**, 73–4, with mid-rail (mainly in W.) from *c.*1500, 62; wavy (ogee), mid-16C to earlier 17C, 62, **67**, 73; square-panel, earlier 15C to late 17C, 53, 73; decorative (and close-panel), *c.*1570 to later 17C,

revived *c*.1900, mass-produced from 1918, **172**, 177, **181**; Functionalist undivided, in horizontal bands, *c*.1930–, 179, 180, **183**; Modernistic often stepped or around corners, 1930–40; panels below, 1945–70, 180, **181**; picture, 182, floor to ceiling, fl. 1955–70, 183, **184**, **185**; rectangular oriels, *c*.1965–, 185, **185**; Post-Modern, circular, round-headed and corner, *c*.1980–86, 186, **187**; see GLAZING
Window Tax: 1697–1851, 110, 121, 146–7

INDEX OF PLACES AND PERSONS

Rural houses are indexed by individual name. Urban houses are indexed by town. Counties are not indexed.

Bury St Edmunds
  Cupola Ho 102
  Moyses Hall 27
Busby, C.A. 145, **147**
Buxton: The Crescent 134–5
Calico Ho, Newnham **87**
Campbell, Colen 118, 120
Candiehead, Stirlingshire **170**
Canterbury: 25, 33, 55; Christchurch
  Priory 28
Cardiff: Greenwich Rd **181**
Carlton Husthwaite, Yorks 65
Carnforth: Hunter St 162
Carr, John 135
Carron Co. 140, 152
39 The Causeway, Steventon 44, **44**
79 The Causeway, Steventon **74**,
  75, 85
83 The Causeway, Steventon 31, **31**
Causeway Fm, Windermere 86
Charles, F.W.B. **43**
Charlton 23
Chaucer, G. 43, 47
Cheddar 22
Cheltenham 152, 157–8
  Berkeley Pl, London Rd 152
  Lyppiatt Terr 155
  Pittville Lawn 158
Chennels Brook Fm, Horsham 42, **42**
Chessor, John 162
Chester: 33–4, 136, 168; Watergate
  St **33**, 34
Church Fm Museum, Skegness 76
Clergy Ho, Alfriston 37, 40
Coade, Eleanor 135, 137, 138
Cogges, Witney 31, **31**
Conisborough Castle 27
Corbusier, Le 179, 183
Costains Co 177, 181
Cottingham, L.B. 152
Coventry: 54; Spon St 56, **56**
Cowdery's Down **10**
Crofton Fm, Orpington 43
Crittal Co 179
Cromford: North St 141, 142
Cross Fm, Westhay 64
Crunden, J. 138
Cubitt, Thomas 153
Cullompton: Willand Rd 180, **181**
Culross: 67, 91
  The Study 89, **90**
Cumming, A. 140
Currie, C. 30
Dale Co 140
Dance, G. II, 133, 134, 146

Darlington 120
Dartmouth: Buttermarket 89
Deanburnhaugh 129
Depden Green 41
Devey, G. 168
Dixon, J. **185**, 186
Dorchester, Dorset: S. Lodge **123**
Dowson, Sir P. 183, **184**
Doyle & Underwood 147
Dunfermline 128
Dunning, G.C. **34**
Dunstable: Middle Row 48, 49
Durham Ho, Great Bardfield 53
E Riddlesden Hall **87**
Ecclefechan 142
Edgar's Fm, Stowmarket 37, **37**, 41
Edgend, Nelson 127, **127**
Edinburgh 67, 117, 142, 143
  Belgrave Cres 162
  Carlton St 144, **144**
  Charlotte Sq 136, 142, 144
  Chessel's Ct, 240
  312–28 Canongate 117
  Gladstone's Land 90, **90**
  High School 151
  John Knox's Ho 68, **68**
  Marchmont area 169
  Mary of Guise's Ho 68
  Milne's Ct 117
  Moray Pl 144, 145
  New Town 142, 143, 144
  39–43 N. Castle St 142
  Royal Terr **143**, 144, **144**
  St Bernard's Cres 151
Elgin 67
  7 High St (Braco's Ho) 90
  103 High St 89
Elland Hall 41
Elsam, Richard 148
Erroll 128
Eveleigh, John 135
Evesham: High St 102
Exeter 46, 48, 50, 54, 70, 102
  16 Fog St (ex-16 Edmund St)
    55–6, **55**
  High St 99
  Tudor Ho 101
  Rosebury Rd 161
Falkland
  Cross Wynd 128
  Key Ho 116
Farnham 133; 90 West St 136
Farrell, Terry 186
Fforest, Brechfa **115**
Fiennes, Celia 15, 109